THE ONLY TELLER

Readings in the Monologue Novel

THE
ONLY TELLER

Readings in the Monologue Novel

HETTY CLEWS

1985

Sono Nis Press

VICTORIA, BRITISH COLUMBIA

Canadian Cataloguing in Publication Data

Clews, Hetty, 1929-
    The only teller

Bibliography: p.
Includes index.
ISBN 0-919203-50-7

1. First person narrative.   2. Fiction — Technique.
I. Title.
PN3383.P64C54 1985   809.3   c84-091412-1

This book has been published with the help of a grant from
the Canadian Federation for the Humanities using funds
provided by the Social Sciences and Humanities Research
Council of Canada.

Published by
SONO NIS PRESS
1745 Blanshard Street
Victoria, British Columbia, Canada v8w 2j8

Designed and printed in Canada by
MORRISS PRINTING COMPANY LTD.
Victoria, British Columbia

To Minnie, my mother
Alan, my husband
Simon, Alison, Margaret and Madeleine
my children —
faithful listeners

ACKNOWLEDGEMENTS

J. K. Johnstone
Leon Edel
Ivan Eyre
Patricia E. Bovey and the Art Gallery of Greater Victoria

"I must go back and tell the story over.
  It is a curious story, not so much in the external
  events which are common enough,
  but in the way it presents itself to me,
  the only teller."

SAMMY MOUNTJOY in *Free Fall*

Contents

Introduction

It is more than a quarter of a century since Margaret Kennedy, seeking to legitimize the novel, began her discussion of the ancient art of story-telling with the observation that "Criticism has never paid to the novel the degree of attention which it has accorded to other kinds of literature."[1]

In the intervening years many responsible critics have sought to pay the novel that degree of attention which they agree it deserves. Their task has been difficult because it is the nature of the novel to be "new," and to renew itself by a diversification which resists the limits of precise definition. Consequently there have been as many kinds of criticism of the novel as there are kinds of novel. Few descriptions of its abiding characteristics can be made with confidence. It is written, it is fiction, it is longer than the short story, and it is a narrative of events befalling recognizable human beings — though not necessarily, as was once held, events arranged in linear time sequence. The novel, however, is more than the sum of these parts, for they alone can scarcely account for its providing the reader with a window to a world he can believe to be real and thus enlarging his vision of life. If the virtual world of the novel is to appear real to the reader it is axiomatic that it appear real to the writer. If what the reader sees through the provided window is to enlarge his vision of life, he must give assent to the significance of the writer's concerns. It is here that the multifarious nature of the novel demonstrates itself, for a novelist's concerns may be historical, moral, political, psychological, philosophic, mythological, social, aesthetic, or any combination of these. Consequently the critic of the novel can oper-

[1] *The Outlaws on Parnassus* (London: Cresset, 1958), p. 1.

11

ate within any of the frames of reference suggested by the substance or the theme of the work.

Recent criticism has developed a poetics for the novel by seeking the source of the reader's experience of virtual reality and significance in the novelist's technique. There is no clearer exposition of what technique means to the novelist than that provided by Mark Schorer:

> For technique is the means by which the writer's experience, which is his subject matter, compels him to attend to it; technique is the only means he has of discovering, exploring, developing his subject, of conveying its meaning, and finally, of evaluating it.
> . . . Technique in fiction is, of course, all those obvious forms of it which are usually taken to be the whole of it, and . . . the uses to which language, as language, is put to express the quality of the experience in question; and the uses of point of view not only as a mode of dramatic delimitation, but more particularly, of thematic definition.[2]

If one adds to this statement the injunction of Ford Madox Ford: "You must have your eyes forever on your Reader. That alone constitutes . . . Technique!",[3] then the text of the novel may be understood as a combination of forms and signs consciously designed by the author to guide the imagination of his reader. Criticism accordingly shifts its focus from the substance of the narrative to the stylistic means of communication whereby the reader is persuaded to enter the imagined world created by the novelist.

It is from this stance, viewing the novel as communication, that I write. My purpose is to examine one kind of technique which seems increasingly evident in twentieth-century novels. In it the author creates a speaker, clearly differentiated from himself, who proceeds to address an audience confidentially in much the same way as the "I" of the dramatic monologue does, but more discursively and over an extended period of time. Such a created speaker will in what follows be termed a "monologuist," and his account of himself and his experiences will be termed a "monologue novel."

In a broad sense, all "I" narrators may be described as monologuists, and the monologue in English literature has a history which extends at least as far back as Chaucer. I do not intend, however, a survey of first-person narration in all its forms. My concern is with

---

[2] "Technique as Discovery," in *Forms of Modern Fiction*, ed. William Van O'Connor (Bloomington: Indiana University Press, 1959), pp. 9-11.

[3] "Technique," *The Southern Review I* (1935), 35. The dots are the author's and are used for emphasis.

the development, in the twentieth-century novel, of a dramatized speaker in a different relationship to his audience from that of the author. His closest forebear in prose is the *persona* of the satirist, who also is recognizable as an entity quite separate from his creator, and through whom also an ironic gap between "speaker" and writer emerges for the delectation of the reader. As in satire, so in the novels here considered, the creation of a mouthpiece is a dramatic act fully as conscious as that undertaken by the author of the dramatic monologue.

To evoke another human being, and to present him concretely in a particular setting of time, place, and relationship with a listener, is the traditional function of the dramatist. Alex Comfort says of drama that it is:

> ... a stylized presentation of a background which the audience shares with the writer, though his individual treatment may be different from theirs, and for it to continue as a major art form the audience must actively participate in the illusion, in the process of composition, and in the acceptance of the result. In our own society there has been a gradual replacement of drama in this sense by dramatized fiction.[4]

My hypothesis builds on Comfort's premise by isolating from his general category of "dramatized fiction" the more specific sub-genre of the monologue novel, and applying to it his description of the audience response that is necessary if the work is to succeed. Active participation in the illusion, the process of composition, and the acceptance of the result — this is precisely what monologue novels require of readers as audience. The stylized presentation of a background which the reader, as audience, shares with the apparent speaker — this is what the monologue embodies. Monologue novels seem to offer compelling evidence of the modern novelist's desire to invite the reader's participation in the act of creation itself, thereby evincing a shift of authority from writer to reader.

Most earlier novels engage the reader chiefly by a tale in the telling, as will be shown in the preliminary chapters of this book. In the history of the novel, narrators have appeared in many guises, but whatever the guise or disguise the reader has commonly recognized the author as the only teller of the tale. For this reason it is possible to have vivid memories of a novel without being able to remember whether its events are recounted in the first or the third person. The substance of each narrator's experiences, as shaped and

---

[4] *The Novel and Our Time* (London: Phoenix House, 1948), pp. 10-11.

13

presented to us by a distinctive author, is what we chiefly recall. We read and re-read the fiction of the eighteenth and nineteenth centuries for what Scholes and Kellogg have called a

... quality of mind transmitted ... through the language of characterization, motivation, description and commentary — the intelligence and sensitivity with which the fictional events are related to the perceivable world or the world of ideas; the accuracy and insight of the artist's picture of the brazen world in which we live, or the beauty and idealism of the golden world created in fiction.[5]

It is this discovered and cherished "quality of mind" which enables us to speak of great novelists from Richardson to E. M. Forster as if they were personal friends, equally known and valued by others.

In those monologue novels considered subsequently, this kind of comfortable security is less readily achieved because the distinctive authorial voice or the quality of mind infusing the narrative is much harder to discern. It is true that the creator is always present in his creation; however, when his first *fiat* is a teller totally distanced from himself, who is offered as "the only teller" of the tale, that creator effectively effaces himself from the substance of his novel to a greater extent than is prescribed even by the poetics of Gustave Flaubert or Henry James. Consequently, his hidden presence works upon the reader as does the presence of the poet in the dramatic monologue as described by Robert Langbaum:

It can be said of the dramatic monologue generally that there is at work in it a consciousness, whether intellectual or historical, beyond what the speaker can lay claim to. This consciousness is the mark of the poet's projection into the poem; and is also the pole which attracts our projection, since we find in it the counterpart of our own consciousness.[6]

In contending that this statement can be helpfully applied to the novel monologue, I submit that instead of becoming engaged by the substance of such a novel, the reader is chiefly engaged by his own projection into it. The monologuist, addressing his reader directly and unequivocally, invites his participation in the re-enactment of whatever tale is to be told. The reader, therefore, entering the dramatization as listener, finds himself collaborating in the actualization of the objective situation which the tale embodies. And whereas he may feel, as he reads, that he is responding directly to the speaker of

[5] *The Nature of Narrative* (London: Oxford University Press, 1966), p. 239. All page numbers in parenthesis are to this edition.
[6] *The Poetry of Experience* (New York: Random House, 1957), p. 94.

the monologue, he is in fact the participant in a dramatization, and the true counterpart of his consciousness is the consciousness which created that speaker.

The several kinds of monologue which I intend to examine have in common the reader's prerogative as maker of meaning. I shall contend that the monologue form excites inquiry and frustrates certainty, so that whatever its generic shape may be, its symbolic shape is that of the question mark. The metaphysically oriented novelist has as his primary concern a felt life which transcends particulars of environment and character, he therefore creates monologuists as vehicles for rhetoric, and what his monologuists say is the question. The empirically oriented novelist makes the truth of what happens inside and outside his monologuist's mind the mystery; what his monologuist knows or does not know is the question. But always there is the question, and the reader, far from being given an answer, is required to furnish his own.

The mystery is a consequence of there being no recorded response to the speaker, and this lack of response is a feature of both monologue and soliloquy. The terms "monologue" and "soliloquy," familiar to the reader of poetry and drama, are not as synonymous as they may at first appear. In drama, the soliloquy is distinguished from the monologue by the absence of an audience within the play; indeed, the soliloquy as it is usually understood occurs only within a play, when a character whose usual mode of self-expression is dialogue communicates intra-personally, debating with himself some unresolved issue, so that the external audience overhears the language of his innermost thought. By extension, however, we may use the term "soliloquy" for any expression of inner thought, wherever it occurs, if it has no external respondent and no function outside those circumstances in which it is addressed by a speaker to himself.

The monologue, conversely, in both drama and poetry, is addressed to a listener whose presence is overtly acknowledged by the speaker. In drama, this silent listener is either physically present, as in Strindberg's *The Stronger*, or assumed to be present, as in Pinter's *Monologue*, by both speaker and audience. In verse, the dramatic monologue signals the presence of the listener in a variety of ways, and its success as communication is largely determined by the degree to which the reader is persuaded to assume the identity of the person addressed. In both, the monologue, unlike the soliloquy, is an organic entity which is independent of the context in which it may be construed to occur.

15

These are the reasons for speaking of novel "monologues" rather than "soliloquies." The works which I characterize as novel monologues present a speaker who formulates his thoughts or his recollections into language designed for a listening audience, or even, it seems, language very selectively designed for a single listener whom the reader is persuaded to become. Furthermore, novel monologues are shaped by a single controlling purpose from beginning to end. The monologuist has something definitive he must say and an audience in mind to whom it must be said.

What he has to say, and the person or group to whom he must say it, are, of course, distinctively different for each monologuist, but there are similarities to be discerned. Out of many possible classifications I have chosen four, one of which is clearly separable from the other three. The categories I have named for exploration are the formalized monologue, and three kinds of mimetic monologues: autobiographic, eyewitness, and confessional.

In distinguishing only four kinds of monologues among many, I acknowledge the need for considerable cross reference. There are, however, several broad generalizations that can be made and certain terms that should be defined. In the chapter entitled "Formalized Monologues" I shall contend that there is a rare kind of novelist for whom rhetoric is more appealing than psychology. Such a novelist creates fictive speakers primarily as multipersonal expressions of his own distinctive voice. His subject is likely to be a reality beyond the empirical world; consequently, he uses poetic design and fashioning to express his own perception of such a metaphysical reality through carefully wrought and comparative monologues. The novelists selected as exponents of the formalized monologue are Virginia Woolf (*The Waves*, 1931) and William Faulkner (*The Sound and the Fury*, 1929, and *As I Lay Dying*, 1930). In both these novelists, despite their interest in experimentation, I find likeness to the memorable novelists of former centuries. They are likely to be remembered for their own "quality of mind" as much as for their unusual use of the monologue form, and they deserve a place in this study because of, or perhaps in spite of, their highly idiosyncratic art.

In considering the achievements of certain novelists whom I distinguish as empirically oriented, I shall use the term "mimetic." By "mimetic monologues" I mean those which convince the reader that they are psychologically accurate representations of individual perceptions of the observable world. There are several discernible forms of the mimetic monologue. I have attempted to isolate three variants

16

for representative analysis. The autobiographic monologue offers the "I" as hero, engrossed in the telling of an apparently authentic life-story and concerned chiefly with his self-image. The eyewitness monologue offers the "I" as observer, seeking to interpret evidence presented to his senses and his judgement, and to share his perceptions with an audience as a means of apparently clarifying them for himself. The confessional monologue offers the "I" as penitent, experiencing in immediacy or in recollection some night of the soul, and striving towards self-knowledge as a means of redemption.

The field of examples of mimetic monologues is wide, and is rapidly increasing as more and more twentieth-century fiction, for reasons I shall suggest as a conclusion, falls into the genre of the monologue novel. I have therefore limited the body of this study to novelists with whom the reader is likely to be already familiar. The autobiographic monologue will be represented by Thomas Mann's Felix, from *The Confessions of Felix Krull, Confidence Man* (1937); Joyce Cary's Gulley Jimson, from *The Horse's Mouth* (1944); and Margaret Laurence's Hagar Shipley, from *The Stone Angel* (1964). The eyewitness monologue will feature Conrad's Marlow, from *The Heart of Darkness* (1902); Henry James's governess, from *The Turn of the Screw* (1898); and Ford Madox Ford's Dowell, from *The Good Soldier* (1915). The confessional monologue will be represented by Dostoevsky's Underground Man, from *Notes from Underground* (1864); Camus's Judge Penitent from *The Fall* (1956); and William Golding's Sammy Mountjoy, from *Free Fall* (1959).

This gallery of monologuists is, I submit, sufficiently diversified to offer some interesting comparisons and contrasts, and sufficiently restricted to allow for some close textual analysis. Peripheral references will be made as they seem necessary, and some more recent monologue novels that seem related to those listed above will also be noted as a means of demonstrating the scope afforded by the monologue in fiction.

The possibilities for the monologuist are too varied to be exhaustively considered in a single book. The speaker to whom we listen can choose from many modes of communication and be motivated by many needs. He can tell an apparently verifiable tale, as in the autobiographical monologue, or he can fantasize freely, as in some eyewitness monologues. He can be a solipsist, as in the confessional monologue, or demonstrably self-effacing in, again, some eye-witness monologues. He can be observer, participant or protagonist, or all three in different degrees at different times. He can be entirely limited to what he has experienced directly; he can supplement his knowledge with what he has learnt from others; or he can conjecture freely and imagine fully. He can quickly earn his listener's trust or he can disclose himself to be partially or totally unreliable. He can follow external or internal time. When, as is customary, his monologue is retrospective, it opens up another ironic gap between the speaker "now" and the speaker "then." The possibilities inherent in self-disclosure are many. But whatever the mode and whatever the motive, the effect of personal interaction is inescapable. The reader cannot avoid being aware of the "I" as a personality to whom he must respond.

The sense that we are being talked to by someone is an important part of our experience of almost any literary work. In the novel, however, this sense can come to us in several ways. It can be forced upon us, more or less obtrusively, by an author openly commenting upon his function as author. It can slowly seep into our consciousness as we read, despite the author's attempt to "disappear," and thus become an awareness we will perhaps extend and enrich by reflection. Or it can be at the outset the very foundation for our experience of the tale that is to be told ("Call me Ishmael!"), preparing us to "listen" to a voice declaring itself in and through every utterance it makes. If I am right in suggesting that this third way is increasingly explored by the writers of modern fiction, then two questions arise from the premise. Why should this be? And what are the different means by which certain novelists have created the speaking presence of their monologuists and have given form to their utterances? These are the questions which will be addressed in what follows.

CHAPTER ONE

Narrators:
Guise and Disguise

In order that the most banal event may become an adventure, it is a necessary and sufficient condition that one should set about relating it. — JEAN-PAUL SARTRE, *La Nausée*

A developing poetics for the novel has traced, during the past two centuries, a complicated pattern of interaction between narrator, narrative, and reader. Crucial to this endeavour is the relationship of author to narrator.

In those eighteenth-century works which are generally regarded as the first novels to be written in English, author and narrator were ostensibly one and the same. This is because in an empirical age the credibility of any tale rested in part on the assurance of its teller that it was indeed "true." A wealth of circumstantial detail by Defoe, or of immediate sensory experience by Richardson, might endorse the reader's impression of truth, but beyond this the author needed to assure the reader that the speaker was indeed recounting personal experience. The original writer of *Moll Flanders*, however subject her work might be to editorial emendation, must be seen to be Moll herself; the writer of all those letters must be believed to be Pamela herself.

Even Fielding, while acknowledging his eclecticism, is at pains to claim that among the romance, drama, and essay content of his "comic epic in prose" he is also presenting "history." His engaging asides as narrator succeed in making him a *dramatis persona* within such history, so that when we have finished reading it we are more likely to be aware of Fielding as a character than we are of his putative hero.

The same is true of subsequent novelists who assert their presence as narrators within their work. The tone of the author as declared

narrator varies considerably from Thackeray ("Come, children!")
to George Eliot ("This is what I undertake to do for you, reader"),
and accounts for at least a measure of the reader's response to the
work. Generally, however, when the author appears openly in the
guise of narrator he does so to win the reader's attention and
co-operation in what he holds to be a necessary contract. As Trollope expresses it:

> And here, perhaps, it may be allowed to the novelist to explain his
> views on a very important point in the art of telling tales. He ventures
> to reprobate that system which goes far to violate all proper confidence
> between the author and his readers. . . . Our doctrine is, that the author
> and the reader should move along together in full confidence with each
> other.[1]

The authorial "I" or "we" of earlier novelists still occurs in some
modern works, but in them it is likely to be tinged with irony in the
manner of Thomas Mann's recounting of the story of Hans Castorp.
The modern novelist, it seems, can no longer assume that narrator
and reader will enjoy full confidence in each other, and the modern
critic is likely to accept the contention of Bradford A. Booth, writing
in 1950, that ". . . the most significant change in the fiction of our
time is the disappearance of the author." Or, beyond this, the modern critic will seek to qualify the term "author" in accordance with
the distinctions made by a later Booth between the man who writes
the book (author), the man whose attitudes shape the book (implied author), and the man who communicates directly with the
reader (narrator):

> The "implied author" chooses, consciously or unconsciously, what
> we read; . . . he is the sum of his own choices. . . . This implied author
> is always distinct from the "real man" — whatever we may take him
> to be — who creates a superior version of himself, a "second self," as
> he creates his work.[2]

In the light of these distinctions we might wish to qualify the
phrase "the disappearance of the author" to read "the apparent dis-

---

[1] *Barchester Towers* (New York: Scribners, 1923), pp. 127-28. All page numbers in parenthesis are to this edition.

[2] Wayne C. Booth, *The Rhetoric of Fiction* (Chicago: University of Chicago
Press, 1961), pp. 74 and 151. All page numbers in parenthesis are to this
edition. Kathleen Tillotson, *The Tale and the Teller* (London: Oxford University Press, 1959), p. 22, points out that Dowden, as early as 1877, had
distinguished between the author and the narrator, calling George Eliot's
narrator "that second self who writes her books."

appearance of the author," but the essential shift from the intrusive narrator to the presumably invisible author is beyond dispute.

For the first statement postulating an invisible narrator we may turn to the author of what might be called the first modern novel. Flaubert's success with *Madame Bovary* was such that over and over again he was forced to disclaim any correspondence between Emma and a living person. The strongest and most elaborated protest occurs in a letter he wrote to Mademoiselle Lerager de Chantepie in 1857:

> Mme. Bovary has no foundation in fact. . . . I have put nothing into the novel of my own feelings or my own life. The illusion (if there is one) arises, on the contrary, from the impersonality of the work. It is one of my principles that one must not *write oneself in*. The artist must stand to his work as God to His creation, invisible and all powerful; he must be everywhere felt but nowhere seen.

As first glance the closing injunction seems remarkably similar to the statement which James Joyce was later to attribute to Stephen Dedalus, enunciating a process whereby "the artist, like the God of creation, remains within or behind or beyond or above his handiwork, invisible, refined out of existence, indifferent, paring his fingernails." There are, however, significant differences. Flaubert speaks for himself in his letter; Joyce speaks for his hero, who is not necessarily his own mature and considered spokesman, in his novel. Flaubert allows the presence of the author as narrator, albeit as a felt rather than a seen presence, in the work; Stephen seems to acknowledge the possibility of completely objective recording, at least in what he calls "the dramatic form." There is a difference between not writing oneself in and refining oneself out, as there is between an impersonalized work and a work produced by an indifferent creator, and as there is between a God who makes Himself felt in the world He has created and a God who concerns Himself only with Himself in whatever relationship He maintains with that world. Yet however we may discern and describe differences in their stated poetics, the art itself, in the case of both Flaubert and Joyce, has seemed to countless readers to bear witness both to God-like power and to the unique presence of the individual narrator. *Madame Bovary* begins in the first person, with the pronoun "we," offering a nameless narrator whose air of authority, once established, can melt into impersonal omniscience. *A Portrait of the Artist as a Young Man* is written consistently from the point of view of the young Stephen, tracing his awareness from the "moocow" of his childhood to the lyrically expressed decision of his maturity; the record ends with a first-person transcription from his diary. The narrators, therefore, assume different guises, but in each case the narrator is there, and the work is what it is because of his "invisible" presence.

Direct communication with the reader, as we have noted in works by Thackeray, Trollope, and George Eliot, does signify the self-conscious presence of the author as narrator. It is not, however, the only means of signifying narrator presence, because manifestations of the narrator, whatever his disguise, occur in every narrative. Unfortunately, much earlier critical discussion of the teller in the tale tended to accept overt self-acknowledgement as the only way in which a narrator makes his presence felt, and consequently directed considerable attention to the presence or absence of what was commonly called the intrusive author. Increasingly, in the present century, "an inordinate amount of time and energy . . . have been given over to celebrating his disappearance."[3] To understand the reason for this preoccupation we must briefly consider the seminal aesthetics of another heir to Flaubert, Henry James.

No other novelist has descanted with such care upon the art of the novel. In essays, reviews and prefaces written over the course of a lifetime devoted to his craft, James worked tirelessly, if tautologically, at his manifesto for novelists. Reduced to its essence his injunction was, in the words of Allen Tate, "Don't state . . . render! Don't tell us what is happening. Let it happen!" Tate's translation is admirably succinct, but James himself explains his technique for so rendering his subject as follows:

> I have already betrayed, as an accepted habit, and even to extravagance commented on, my preference for dealing with subject matter, for "seeing my story," through the opportunity and sensibility of some more or less detached, some not strictly involved, though thoroughly intelligent and interested, witness or reporter, some person who contributes to the case mainly a certain amount of criticism and interpretation of it. . . . Again and again, on review, the shorter things in especial that I have gathered into this series have ranged themselves not as my own impersonal account of the affair in hand, but as my account of somebody's impression of it . . . the impersonal author's concrete deputy or delegate, a convenient substitute or apologist for the creative power otherwise so veiled and disembodied. . . . I have . . . constantly inclined to the idea of the particular attaching case *plus* some near individual view of it; that nearness quite having thus to become an imagined observer's, a projected, charmed painter's or poet's — however avowed the "minor" quality in the latter — close

³ Walter J. Slatoff, *With Respect to Readers* (New York: Cornell University Press, 1970), p. 110. All page numbers in parenthesis are to this edition.

and sensitive contact with it. Anything, in short, I now reflect, must have seemed to me better — better for the process and the effect of representation, my irrepressible ideal — than the mere muffled majesty of irresponsible "authorship."[4]

Here James evidently equates "the mere muffled majesty of irresponsible 'authorship'" with the authorial "I," and names his irrepressible ideal as "the impersonal author." Like Flaubert, he conceives of the creative power as felt but not seen, but this power, we should note, is not refined out of existence since it is attached to a surrogate, elsewhere called a "reflector" or a "centre," speaking or interpreting, in fact narrating, within the story. As for the story itself:

> ... if it represents anything, [it] represents the subject, the idea, the *donnée* of the novel, and *there is surely no "school" ... which urges that a novel should be all treatment and no subject.* . . . This sense of the story being the idea, the starting-point of the novel, is the only one that I see in which it can be spoken of as something different from its organic whole, . . . in proportion as the work is successful the idea permeates and penetrates it, informs and animates it.[5]

I have italicized the reference to a "school" because, ironically enough, James was to become the unwitting founder of a fraternity which came close to requiring that a novel should be "all treatment and no subject." His critical remarks have been collected and annotated to become restrictive rules for the treatment of material, rules which largely apply to the management of point of view and which form a basis for the assessment of all other novels in comparison with *The Ambassadors.*

The precepts which have come to be called "Jamesian" were first set forth categorically by Percy Lubbock, who demonstrates his prescriptive interpretation of James's methods in this comment: "The art of fiction does not begin until the novelist thinks of his story as a matter to be 'shown', to be so exhibited that it will 'tell' itself. The thing has to look true and that is all. It is not made to look true by simple statement."[6]

Such a dictum denies that a host of earlier novelists were indeed practising the art of fiction. It rests upon the assumption that a responsible author tells nothing, but shows all. And for good or ill

---

[4] *The Art of the Novel*, ed. R. P. Blackmur (New York: Scribners, 1947), pp. 327-28. All page numbers in parenthesis are to this edition.

[5] *The Art of Fiction* (New York: Oxford University Press, 1948), p. 18. All page numbers in parenthesis are to this edition.

[6] *The Craft of Fiction* (London: Cape, 1921), p. 62.

23

the simplistic distinction between "telling" and "showing," without consideration of "telling" as a way of "showing" and "showing" as a form of "telling," has been with us ever since. As for making a thing "look true," how is this accomplished? Is showing, as opposed to telling, the guarantee of demonstrated truth? And to whom must it "look true"? A reader's belief is neither simply nor universally assured, and the inference that the success of a work of fiction is to be measured only by the reader's "belief" in it is highly dubious. A novel is the product of a tacit compact between reader and writer, and in whatever ways this compact may be affected by the Time Spirit, its essence is always the readiness of the reader to allow the teller of the tale his own way of telling in return for being shown something about human experience that is meaningful and memorable. One who requires only "real life" will not read a novel at all, but simply look about him.

Lubbock, however, was not alone in believing that "truth," in art, is a matter of creating the illusion of reality, and that an author commenting openly upon the motives and fortunes of his created characters vitiates such an illusion. In his survey of contemporary exponents of "point of view" theories, Friedman notes the agreement of Edith Wharton, Joseph Beach, Allen Tate, Mark Schorer, Ellen Glasgow, and Bernard de Voto with Lubbock's contention.[7] The sole demurral listed issues from E. M. Forster. In effect, Friedman's essay testifies to the rapid growth of a school comprising critics and novelists alike, and approves the body of criticism which seems to have sprung up in answer to the appeal of Phyllis Bentley: "The gradual decline in the use of direct comment, till at last heaved overboard with a splash by the twentieth century, is a fascinating study which should be attempted by a contemporary critic."[8]

This is an amusing metaphor, but on reflection it is less apt than it appears. The more recent critics to whom I am indebted have exposed other uses of direct comment than those signalled by address to the "dear Reader." In *The Rhetoric of Fiction*, 1961, Wayne Booth effectively demonstrates the ways in which a presumably invisible author may intrude to instruct the reader. In *With Respect to Readers*, 1970, W. J. Slatoff shows the limitations of preoccupation with "point of view" and extends Booth's discussion of the "implied author" to embrace a presence "more directly felt, and

[7] Norman Friedman, "Point of View in Fiction," *PMLA*, 70 (1955), 1166-68.
[8] Phyllis Bentley, *Some Observations on the Art of Narrative* (London: Home and Van Thal, 1946), p. 35.

distinctly human, than the total set of 'norms and choices' in a work." And in *The Teller in the Tale*, 1967, Louis Rubin argues the inescapable presence of the narrator, whatever guise or disguise the author chooses, consciously or subconsciously, for him. In a central chapter, Rubin analyzes the way Henry James himself makes direct comment in several novels, *The Ambassadors* included. He notes of this novel: "James considers it important for us to realize that Strether's first impression of Chad is going to remain with him for some time to come. So the author 'intrudes' and addresses the reader directly." Rubin then refers his reader to this excerpt:

Our friend [that is, James's and the reader's friend] was to go over it afterwards again and again — he was going over it much of the time that they were together, and they were together constantly for three or four days: the note had been so strongly struck during the first half-hour that everything happening since was comparatively a minor development.

It is this kind of authorial insistence that we see and remember things *his* way, which is only incidentally the way of his chosen centre, which prompts Rubin to exclaim: "The idea that Henry James, of all people, practised the art of fiction as if the personality of the novelist were not part of it, as if novels were not to appear to be 'written', has always seemed incredible to me. James not 'in' his novels? No novelist who ever wrote is more 'in' his novels than Henry James!"[9] And the studies of irony and ambiguity in James's novels that have been produced since Friedman's essay testify also to the presence of the author, however strenuous his attempts at self-effacement, in even the most dramatized "renderings" of experience.

The second half of the twentieth century has produced an increasing volume of criticism challenging the concept of the disappearing author, and returning to the respected views of E. M. Forster. Such challenges usually take account of what has happened to James in the hands of Jamesians, because James is central to any discussion of narrative guises, but they are informed largely by those considerations of reader response which have found articulation in the words of Wayne Booth, namely, that since literature does communicate attitudes and value systems which gratify the reader's need "to know where, in the world of values, he stands — that is, to know

---

[9] *The Teller in the Tale* (Washington: University of Washington Press, 1967), pp. 91-92. All page numbers in parenthesis are to this edition. Cf. Slatoff, p. 110. "I am more acutely and meaningfully aware of the presence narrating *The Ambassadors* than the narrator of *Vanity Fair*."

where the author *wants* him to stand," then literature does serve as an expression of what the author wants from his reader. To this extent, at least, the author makes himself known. He can no more disappear from this contract than the reader can.

I accept, therefore, the contention of these last-named critics that the author is always present, in one guise or another, in the work he creates. As a means of demonstrating this contention, and in deference to Lubbock's urging to "show" rather than "tell," we may look at some samples of the way in which different kinds of narrators have narrated the same story — the account of a proposal of marriage.

We have already noted Trollope as a self-acknowledged "intrusive" author, one of the masters of direct comment. Readers of *Barchester Towers* will doubtless recall that in his first abortive attempt to declare his love for Eleanor Bold, Mr. Arabin made the serious error of inquiring into her intentions with regard to the odious rival, Mr. Slope. The narrator did not hesitate to chide, demonstrating his sense of fun the while:

Poor Mr. Arabin — untaught, illiterate, boorish, ignorant man! — that at forty years of age you should know so little of the workings of a woman's heart! (288)

In narrating the second attempt, the archness of this voice is tempered with sentiment — to its detriment, some readers may find. Furthermore, there is very little action in the account of the successful proposal, and a great deal of commentary. In the ten pages devoted to it, a mere forty lines record the dialogue of the lovers, and the rest offers the narrator's description of the emotions accompanying this dialogue, or his comments upon so interesting a situation:

"Eleanor!" he again exclaimed; and in a moment he had her clasped to his bosom. How this was done, whether the doing was with him or with her, whether she had flown thither conquered by the tenderness of his voice, or he with a violence not likely to give offence had drawn her to his breast, neither of them knew. Nor can I declare. There was now that sympathy between them which hardly admitted of individual motion. They were one and the same, — one flesh, — one spirit, — one life. (466)

This is a narrator who is happy to indulge in the new-found happiness of the lovers whom he, as author, has created. Later, when others of the family circle have been drawn into the secret, he continues to comment at length on the prize such lovers share:

And now it remained to them each to enjoy the assurance of the other's love. How great that luxury is! How far it surpasses any other pleasure which God has allowed to his creatures! And to a woman's heart how doubly delightful!

When the ivy has found its tower, when the delicate creeper has found its strong wall, we know how the parasite plants grow and prosper. They were not created to stretch forth their branches alone, and endure without protection the summer's sun and the winter's storm. . . . What is the turret without its ivy, or the high garden-wall without the jasmine which gives it its beauty and fragrance? The hedge without the honeysuckle is but a hedge.

There is a feeling still half existing, but now half conquered by the force of human nature, that a woman should be ashamed of her love till the husband's right to her compels her to acknowledge it. We would fain preach a different doctrine. A woman should glory in her love; but on that account let her take the more care that it be such as to justify her glory. (470)

Thus speaks the intrusive narrator, ubiquitous and garrulous, openly delighting in the behaviour of his fictive lovers and preaching the doctrine he derives therefrom.

How different, indeed, when the narrator exhibits the reticence of Jane Austen. Long before Trollope indulged in what James called the habit of "giving himself away, which must often bring tears to the eyes of people who take their fiction seriously" (*The Art of Fiction*, p. 80), and even longer before James himself strove in *The Ambassadors* to dramatize the consciousness of Strether, Jane Austen was writing her stories in a remarkably impersonal manner and on the whole from a single point of view. Ubiquitous, within her narrow world, she might be, garrulous she might for dramatic reasons become, but sententious she never was.

Consider the account Jane Austen gives of Mr. Knightley's proposal to the newly chastened Emma:

While he spoke, Emma's mind was most busy, and with all the wonderful velocity of thought, had been able — and yet without losing a word — to catch and comprehend the truth of the whole. . . . She spoke then, on being so entreated. What did she say? Just what she ought, of course. A lady always does. She said enough to show there need not be despair — and to invite him to say more himself.[10]

Here we find Jane Austen eschewing direct dialogue, which elsewhere she uses impeccably, for an artistic purpose. Earlier she has presented a scene in which the pair converse about the fortunes of

[10] *Emma* (Boston: Houghton Mifflin, 1957), p. 338. All page numbers in parenthesis are to this edition.

others, having carefully prepared a setting in time and place for such a conversation. By this point in the action of the novel we are thoroughly acquainted with the characters of Emma and Mr. Knightley, though our perceptions of the latter have been formed largely through the refracted vision of the former. Consequently, at a first reading of the novel we are only slightly more prepared for his description of himself as a lover, however "indifferent," than is Emma herself. The effect of his declaration that she is his "dearest," his "most beloved Emma" is as strong on the reader as it is on Emma herself. It gives us pause, and the pause necessary to such a *dénouement* is marked by the author through a return to commentary. The emotional effect of Jane Austen's shift of method at this moment is strong, stronger than it would have been had she continued to record the words spoken by the woman she stands behind. The commentary goes on to explain and amplify the inner thoughts of her heroine, and then shifts again to an omniscient elaboration of a kind used later by George Eliot:

Seldom, very seldom, does complete truth belong to any human disclosure; seldom can it happen that something is not a little disguised, or a little mistaken; but where, as in this case, though the conduct is mistaken, the feelings are not, it may not be very material. Mr. Knightley could not impute to Emma a more relenting heart than she possessed, or a heart more disposed to accept of his. (339)

Having shifted her narrative stance to comment in this way, Jane Austen returns to the mind of Emma Woodhouse until she closes the chapter — and the most critical scene in the novel — with a final authorial assertion that "she was his own Emma, by hand and word, when they returned into the house" (340). A proposal has been made and accepted, and the dramatic realization of the act has been withheld from us; yet the comments of the author, alternately reticent and discursive, are of such charm and penetration that the reader is completely satisfied. He might even remember this as one of the great love scenes in literature, quite unaware of how little it is played out for him in the telling.

Henry James approaches the task of narrating a similar scene through what is commonly called "the dramatic method." For his own description of what is entailed in the pursuit of objectivity we may refer again to the Prefaces. In commenting upon his experiment in *The Awkward Age*, which Lubbock has praised as his most fully "dramatic" novel, James declares that the objectivity he achieved in a series of "scenes":

... came from the imposed absence of that "going behind" to compass explanations and amplifications, to drag out odds and ends from the "mere" storyteller's great property-shop of aids to illusion: a resource under denial of which it was equally perplexing and delightful, for a change, to proceed. ... I myself have scarcely to plead the cause of "going behind," which is right and beautiful and fruitful in its place and order. ... To make the presented occasion tell all its story itself, remain shut up in its own presence and yet on that patch of staked out ground become thoroughly interesting and remain thoroughly clear, is a process not remarkable, no doubt, so long as a very light weight is laid on it, but difficult enough to challenge and inspire great adroitness so soon as the elements to be dealt with begin at all to "size up." (*The Art of the Novel*, p. 111)

A discussion of Ibsen follows, interesting for its views of *A Doll's House*, *The Wild Duck*, and *Hedda Gabler*, in that James evaluates them according to whether light or heavy weight is laid upon the process of each. The return to his own novel is marked in these words:

The spectator or reader of Ibsen is to be caught at the worst in the act of attention, of the very greatest attention, and that is all, as a precious preliminary at least, that the playwright asks of him, besides being all the very divinest poet can get. I remember rejoicing as much to remark this, after getting launched in "The Awkward Age," as if I were in fact constructing a play; just as I may doubtless appear now not less anxious to keep the philosophy of the dramatist's course before me than if I belonged to his order. ... I tasted to the full the bittersweetness of his draught — the beauty and the difficulty ... of escaping poverty *even though* the references in one's action can only be, with intensity, to each other, to things exactly on the same plane of exhibition with themselves. Exhibition may mean in a "story" twenty different ways ... and the novel, as largely practised in England, is the perfect paradise of the loose end. The play consents to the logic of but one way, mathematically right. ... We are shut up wholly to cross relations, relations all within the action itself; no part of which is related to anything but some other part — save of course by the relation of the total to life. (113-14)

This exposition is very useful to our purpose. It makes clear that James fully understood the art of the drama, and was highly conscious in his use of a dramatic method within a novel form. The difficulties and the delights of the dramatist are equally savoured. But above all, James pinpoints the peculiar task of the dramatist, imprisoned within his form, to "make the presented occasion tell all its story itself," and to present action through dialogue without ever "going behind" his characters to explain or amplify. This is the task of showing without telling. Drama is meant to be played out, either in the arena of the reader's mind or better still on the stage itself. Explanations and amplifications are to be provided either by the imagination of the reader or by the collaborative efforts of a director and actors. The power of drama is in the "here and now" of the playing out, in the immediacy of action. As readers we find scenes in a novel to be "dramatic" when they appear to us as on a stage, as being "played out" while we read. They catch us "in the act of attention, of the very greatest attention."

In *The Spoils of Poynton*, there is a scene which may capture our attentiveness, though on reflection we may discover that "the presented occasion" tells less of the story than does the narrator presenting it:

"Have I kept you off today?" Fleda sadly shook her head, raising her arms a little and dropping them.

Her gesture of resignation gave him a pretext for catching at her hand, but before he could take it she had put it behind her. They had been seated together on Maggie's single sofa, and her movement brought her to her feet, while Owen, looking at her reproachfully, leaned back in discouragement. "What good does it do me to be here when I find you only a stone?"

She met his eyes with all the tenderness she had not yet uttered, and she had not known till this moment how great was the accumulation. "Perhaps, after all," she risked, "there may be even in a stone still some little help for you."

Owen sat there a minute staring at her. "Ah, you're beautiful, more beautiful than any one," he broke out, "but I'll be hanged if I can ever understand you! On Tuesday, at your father's, you were beautiful — as beautiful, just before I left, as you are at this instant. But the next day, when I went back, I found it had apparently meant nothing; and now, again, that you let me come here and you shine at me like an angel, it doesn't bring you an inch nearer to saying what I want you to say." He remained a moment longer in the same position; then he jerked himself up. "What I want you to say is that you like me — what I want you to say is that you pity me." He sprang up and came to her. "What I want you to say is that you'll *save* me."

Fleda hesitated. "Why do you need saving, when you announced to me just now that you're a free man?"

He too hesitated, but he was not checked. "It's just for the reason that I'm free. Don't you know what I mean, Miss Vetch? I want you to marry me."

Fleda, at this, put out her hand in charity; she held his own, which quickly grasped it in a moment, and if he had described her as shining at him it may be assumed that she shone all the more in her deep, still smile.[11]

[11] Henry James, *The Spoils of Poynton* (Norfolk, Conn.: New Directions, 1924), pp. 222-23.

30

The dialogue recorded here is accompanied by two distinct modes of describing the behaviour of the speakers. In the descriptions of action there are movements and gestures which could be readily converted into stage directions if the text were dramatized thus:

(OWEN and FLEDA are seated together on the sofa.)

Fleda: (shaking her head.) Have I kept you off today? (rises.)

Owen: (attempting to catch her hand.) What good does it do me to be here when I find you only a stone?

Fleda: (regarding him tenderly.) Perhaps. After all, there may be even in a stone still some little help for you.

(Pause. OWEN stares at her.)

Owen: Ah, you're beautiful. . . .

and so on.

But there is another kind of narrative description incorporated into the passage under question. It is a kind which may not be translated into the terms of stage direction, but which resembles rather the story-teller's "exhibititon" that we have seen James speak of. The author, seeking to amplify what interests him most (the heroine's state of mind), augments the regard she bends upon her suitor with the observation that it holds "all the tenderness she had not yet uttered, and she had not known till this moment how great was the accumulation." This, again in James's terms, "goes behind" Fleda to explain what cannot be dramatized. Further, the author ends the scene here isolated with a commentary reminiscent of Jane Austen's: ". . . if he had described her as shining at him it may be assumed that she shone all the more in her deep, still smile." The "it may be assumed that" is James's concession to the reader, an admission that he has parted company with the dramatic method in favour of an elaboration not to be accommodated by it. The resultant weaving together of dramatization and narration is as artful in his hands here as it is anywhere in his work. As Rubin has said, "When the technique of dramatization, for all its great advantages is revealing a situation, got in the way of the reader's being told what he needed to know, James did not scruple to violate it" (*The Teller in the Tale*, p. 99).

In reviewing these three samples of narration, we may trace a progress from obtrusive to unobtrusive commentary, or, in the critical terms noted, from the "intrusive" to the "implied" author. The unabashed authorial "I" of Trollope is certainly a more assertive narrator than are the others, but Jane Austen makes her less overt presence strongly felt. Indeed, some readers may agree with Slatoff that:

> ... her most devoted admirers ... may not be able to avoid becoming more aware of the narrator than of Emma and Mr. Knightley at the moment when, flustered by her own love scene, Jane Austen retreats wildly and gives Emma's answer to Mr. Knightley in the form of "What did she say? — Just what she ought, of course. A lady always does." (*With Respect to Readers*, p. 72)

As for Henry James, it may appropriately be said that he appears, in even his more "dramatic" scenes, as a disguised narrator. This is not to underestimate his perfecting of the point of view of the single character, or to deny that modern psychological fiction owes much to his insistence on the exploration of a single consciousness. It is rather to emphasize that his most acclaimed work, *The Ambassadors*, is in a fundamental respect as autobiographical as is Joyce's *A Portrait of the Artist as a Young Man*, since in it he dramatized his own conflicts as an artist caught between two civilizations and ways of life. And it is to reiterate that the teller is, in any case, always present in the tale.

If this is indeed so, then it follows that the novelist who knows it to be so, and who wishes to efface himself as much as possible, will seek those ways of telling which most effectively disguise his presence. One such way is that of "confronting the reader with the direct mental experience of the characters" peopling his work.[12] This is the way of what is now called the psychological novel, and its most characteristic component is the interior monologue. In his discussion of the way in which disparate emotional and sensory experience has been rendered in the fiction of the early part of the twentieth century, Leon Edel has commented definitively on what he describes as the "organized monologue," and on its raw material "the stream of consciousness," in the novels of Proust, Joyce, Dorothy Richardson, and Virginia Woolf. Edel relates the achievements of all these writers to "the new way of statement" which Dorothy Richardson found in the novels of Henry James. His significant contribution to criticism of the novel has since been augmented on a massive scale by Wayne Booth's *The Rhetoric of Fiction*, which

---

[12] Leon Edel, *The Psychological Novel* (London: Rupert Hart-Davis, 1955), p. 14. All page numbers in parenthesis are to this edition.

has become a necessary point of reference for any discussion of narrative techniques.

The other way of self-effacement for the novelist is the way I have chosen to examine — the way of substituting a surrogate narrator for the whole of the tale that is told and thereby producing a single and coherent "organized monologue." In conducting this examination my debt to both Edel and Booth is considerable, but my intention is not to extend what they have so intensively analyzed. The concern of this study is a tributary of the mainstream of twentieth-century fiction — novels in which the author's first creative act is the provision of a narrator who speaks as "I," but whose voice is emphatically and distinctively separated from that of the author himself. These are novels in which monologue is more than a component, in which it is intrinsic and continuous, and in which, to allude to James once more, the narrating "centre" is itself the *"donnée."* The writers of such novels undertake a task larger than detachment, and at the same time opposed to impersonalization — detachment and impersonalization being, as we have seen, less readily achieved than they are striven for. Theirs is a dramatic endeavour comparable to that of Browning in "Caliban upon Setebos" or Beckett in *Krapp's Last Tape*, requiring that the writer detach himself from his own experience and perception and immerse himself in those of a created other. Success in such dramatization in a work as extended as a novel is difficult to achieve, but perhaps less difficult than the task of preserving anonymity in narration. The ultimate disguise of the narrator occurs when he assumes the role of another person, and it may be the only truly effective disguise possible.

33

CHAPTER TWO

Incidental Monologues

I am a bad speaker, and the oration which I seem to render word by word did not flow with the lissom glide it has on paper. — VLADIMIR NABOKOV, *Despair*

The inner life of characters has always been a concern of fiction. Like the soliloquy in drama, the incidental monologue in the novel, whether reported or directly rendered, allows the reader access to motivation and deliberation otherwise unavailable to him.

The interior monologue is consequently a common feature of third person narration. It occurs whenever the narrator wishes to offer the reader a glimpse into the unspoken mental processes of a character — usually the protagonist — in his story. This he can do in one of three ways. He can offer narrative analysis, in which the character's thoughts are filtered through the mind of the narrator with some interpretive commentary; he can present the interior monologue directly by dramatizing the consciousness of the thinker; or he can fuse the two techniques together. The past two centuries have produced novels in which all three methods can be seen, and the twentieth century has seen some notable attempts to dramatize consciousness by means of what has been called the "stream of consciousness" technique.

The reported monologue, from the epic on, has been one of the instruments of the omniscient author, who verbalizes the private mental process of his created consciousness as if it were an oration prepared for an audience — which, indeed, it is.[1] Such a monologue

---

[1] In *The Nature of Narrative*, p. 179 f., Scholes and Kellogg distinguish between what they call the "rhetorical monologue" and the "psychological monologue." They relate the first of these to the epical formula used by Homer: *alla ti e moi tauta philos dielexate thymos* ("but why does my own

is of a piece with the narrative enclosing and supplementing it, and as such it echoes the authorial voice. The reader accepts paraphrase with commentary as a convincing digest of what may well have happened within the deeper wells of a human psyche, for it is a component in an organic rhetorical whole.

An example of this kind of reported monologue is found in a sequence from Stendhal's *The Red and the Black*:

"She leaned upon my arm in the strangest fashion!" Julien said to himself. "Am I a fool, or can it be true that she has a liking for me? She listens to me so meekly even when I confess to her all the sufferings of my pride! She, who is so haughty with everyone else! . . .

"It would be amusing if she loved me! Whether she loves me or not," Julien went on, "I have as my intimate confidant an intelligent girl before whom I see the whole household tremble, and most of all the Marquis de Croisenois. . . .

"But no, either I am mad, or she is making love to me; the more I shew myself cold and respectful towards her, the more she seeks me out. . . . My God, how handsome she is! How I admire her great blue eyes, seen at close range, and looking at me as they often do! What a difference between this spring and the last, when I was living in misery. . . ."

In moments of depression: "That girl is making a fool of me," Julien would think. "She is plotting with her brother to mystify me. . . .

"On the other hand, when Mademoiselle de La Mole fastens her great blue eyes on me with a certain strange expression, Comte Norbert always moves away. That seems to me suspicious; ought he not to be annoyed at his sister's singling out a *domestic* of their household? For I have heard the Duc de Chaulnes use that term of me."

At this memory anger obliterated every other feeling. "Is it only the love of old-fashioned speech in that ducal maniac?

"Anyway, she is pretty!" Julien went on, with the glare of a tiger. "I will have her. . . ."

At all hours of day, when he sought to occupy his mind with some serious business, his thoughts would drift into a profound meditation, and he would come to himself a quarter of an hour later, his heart throbbing with ambition, his head confused, and dreaming of this one idea: "Does she love me?"[2]

---

heart dispute with me thus?") and thence to the *agon*, oratory and soliloquy. They relate the second, which they find emergent in the works of Defoe, Richardson, and Sterne, to mimetic expressions of the mind in the process of formulating ideas and registering perceptions, and thus to stream of consciousness techniques.

[2] Stendhal, *The Red and the Black*, trans. C. K. Scott-Moncrieff (New York: Heritage, 1947), pp. 272-74. All page numbers in parenthesis are to this edition.

Thus ends a chapter in which Julien does a great deal of talking to himself. His thoughts are as carefully articulated as if he were speaking to someone else, or as if he were keeping a journal. Moreover, the account of his thoughts is accompanied with occasional stage directions ("with the glare of a tiger"); and repetitions ("her great blue eyes") endorse the narrator's contention, which is also reinforced by the summarizing final paragraph, that these were habitual preoccupations for Julien's consciousness at this time. And for good balance in a perfectly balanced novel, the succeeding chapter takes us into the mind of Mathilde, reciprocally contemplating the relationship:

Suddenly an idea dawned upon her: "I have the good fortune to be in love," she told herself one day, with an indescribable transport of joy. "I am in love, I am in love, it is quite clear! At my age, a young girl, beautiful, clever, where can she find sensations, if not in love? I may do what I like, I shall never feel any love for Croisenois, Caylus, *e tutti quanti*. They are perfect, too perfect perhaps; in short, they bore me." (276)

The rest of the chapter is occupied with her reflections upon her discovered condition, reflections exquisitely phrased in polished rhetoric that owes something to those descriptions of passion found in the literature she turns over in her mind, *Manon Lescaut, La Nouvelle Héloise*, the *Letters of a Portuguese Nun*, and so forth (276). She even formulates phrases used by her father, the narrator intervenes to explain to us, in the course of her carefully composed speeches to herself (277).

The characters depicted in these rhetorical interior monologues are highly individualized versions of recognizable social types. Their antecedents are to be found in ancient tragic drama, but the monologue device reveals them to us more intimately and more memorably than narrated descriptiton or dialogue can do.

Intimate and memorable revelation through monologue occurs also in another example from the realistic novels of the nineteenth century, Dostoevsky's *Crime and Punishment*. But in this novel we may note a fusion of interpretive and dramatizing techniques. Furthermore, what seems at first to be aptly termed the incidental monologue later assumes a greater significance within the narrative than occasional entries into a central consciousness would imply.

The novel begins in traditional fashion:

One sultry evening early in July a young man emerged from the small furnished room he occupied in a large five-storied house in Sennoy Lane, and turned slowly, with an air of indecision, towards the Kalinsky bridge.[3]

After only one more paragraph of exposition we are introduced to the thoughts of this young man, and they are indicative not only of his present state of mind, but of a predisposition to talk to himself which will continue throughout the novel:

> "Why should I be alarmed by these trifles when I am contemplating such a desperate deed?" thought he, and he gave a strange smile. "Man holds the remedy in his own hands, and lets everything go its own way, simply through cowardice — that is an axiom. I should like to know what people fear most: whatever is contrary to their usual habits, I imagine. But I am talking too much. I talk and do nothing, though I might just as well say I do nothing and so I talk. I have acquired this habit of chattering during the last month, while I have been lying for days together in a corner, feeding my mind on trifles. Why am I taking this walk now? Am I capable of *that*? Can *that* really be serious? Not in the least. These are mere chimeras, idle fancies that flit across my brain!" (2)

Our curiosity is engaged. Our memories of Hamlet are revived. And whereas we may note fleetingly that the author is using this monologue for an expository purpose, we are primarily aware of meeting a troubled soul directly through his introspection. The psyche in which this narrator interests himself is a disordered one, and commands our greatest attention.

Dostoevsky continues his story by means of a fusion of direct and indirect method. He tells us that heat, overcrowding, and odour combine to irritate his young man's already excited nerves. He tells us that his fierce disdain has reached such a pitch that he cares nothing about being seen in the street in tattered clothing and a "frightful" hat. Then, when passers-by deride his appearance, the monologue begins again:

> "I suspected this," muttered he, uneasily, "I foresaw it. That's the worst of it! Some trifle like this might spoil it all. Yet, this hat is certainly too remarkable; it looks so ridiculous. I must get a cap to suit my rags; any old thing would be better than this horror. Hats like these are not worn; this one would be remembered; people would think of it again some time later, and it might furnish a clue. I must attract as little attention as possible just now. Trifles become important, everything hinges on them." (3)

---

[3] Dostoevsky, *Crime and Punishment*, trans. Princess Alexandra Kropotkin (New York: John Winston, 1953), p. 1. All page numbers in parenthesis are to this edition.

At this point a pattern seems to emerge. We may notice that the two monologues have inscribed a circle; the opening question is resolved by the closing statement, and the preoccupation of this speaker with "trifles" has taken on a more sinister meaning. The contemplated "desperate deed," the mystifying "that," have become linked with an act to be performed in secret, for which it is important not to be noticed, and not to provide any tell-tale clue — in short, an act which is also a crime. From the evidence furnished by the monologues we may go on to observe that the narrator, while he comments on the strange behaviour of his agent, does not provide any information about the enterprise afoot. Only the words of the monologue do this:

> Although he reproached himself throughout his soliloquies with ir-
> resolution and a want of energy, he had accustomed himself, little by
> little, and, indeed, in spite of himself, to consider the realization of his
> dream a possibility, though he doubted his resolution. He was now
> rehearsing his enterprise, and his agitation was increasing at every
> step. (3)

Whereas this authorial comment confirms the knowledge we have received from the "soliloquies," it does not augment it. As the narrative proceeds, we depend more and more on the expressed thoughts of Raskolnikoff for enlightenment. The narrative describes his visit to the old woman, but the expressed thoughts demonstrate his interest in the whereabouts of her keys and her strongbox. The narrative reports the dialogue between student and usurer, but the expressed thoughts convey his loathing and horror as he leaves the place. The narrator will frequently confirm what we have learned from the monologues, but he will never anticipate their disclosures.

This dependence upon the monologue diminishes once the introduction of Raskolnikoff and his contemplated crime is accomplished, and once the enactment of the "dream" occurs. However, the protagonist's mental processes continue to occupy the narrator and the reader intermittently between action and dialogue. Frequently they melt into dreams, or nightmares rather, which seem real to reader as to dreamer (89-90, 200-03), and as frequently the interweaving of direct speech and interpretive analysis becomes so subtle as to be unnoticed. But Dostoevsky's use of monologue is beautifully adapted to the pattern of his plot. In chapter thirty-eight, which ends with Raskolnikoff's final confession, there is a street scene counterpoised to the one we have noted in chapter one. The monologue begins once more with a question, and ends once more in self-reproach

(388). The sequel to it is again inspired by the jostling of the crowd, and again he is jeered at — this time not because of his appearance, but because of his behaviour when, recalling Sonia's words, he kisses the earth at his feet. In the first scene he was on his way to the old woman's lodgings, now he makes his way to the police office. As he mounted the stairs to his victim, his thoughts were, "If I feel so timid now, what will it be when I come to put my plan into execution?" (4). Now he says to himself, "Supposing I were to go instead to the home of the superintendent of police and tell him everything in a private conversation? No, no! I will tell it to Powder; it will be over all the sooner" (390). The parallels are worked out in fine detail, and the monologues undergird the structure in perfect symmetry.

There is one final pattern to observe. The last words spoken in interior monologue by Raskolnikoff are very brief. A single sentence occurs two paragraphs before the end of the Epilogue: "He thought of this change, and said, 'Perhaps everything will now change!'" (407). Then the narrator continues from within the mind of Raskolnikoff, shifting unobtrusively from the third to the first person and back again:

He recollected how he had treated Sonia, but these memories hardly troubled him. . . . Under his pillow lay the New Testament. The book belonged to Sonia, it was the same from which she had read to him of the raising of Lazarus. . . .
He did not open it now, but one thought burned within him. Her faith, her feelings, may not mine become like them? Sonia was so happy that nothing could mar her joy. Seven years — only seven years! At the commencement of the happiness they were ready to look upon these seven years as seven days.   (407-08)

This leads to the culminating sentence, which points the reader to a new history — "a story of the gradual renewing of a man" — which lies outside the pages of the story of his crime and punishment. At the end, as at the beginning, Dostoevsky has allowed his protagonist to voice the truth which he, as author, can only corroborate. In his hands the "incidental monologue" has become a structural principle for the work which embodies it.

Dostoevsky's use of the interior monologue in this novel merits close scrutiny because the art with which he composes and incorporates Raskolnikoff's soliloquies may well have been refined by his earlier *Notes from Underground*, a monologue novel to which we shall return. The inner debate in which Raskolnikoff engages is couched in language less refined than that of Julien Sorel; it is formulated clearly, as if for the pen, but the impression of inchoate, dream-like perceptions accompanies each articulation to engage our imagination as well as our intellect, and to ensure a high degree of emotional involvement. Wayne Booth fiinds that:

Dostoievski [*sic*], like Shakespeare, derives some of his pre-eminence from his ability to show what a murky business the moral world really is while still keeping the lines of our moral sympathies clear. His criminals remain deeply sympathetic because he knows, and makes us know, why they are criminals and why they are still sympathetic. Not genuine ambiguity, but rather complexity with clarity, seems to be his secret. (*The Rhetoric of Fiction*, p. 135)

One way that he "makes us know" is, I think, through his use of the monologue, which serves to clarify the complexity for us.

Another modern note in the use of the monologue is sounded in Tolstoy's *Anna Karenin*. Tolstoy customarily dramatizes mental processes directly; a typical example of his use of the interior monologue is found when Darya Aleksandrovna looks back upon the fifteen years of her marriage:

"[I recall] the pregnancy, nausea, dullness of mind, indifference to everything, and, above all, homeliness. Even Kitty, young, pretty Kitty, looks worse, but I become positively homely when I am pregnant, — I know it."[4]

Darya's monologue, enumerating the sorrows of motherhood, runs on for four pages, leads to thoughts of Anna, and ends on the humorous note which is one of Tolstoy's gracious gifts to his reader:

"Anna has acted nicely, and I will not reproach her for anything. She is happy, is making another man happy, and is not crushed, like myself, but is, no doubt, as fresh as ever, brilliant, open to everything," thought Darya Aleksandrovna, and a cunning smile puckered her lips, especially because, thinking of Anna's romance, she thought in parallel lines of her own romance of nearly the same character with an imaginary, collective man, who was in love with her. She, like Anna, made a full confession of it to her husband. And Stepan Arkadevich's surprise and perplexity upon hearing that bit of news made her smile. (91)

The variation in method which marks Anna's interior monologue prior to her suicide is striking. Tolstoy abandons the fairly logical, coherent rhetoric he has used in such reflections as Darya's when he attempts to depict the disordered mind of his poor heroine as she approaches self-destruction. For four chapters at the close of Part

4 Tolstoy, *Anna Karenin*, trans. Leo Wiener (Boston: Dana Estes, 1904), III, 88. All page numbers in parenthesis are to the third volume of this edition.

Seven we are presented with a steadily disintegrating consciousness; Anna recollects the past, plans the present and the future, attempts to analyze her situation rationally, and all the time receives and records immediate sensory impressions; and the resultant jumbled expression employs the associative patterns of stream of consciousness:

"Yes, what was the last good thought I had?" she tried to recall it. "Tyutkin *Coiffeur*? No, not that. Yes, the thing that Yashvin talked about: the struggle for existence and hatred are the only things that unite people. Yes, you are driving there in vain," she mentally turned to a company of people in a four-in-hand, who were apparently driving out of town to have a good time. "The dog that you are taking with you will not help you. You can't run away from yourselves. . . . Yes, in Vronski was the triumph of a successful ambition. Of course, there was also love, but the greater share fell to the pride of success. He boasted of me. Now it is past. There is nothing to boast of. There is nothing to pride himself on, but much to be ashamed of. . . .

"My love is growing more passionate and selfish, and his is going out and going out, and that is why we are separating," she continued to think. "And it cannot be helped. For me everything is in him, and I demand that he should give himself more and more to me. But he wants to get farther and farther from me. That's it: before our liaison we kept going all the time toward each other, and since then we have been irresistibly going in various directions. And this cannot be changed. . . . He has not been loving me for quite a while. Where love ends, hatred begins. I do not know these streets at all. There are mountains and houses and houses — And in the houses are people and people — How many there are, — there is no end of them, — and all of them hate each other. Suppose I discover that which I wish in order to be happy. Well? I get a divorce. . . .

"Well, I get a divorce, and am Vronski's wife. Will Kitty cease looking at me the way she looked at me today? No. . . . Impossible! We diverge in life and I cause his unhappiness, and he mine, and it is impossible to change him and me. Every possible attempt has been made, — the screw is loose. Yes, a beggar with a child. She thinks that she ought to be pitied. Have not all of us been thrown into this world simply to hate each other, and, therefore, to torture ourselves and others? Gymnasiasts are walking there, and laughing. Serezha?" she recalled. . . . And the clearness with which she now saw her own life and that of others gave her pleasure. "Such am I, and Peter, and coachman Fedor, and that merchant, and all those people who live near the Volga, whither these advertisements invite to go, and everywhere, and at all times," she thought, just as she was nearing the low structure of the Nizhne-Novgorod station, and porters rushed out towards her. (324-27)

So Anna approaches her end. Her impressions of humanity, formed with increasing misanthropy and hopelessness as she observes a variety of people at the station and in the train, are refracted through her inner torment until she asks herself, "Why not put out the candle when there is nothing more to look at, when it is an abomination to look at all this?" (330). And inexorably we follow her until the moment the narrator describes for us, when "the candle, at which she had been reading the book that was filled with tribulation, deceits, sorrow and evil, flickered with a brighter light than ever, illuminated for her everything which had been in the darkness, began to crackle and grow dim, and went out for ever" (333).

The "yes" which frequently punctuates Anna's inner statements is not the only feature which reminds us here of Molly Bloom. In fact one reader has gone so far as to say:

... although Molly's culminating monologue in *Ulysses* is essentially comic, its technical affinities with Anna Karenina's culminating monologue are uncanny. The knowledge of feminine psychology which Jung praised in Joyce owes much to Joyce's sensitivity and to his marriage, no doubt, but also owes something to Tolstoy.   (*The Nature of Narrative*, p. 195)

However, before turning to Joyce, it is profitable to note the way in which Henry James explores the feminine psyche. His is the way we enumerated first, the way of the narrator's interpretive analysis. He commonly explores the monologue at second hand, filtering the thoughts of his hero or heroine through a benign and elucidating reportage. This he does, for example, in the case of Isabel Archer (now Osmond) in the scene which he himself calls "the best thing in the book" (*The Art of the Novel*, p. 57).

Isabel sits alone by a dying fire late into the night and reviews the experiences of her marriage. Her "exciting" inward life gathers itself into an "extraordinary meditative vigil" in the course of which she clarifies for herself, like Anna, her relationship with the man to whom she has bound herself. And like Anna, she sees "the whole man" where formerly she had seen only half, and recognizes her inability to become what he would have her be:

She knew of no wrong that he had done; he was not violent, he was not cruel; she simply believed that he hated her. That was all she accused him of, and the miserable part of it was precisely that it was not a crime, for against a crime she might have found redress. He had discovered that she was so different, that she was not what he had believed she would prove to be. He had thought at first he could change her, and she had done her best to be what he would like. But she was, after all, herself — she couldn't help that; and now there was no use pretending, playing a part, for he knew her and he had made up his mind.[5]

Now, taken out of its context in the chapter, there is nothing in this passage to suggest that we are sharing a mental process. This could just as well be a "direct comment" by an omniscient author. The chapter, however, begins with Isabel left alone to reflect on the injunction her departing husband has made; "Osmond had told her to think of what he had said; and she did so indeed, and of many other things" (370).

She thinks for eleven pages, and then we are told:

> She heard the small hours strike, and then the great ones, but her vigil took no heed of time. Her mind, assailed by visions, was in a state of extraordinary activity, and her visions might as well come to her there, where she sat up to meet them, as on her pillow, to make a mockery of rest. *As I have said*, she believed she was not defiant. . . . When the clock struck four she got up; she was going to bed at last. (380-81)

I have italicized the words which indicate the presence of the narrator. During the reported meditation he has intervened, occasionally and tactfully, to indicate a change in the direction of her thinking, or a motivation for a new thought. And occasionally the interpreted monologue contains a word or a phrase we can imagine coming from the lips of Isabel, were she speaking her thoughts aloud:

> What was coming — what was before them? . . .
> What would he do — what ought she to do? . . .
> Ah, yes, if Gilbert was jealous of her there was perhaps some reason. . . .
> How could he have known? What a mystery! What a wonder of wisdom! (379-80)

These questions and statements, translated into the present tense and given an I-narrator, would have the stamp of Isabel's immediate consciousness. But this is not the Jamesian method. What he gives is the point of view of the mind, not the mind itself at work; his concern is the representatiton of an inner vision, not the presentation of felt thought. "In studying the problems of his fixed and varying centres of consciousness," says Leon Edel, "Henry James was preparing the way for those who would follow and carry this technique to its logical conclusion: to record the action of the mind itself."

[5] Henry James, *The Portrait of a Lady* (London: Macmillan, 1882), p. 372. All page numbers in parenthesis are to this edition.

It seems we can detect both Tolstoy and James behind the achievements of James Joyce, for if the dramatic monologues of Anna are an influence on the monologue of Molly Bloom, then the methods of James may equally be an influence on Joyce's management of point of view in *A Portrait of the Artist as a Young Man.*

The opening sentences of Joyce's first novel quickly introduce us to a focus of consciousness who is remembering the experiences the story will contain. This focus is a "he," and not an "I," but he might as well be "I" because everything is narrowed down to his perceptions. And it is entirely appropriate, since the title of the work arouses expectations of the early life of an artist, that the first remembered experiences should belong to childhood, and that the first remembered activities of the "he" should pertain to the arts of storytelling and poetry.[6]

Another idea rapidly occurs to the reader coming to this novel for the first time. The teller is evidently selecting memories in no random fashion, for they are presented economically and chronologically — presented, in fact, as the shaping hand of the artist presents his material. A story of a young boy destined to be an artist is, it appears, being told by the artist he has become.

There seems no room for doubt by the beginning of the second section of chapter one. The "he" is now at school, playing football — or at least running fitfully along the fringes of the game. The author describes the evening air and the flight of the ball, "a greasy leather orb," in terms beyond the vocabulary of a small boy. Then a change of syntax occurs. "... his eyes were weak and watery. Rody Kickham was not like that: he would be captain of the third line all the fellows said" (8).[7] At this point the thoughts of the boy are couched in the language of the boy — they are monologuized. But the author who so accurately reproduces the responses of the child Stephen is a recorder who himself recalls the way a ball travelled the air "like a heavy bird through the grey light." The relationship between the Stephen who is the character, or perhaps *persona* would be a more accurate term, and the artist who is retrospectively inside his consciousness, is fused; it can only be an autobiographical relationship.

[6] James Joyce, *A Portrait of the Artist as a Young Man* (Harmondsworth: Penguin, 1960), p. 7. All page numbers in parenthesis are to this edition.

[7] In *The Teller in the Tale*, p. 157, Rubin cites this passage as evidence of his contention that Joyce is herein reinforcing his reader's awareness of the autobiographical mode, and enacting the role of "implied author" as described by Wayne Booth.

The question why, if this is so, Joyce chose to eschew I-narration, does not tease the reader for long, because Stephen's responses have an immediate quality more convincing than I-narration necessarily produces. Many of the recorded thoughts have no pronoun in any case:

How cold and slimy the water had been! A fellow had once seen a big rat jump into the scum. Mother was sitting at the fire with Dante waiting for Brigid to bring in the tea. She had her feet on the fender and her jewelly slippers were so hot and they had such a lovely warm smell! Dante knew a lot of things. (10-11)

Or sometimes a "you" is used:

It was green and wettish. But soon the gas would be lit and in burning it made a light noise like a little song. Always the same: and when the fellows stopped talking in the playroom you could hear it. (11-12)

Furthermore, the portrait continues to be painted through a kind of double vision. There are two Stephens discernible in the work: the actual Stephen whose daily experiences are reported in this factual way, and the incipient Stephen whose soul is sprouting and spreading wings. The rhetoric of the first Stephen is a spare, concrete prose:

In a few moments he was barefoot, his stockings folded in his pockets and his canvas shoes dangling by their knotted laces over his shoulders and, picking a pointed salt-eaten stick out of the jetsam among the rocks, he clambered down the slope of the breakwater. (170-71)

The rhetoric of the second Stephen is lyrical and highly self-conscious rhythmic prose:

The water of the rivulet was dark with endless drift and mirrored the high-drifting clouds. The clouds were drifting above him silently and silently the sea-tangle was drifting below him and the grey warm air was still and a new wild life was singing in his veins. (171)

These two styles alternate in close proximity, as above, or they melt into each other, as in the case of the first example cited. We may observe that the prose rhetoric is used for the actions of the young man, the poetic rhetoric is reserved for the reflections of the developing artist. This is clearly seen in the passage that follows, where waking memories prompt the young dreamer to write his dreamt villanelle down:

45

An enchantment of the heart! The night had been enchanted. In a dream or vision he had known the ecstasy of seraphic life. Was it an instant of enchantment only or long hours and years and ages?

The instant of inspiration seemed now to be reflected from all sides at once from a multitude of cloudy circumstances of what had happened or of what might have happened. The instant flashed forth like a point of light and now from cloud on cloud of vague circumstance confused form was veiling softly its afterglow. . . .

The veiled windless hour had passed and behind the panes of the naked window the morning light was gathering. A bell beat faintly very far away. A bird twittered; two birds, three. The bell and the bird ceased; and the dull white light spread itself east and west, covering the world, covering the roselight in his heart.

Fearing to lose all, he raised himself suddenly onto his elbow to look for paper and pencil. There was neither on the table; only the soup plate he had eaten the rice from for supper and the candlestick with its tendrils of tallow and its paper socket, singed by the last flame. He stretched his arm warily towards the foot of the bed, groping with his hand in the pockets of the coat that hung there. His fingers found a pencil and then a cigarette packet. He lay back and, tearing open the packet, placed the last cigarette on the window ledge and began to write out the stanzas of the villanelle in small neat letters on the rough cardboard surface.   (216-18)

Such transitions from an enchantment of the heart to the mundane realities of the flesh are common throughout the novel. The reader comes to accept unquestioningly the double picture of a youth who drains "his third cup of watery tea to the dregs" one moment and remembers "pale sorrows and the fragrance falling from soft branches" the next, or who listens to his belly counselling him to stuff greasy stew into it prior to listening to the music of Shelley and experiencing a "cold lucid indifference in his soul" (173-75, 102-03). It is as if the poet in embryo, the true centre of the work, is held in tension between the weak-eyed boy growing up in Dublin and the mature, fully-fledged artist who contemplates him.

Perhaps this tension is due to Joyce's desire to achieve in this work what he himself described, first in *Stephen Hero*, as "epical form." He expresses this idea through Stephen's exposition in *A Portrait*:

The simplest epical form is seen emerging out of lyrical literature when the artist prolongs and broods upon himself as the centre of an epical event [such as the story of Icarus and Daedalus?] and this form progresses till the centre of emotional gravity is equidistant from the artist himself and from others. The narrative is no longer purely personal. The personality of the artist passes into the narration itself, flowing round the persons and the action like a vital sea.   (214)

Had Joyce chosen the customary autobiographical convention of I-narration for his own story, the narrative would have taken on a "purely personal," or lyrical, form. On the other hand, a work which is in its nature self-reflective cannot be expressed in the dramatic form as he defines it. Therefore, discussions of how far he has achieved his ideal of the dramatic form (if such it be) in *A Portrait* seem misguided. As it is, the fledging and flight of Stephen Dedalus can be seen to be "the centre of emotional gravity" in the novel, equidistant from the artist who presents it and the reader who considers it. Or, to express it in Joyce's other way, the image of the emergent artist is seen in mediate relation to the writer and to the reader. Certainly the personality of the artist, Joyce's "second self" as Booth designates it, passes into the narration itself to flow around persons and action like a vital sea, for Joyce's very conscious use of water imagery endorses the metaphor.

There is one other statement in Stephen's description of the epical form which merits attention. It is the only form for which he offers an example: "This progress [from lyrical to epical] you will see easily in that old English ballad *Turpin Hero* which begins in the first person and ends in the third person" (214).

Perhaps attention should be drawn to the similarity between the title he cites and the title of Joyce's first draft of *A Portrait, Stephen Hero*. Perhaps this similarity demonstrates that Joyce was consciously striving for the effects he attributes to epical form in his autobiographical novel. An interesting twist is provided to the analogy of *Turpin Hero* in that *A Portrait* begins in the third person and ends in the first person. Are we to deduce anything from this?

We can at least observe that the device of the journal grants the writer the privilege of true interior monologue, while at the same time finally reducing the distance between himself and his protagonist. In fact there is a *double-entendre* in the journal entry for March 24, "Crossing Stephen's, that is, my green..." (249). And the journal provides not only a recapitulation for themes and epiphanies recorded earlier, but a duplication of the two Stephens we have previously discerned. The one dispassionately records meetings with Davin, with Cranly, with Lynch, with Mulrennan. The other lyrically reflects upon a dream, upon "wild spring," upon the sound of hoofs in the night, upon the spell of arms and voices calling him away. And finally the Stephen whom we first encountered listening

47

to a story told by his father becomes the Stephen who addresses his old, his primordial father, the artificer (253).

The dual aspects of Stephen Dedalus, body and spirit, are drawn together less extricably in the interior monologues of *Ulysses*. It is in this great work that Joyce takes the reader on the journey that was mapped out and signposted in *A Portrait* — the journey into the mind itself at the moment of thought, conscious and even subconscious. And in Stephen's interior monologues the transition between spiritual and physical can take place literally with the speed of thought.

> They are coming, waves. The whitemaned seahorses, champing, brightwindbrindled, the steeds of Mananaan.
> I mustn't forget his letter for the press. And after? The Ship, half twelve. By the way go easy with that money like a good young imbecile. Yes, I must.[8]

To the reader who comes to *Ulysses* from *A Portrait* there is no doubt about the identity of Stephen. Not only are his name and his ash plant familiar, familiar also is his relationship to the authorial voice continuing his story. What is new is the gradual, almost imperceptible shift from "he" to "I." In the first two sections of chapter one, in dialogue with Mulligan and Haines and in discharge of his teaching duties, the "I" of Stephen appears fitfully. But by the third or "Proteus" section the flickering candle, to use Tolstoy's metaphor for Anna's consciousness, has become what Virginia Woolf called "that innermost flame." We are ineluctably within the mind of Stephen Dedalus, and that modality will shape our response to his world.

When Joyce was asked about his use of the stream of consciousness technique in *Ulysses*, he always referred to the monologue novel he had read in his twenties, *Les lauriers sont coupés* by Edouard Dujardin (1888). Doubt has been cast upon the seriousness of Joyce's tribute, but Dujardin responded gratefully, and half a century after his novel had been published he defined his technique in words quoted by Edel in *The Psychological Novel*, p. 54:

> The internal monologue, in its nature of the order of poetry, is that unheard and unspoken speech by which a character expresses his inmost thoughts, those lying nearest the unconscious, without regard to logical organization — that is, in their original state — by means of direct sentences reduced to a syntactic minimum, and in such a way

---

[8] James Joyce, *Ulysses* (Harmondsworth: Penguin, 1968), p. 44. All page numbers in parenthesis are to this edition.

as to give the impression of reproducing the thoughts just as they come into the mind.

As Edel goes on to point out, this description owes more to Dujardin's reading of Joyce than it does to consideration of his own novel, in which the continuous present tense unfolding of his protagonist's consciousness impedes any objective narrative flow and thus creates frequent awkwardness. Joyce solves this problem by maintaining an authorial position outside Stephen sufficiently to enable us to digest external changes of time and place. We are made to see with Stephen, and to follow the associations in his mind, but we are also invited to watch his walk along the shore from the outside.

> His feet marched in sudden proud rhythm over the sand furrows.
> ... He stared at them proudly, piled stone mammoth skulls. ...
> He had come nearer the edge of the sea and wet sand slapped his boots. ... Here, I am not walking out to the Kish lightship am I? He stood suddenly, his feet beginning to sink slowly in the quaking soil. Turn back. (48-49)

Nor is it Stephen Dedalus alone whom we accompany in this double way. Once we have left him on the seashore we immediately encounter another and quite different consciousness. Leopold Bloom is a good man, a lovable man, but his perceptions are limited, and it is important that we recognize his limitations lest we accept his own evaluation of his experiences in the way we accept the less lovable Stephen's. Consequently, we quickly discover in his thought patterns a sensory emphasis. He feeds the cat and feeds his wife and feeds himself. He lusts after a girl and protectively loves his own girl. He defecates between thoughts of fertilizing the garden and dressing with Molly. Then, when his peregrinations through Dublin have begun, his monologues are interrupted by snatches of conversation with friends and neighbours which show an increasing discrepancy between what he thinks is going on and what is actually happening. When he gives Bantam Lyons the newspaper it is clear to the reader that Bantam understands something quite unknown to Bloom (87). When he sits musing about Paddy Dignam's death it is clear that his more insensitive fellow mourners see him very differently from the way he sees himself (89-102). When he finally tends to Stephen after the street brawl, the divergence between his awareness and Stephen's awareness of the situation creates the relationship towards which the entire double voyage has been moving (539-85).

49

Louis D. Rubin suggests that Joyce shows us Bloom "from above" for a definite purpose:

> ... compared with Stephen's monologue, that of Bloom flows much less smoothly from within, and is interrupted with much greater frequency in order that we may look at Bloom. In part this is because Bloom is a much more richly comic character, but that too is significant, for by its very nature comedy precludes identification with a character, and demands that we view the character from outside and above. For the success of the Bloom episode it is important that our view be from above, so that we see Bloom both as he appears to the others, as he appears to himself, and as he really is. (*The Teller in the Tale*, p. 167)

Rubin goes on to postulate that we sympathize with Bloom, but we identify with Stephen, whose veracity is never in doubt. With this I cannot agree, but there is indeed a differentiation in the technique of presentatiton which encourages the reader to identify Stephen with the implied author and to regard Bloom as a more detached creation. Bloom appears to be viewed "from outside and above" more frequently and in clearer perspective than Stephen needs to be. Even his longest and most expansive interior monologue is prefaced by the saccharine prose of "Nausicaa" in which he plays his part as a figure before he takes centre stage as monologuist.

It is in this scene, however, that Bloom's monologue slides into the fragmentary pastiche of ideas and images characteristic of stream of consciousness writing. He is sleepy, enervated by his spontaneous ejaculation. His erotic dreams are none the less unexhausted, and they revolve as always around Molly. The events of the day flicker in and out of the present lassitude in elusive associations which the patient reader can seek to trace, until sleep overtakes him:

> We'll never meet again. But it was lovely. Goodbye, dear. Thanks. Made me feel so young.
> Short snooze now if I had. Must be near nine. Liverpool boat long gone. Not even the smoke. And she can do the other. Did too. And Belfast. I won't go. Race there, race back to Ennis. Let him. Just close my eyes a moment. Won't sleep though. Half dream. It never comes the same. Bat again. No harm in him. Just a few.
> O sweety all your little girlwhite up I saw dirty bracegirdle made me do love sticky we two naughty Grace darling she him half past the bed met him pike hoses frillier for Raoul to perfume your wife black hair heave under embon *senorita* young eyes Mulvey plump years dreams return tail end Agendath swooney lovey showed me her next year in drawers return next in her next her next. (379)

In the last paragraph of this sluggish stream we see prefigured a device which is used at the end in Molly's monologue. This, the longest interior monologue in the novel, runs for forty-five pages without interruption or punctuation. In it the faithless Penelope unweaves the tapestry of the day's events from the changeless loom of the earth mother, and the reader must untangle the threads by providing syntax as best he may. It is worth the effort. The absence of punctuation corresponds to the absence of inhibition; the absence of any interpretive comment allows a full-spated flow which becomes a torrent.

In the monologues of Stephen and Bloom the narrator continued to be present, as we have noted, to record the movements of the thinkers and to allow us an accompanying external view, especially of Bloom. But Molly scarcely moves. She is supine, in the quiescent state favoured by psychoanalysts when they seek to liberate free association in their patients — a couch, darkness, silence. Such movements as she does make — from bed to chamber pot and back — are incorporated into the flow of her thought (690-93); such external stimuli as exist in the darkened bedroom — Poldy's snores (699), the recurrent train whistle (675, 683, 684), and the sound of George's church bells (693) — are woven into the free associative patterns created by Molly's libido.

The result is a unity unparalleled elsewhere in *Ulysses*. The monologue is free, in that no external constraints of any kind are placed upon it, but it is also a form, an organic whole from its opening "yes" to its closing "yes," a cohesive declaration of affirmation. It can be isolated and examined as an expression of what Lawrence called the "underconsciousness," and what Freud has made familiar as the "subconscious." It can also be compared to the prayer in ancient narratives, or the soliloquy in Elizabethan drama, as a self-revelation which holds absolute validity for those who overhear it. Finally, it can be seen as the expression of thoughts which not even Molly Bloom would verbalize openly, and as such it sets a seal on Joyce's exploration of the way individuals move in their own spheres of consciousness. *Ulysses* offers us three individual consciousnesses which can be grasped only through their interior monologues; Stephen actively abstracting and synthesizing experience, Bloom passively recording and tabulating perceptions, and Molly receiving and integrating sensations.

More recent novelists, inheriting examples of the monologue such as the above and seeking to render experience which is inner as well as outer, psychological as well as circumstantial, have a variety of forms and techniques from which to choose. They can report in Stendhal's way, rhetorically developing an organized monologue. They can follow the model provided by Dostoevsky, and use directly rendered "soliloquies" as a principle of formal cohesion. They can present an ordered synopsis of musings in the fashion of Henry James, or trace shifting and fragmented perceptions in the fashion of Tolstoy and Joyce. But Scholes and Kellogg find that one of the major trends in twentieth-century characterization is "away from the attempt to penetrate the individual psyche," and toward a focus on the apprehension of "impressions which claim no absolute validity as facts." They share Auerbach's distrust of methods "which dissolve reality into multiple and multivalent reflections of consciousness," and maintain that interior monologues as a means of characterization have been largely abandoned of late because "writers have lost faith in the realness of realism. . . . A consciousness of a gap between the apprehendable and the true . . . makes realistic presentation of character far less necessary than it had seemed in the previous century" (*The Nature of Narrative*, p. 203).

Auerbach's questioning of the modern movement away from objective reality is not applicable to *Ulysses*, because Joyce, as we have seen, carefully preserves "a viewpoint outside the novel from which the people and events within it are observed." His suggestive comments occur in the final chapter of *Mimesis*, where he considers the method of Virginia Woolf to conclude that it is a technique which gives us "not merely one person whose consciousness (that is the impressions it receives) is rendered, but many persons, with frequent shifts from one to the other. . . . It basically differs from the unipersonal subjectivism which allows only a single and generally very unusual person to make himself heard."[9]

Some have described Virginia Woolf as an exponent of stream of consciousness, while some have described her as a writer of reported internal monologues, and others have denied either description. So far I have assumed with Booth, Friedman, and Hoffman that the terms may be interchangeable.[10] But Auerbach's description of *To*

9 Auerbach, *Mimesis* (Princeton: Princeton University Press, 1953), pp. 534-36.

10 *The Rhetoric of Fiction*, p. 54. Cf. also Melvin Friedman, *Stream of Consciousness: A Study in Literary Method* (New Haven: Yale University Press, 1955), and Frederick Hoffman, *Freudianism and the Literary Mind* (Baton Rouge: Louisiana State University Press, 1945), pp. 126-29. Divergent views should be noted in James Hafley, *The Glass Roof: Virginia Woolf as Novelist*

the Lighthouse as a "multipersonal representation of consciousness" introduces a new idea for consideration. Certainly when we compare Virginia Woolf's achievements with those of Joyce, to whom she so frequently is compared, there is a notable difference in the way she approaches the expression of consciousness. Perhaps the difference stems from her dislike of the "egoistic" quality which she discerned in Richardson and Joyce, or perhaps from her concern for a transcendent reality beyond the self. Her famous dictum about recording "the atoms as they fall upon the mind in the order in which they fall" occurs in an essay in which she discusses the method of Joyce — a method which she herself rejects for reasons she gives a few lines later:

> Is it the method that inhibits the creative power? Is it due to the method that we feel neither jovial nor magnanimous, but *centred in a self which, in spite of its tremor or susceptibility, never embraces or creates what is outside itself and beyond?* ... This method has the merit of bringing us closer to what we are prepared to call life itself; did not the reading of *Ulysses* suggest how much of life is excluded or ignored, and did it not come with a shock to open *Tristram Shandy* or even *Pendennis* and be by them convinced that there are not only other aspects of life, but more important ones into the bargain.[11] (My italics)

When we consider statements by Virginia Woolf herself, the method she develops from *Jacob's Room* to *The Waves* seems to be an attempt to embrace or create what is outside the self or beyond it. When we examine that method through the analysis of Robert Humphrey, it seems to be simply an indirect, as opposed to a direct, treatment of monologue.[12]

Humphrey discards Dujardin's definition of stream of consciousness, quoted earlier in this chapter, and suggests that we should examine the work of four so-called stream of consciousness writers, Joyce, Woolf, Dorothy Richardson, and Faulkner, to discover what they have in common. This inductive procedure can lead to only one conclusion, that stream of consciousness is less a method than a subject matter. For Humphrey, stream of consciousness is one kind

---

(Berkeley: University of California Press, 1954) and Walter Allen, *The English Novel: A Short Critical History* (New York: Dutton, 1954), p. 336.

[11] Virginia Woolf, "Modern Fiction," in *Collected Essays*, Vol. 2 (London: Hogarth, 1966), pp. 107-08.

[12] Robert Humphrey, *Stream of Consciousness in the Modern Novel* (Berkeley: University of California Press, 1954). All page numbers in parenthesis are to this edition.

of psychological fiction, distinguished from the works of James or Proust "precisely in that it is concerned with those levels of consciousness that are more inchoate than rational verbalization — those levels on the margin of attention" (2-3). Technical differences are accounted for as divergent means towards the same end. These differences he separates into four categories.

The first technique to be enumerated Humphrey calls the "direct interior monologue." He describes such a monologue as dramatic and unedited, with no sign of authorial presence. The last chapter of *Ulysses* is a perfect example of such a monologue.

The second technique, the "indirect interior monologue," allows for third-person treatment and the occasional interpolation from the author. Such would be the appellation Humphrey would give to Tolstoy's treatment of Anna in the excerpt we have noted, and he cites *Mrs. Dalloway* and *To the Lighthouse* as examples of the indirect interior monologue in the work of Virginia Woolf.

The third technique Humphrey calls the "omniscient technique." In it, the author stands between the reader and the character and describes consciousness in the third person. But his subject is stream of consciousness, not event, and is therefore essentially disorganized. Humphrey cites Dorothy Richardson as an exponent of this technique, noting that in *Pilgrimage* Miriam's consciousness is represented in all its "unformulated, unspoken, incoherent state" (34).

The fourth and final major technique Humphrey calls "soliloquy." This, he says, presents "the psychic content and processes of a character directly from character to reader without the presence of an author, but with an audience tacitly assumed.... The point of view is always the character's, and the level of consciousness is usually close to the surface" (36). As examples of this method he cites *The Waves* and Faulkner's *As I Lay Dying*, which I propose to consider separately as rhetorical, or formalized, monologues.

All four methods are unified, in Humphrey's analysis, by "the actual texture of consciousness," which the author presents mimetically, by whatever means of imagery, free association, and discontinuity he finds to suit his purpose of rendering the "inchoate" nature of the subject (63). And an attempt is made in all stream of consciousness writing to suggest a record of thought *as it occurs*, within circumstantial context, deep within a private layer of the mind.

Humphrey's differentiations stem from his classification of stream of consciousness as genre and interior monologue as technique, and the resultant thesis that there are many technical variations possible within the stream of consciousness form. The names he gives to those variations he describes are debatable, particularly in the case of the term "soliloquy," which I have already suggested belongs properly in the context of drama, where there are two audiences predicated. However, his concept of variant forms of monologue is useful, especially where so distinctive an artist as Virginia Woolf is concerned. The "multi-personal representation" to which Auerbach has drawn attention in his analysis of *To the Lighthouse* becomes in Humphrey's schema "indirect interior monologue," which is described as allowing authorial interpretation and variable viewpoints.

The shifting stance which Auerbach traces in "The Brown Stocking" sequence of *To the Lighthouse* is quickly discernible in the opening pages of *Mrs. Dalloway*. The first chapter begins with a single statement of reported speech, "Mrs. Dalloway said she would buy the flowers herself," and at once the leap is made, through Virginia Woolf's favourite transitional device "For," into the mind of Clarissa. A stabilizing interjection, "thought Clarissa Dalloway," confirms this movement, and then we are away:

> What a lark! What a plunge! For so it had always seemed to her when, with a little squeak of the hinges, which she could hear now, she had burst open the French windows and plunged at Bourton into the open air. How fresh, how calm, stiller than this of course, the air was in the early morning; like the flap of a wave; chill and sharp and yet (for a girl of eighteen as she then was) solemn, feeling as she did, standing there at the open window, that something awful was about to happen.[13]

With unobtrusiveness Virginia Woolf achieves several effects in these opening paragraphs. She makes it clear that Clarissa Dalloway's thoughts are her subject. She suggests the scene — a lady leaving her house after an exchange with her maid. She distinguishes past from present to introduce a reverie. But in reporting the reverie — and it is a report in the third person, not a transcription in the first person — she occupies a position at once within and without the mental process she describes. As author she interjects "thought Mrs. Dalloway," but how much of what follows is her voice rather than Clarissa's? Who says, "For so it had always seemed to her ...," "... which she could hear now ...," "for a girl of eighteen

---

[13] Virginia Woolf, *Mrs. Dalloway* (London: Hogarth, 1933), p. 7. All page numbers in parenthesis are to this edition.

55

as she then was . . ."? Are these the reflections of Clarissa or inter-pretive statements by the author?

This passage is so apt an illustration of Humphrey's "indirect interior monologue" that it is the one he quotes in support of his definition. It contrasts sharply with Joyce's use of monologue, where every atom is indeed recorded as it falls in the random order in which it falls. As we read *Mrs. Dalloway* it is the narrating con-sciousness which makes its presence felt, rather than the individual psyches which it enters. For as the novel proceeds, the same ambig-uous veiling of the recorded thoughts covers thinkers other than Clarissa. It covers Peter Walsh:

> Well, I've had my fun; I've had it, he thought, looking up at the swinging baskets of pale geraniums. And it was smashed to atoms — his fun, for it was half made up, as he knew very well; invented, this escapade with the girl, made up, as one makes up the better part of life, he thought — making oneself up; making her up, creating an exquisite amusement, and something more. But odd it was, and quite true; all this one could never share — it smashed to atoms. (83)

Peter's reflections, like those of Clarissa, melt into the reflections of the narrator, and are expressed in the same language, so that as he walks on up the street a transition to narration is effected in a perfect rhythmic flow. So imperceptible are the shifts from interior to ex-terior that the lulled reader assimilates the narrated passages as part of the same steady stream of reflection, the leaden circles of expo-sition dissolving, as it were, in the air of contemplation.

Not only is it difficult to distinguish external from internal in *Mrs. Dalloway*, it is also frequently impossible to distinguish one character from another by the manner of his thinking. The single authorial voice permeates all the scenes which in conventional novels would be presented through dialogue. There is a double distancing from the spoken words as they are recorded, for they are refracted through the consciousness of the speaker, and then through the consciousness of the narrator. One example of this occurs in the tea-shop scene between Miss Kilman and Elizabeth:

> She did not much like parties, Elizabeth said. Miss Kilman opened her mouth, slightly projected her chin, and swallowed down the last inches of the chocolate eclair, then wiped her fingers, and washed the tea round in her cup.
> She was about to split asunder, she felt. The agony was so terrific. If she could grasp her, if she could clasp her, if she could make her hers absolutely and for ever and then die; that was all she wanted. But to sit here, unable to think of anything to say, to see Elizabeth

turning against her; to be felt repulsive even by her — it was too much; she could not stand it. The thick fingers curled inwards.

"I never go to parties," said Miss Kilman, just to keep Elizabeth from going. "People don't ask me to parties" — and she knew as she said it that it was this egotism that was her undoing; Mr. Whittaker had warned her; but she could not help it. She had suffered so horribly. "Why should they ask me?" she said. "I'm plain, I'm unhappy." She knew it was idiotic. But it was all those people passing — people with parcels who despised her — who made her say it. However, she was Doris Kilman. She had her degree. She was a woman who had made her way in the world. Her knowledge of modern history was more than respectable.

"I don't pity myself," she said. "I pity" — she meant to say "your mother," but no, she could not, not to Elizabeth. "I pity other people much more."

Like some dumb creature who has been brought up to a gate for an unknown purpose, and stands there longing to gallop away, Elizabeth Dalloway sat silent. Was Miss Kilman going to say anything more?

"Don't quite forget me," said Doris Kilman; her voice quivered. Right away to the end of the field the dumb creature galloped in terror.

The great hand opened and shut.

Elizabeth turned her head. The waitress came. One had to pay at the desk, Elizabeth said, and went off, drawing out, so Miss Kilman felt, the very entrails of her body, stretching them as she crossed the room, and then, with a final twist, bowing her head very politely, she went. (199-200)

Throughout this scene Elizabeth's words are reported indirectly, as heard by her companion. This should mean we are inside the consciousness of Miss Kilman, but no, we are sometimes outside the greedy and suggestively sinister figure as she consumes an eclair and flexes her thick fingers. Is this the picture of her Elizabeth sees? Does Elizabeth consciously compare herself to a dumb creature at a gate? Or is this how Miss Kilman sees her? Or is it, like the analogy of "the solitary traveller" (87), what the narrator sees as she contemplates both? The torments of feeling split asunder, and of having her entrails drawn across the room, we can confidently attribute to the consciousness of Doris Kilman, as coming from a level beneath that which is readily verbalized. But is it the same suffering creature who notices the turn of the head, the advent of the waitress, the final polite bow across the room? We are not sure, nor does it matter. The spoken words of dialogue occupy fewer than eight lines in a five-page sequence, and of them at least three can be construed as Miss Kilman's habitual self-reflection. What she says to Elizabeth Dalloway is in any case relatively insignificant. The important re-

57

actions all take place in three minds — Kilman's, Elizabeth's, and the narrator's — and which is where is seldom determinable.

The novel presents many such scenes in which the author renders the interplay between characters indirectly, so that objective events are distilled for the reader through a funnel of subjectivity. This is the unique technique of Virginia Woolf; no other novelist so interfuses the flow of multiple consciousness with his own distinctive voice, or renders multipersonal experiences as though they were washed over by water. The meeting and interchanging of personal identity in some elemental form of life — mist above the trees (16) — the collect and fall of waves on the shore (61) — the solemn, ashen-pale sky (280) — lends to her stream of consciousness novels the aura of a continuous monologue, and it is the monologue of the artist herself. For as an artist Virginia Woolf is distinctively capable of providing the bridge from incidental monologues to the monologue novel itself.

CHAPTER THREE

Formalized Monologues

But first, Reader, I will give you a word of warning. This is a foot-off-the-ground novel that came by the left hand. And the thoughts come and go and sometimes they don't quite come. . . . For this book is the talking voice that runs on, and the thoughts come, the way I said, and the people come too, and come and go, to illustrate the thoughts, to point the moral, to adorn the tale. — STEVIE SMITH, *Novel on Yellow Paper*

From the monologue as a constituent of the novel, we turn to the novel constituted by monologue. All the novels discussed hereafter are termed "monologue novels," which is to say that they are novels in which monologue is the major, if not the sole, means of narration. In such novels the author provides a voice or voices which he has created as "I" speakers, and the voice(s) can be either mimetic or rhetorical.

Once more we should note the difference between a psychological and a rhetorical concern in the monologue. Those monologue novels which I consider psychological work through mimesis; in them the speaker is single and is characterized, through what he says and his manner of saying it, as the discrete purveyor of his own experience. As such he may appear sympathetic or antipathetic, clear-sighted or confused, honest or self-dramatizing, but he is above all convincingly human, and clearly distinguishable from the author of the work.

Rhetorical monologues, or "soliloquies" in Humphrey's terminology, are less concerned with psychological accuracy than they are with a memorable expression of some perceived truth which is metaphysical, transcending particulars of time, place and circumstance. Such monologues seem to derive from the writer's impulse to understand, and to cause the reader to understand, the true nature of some part of universal human experience. Therefore they have as their focus less the character speaking than the audience addressed, and mimetic verisimilitude yields to rhetorical effect. I have termed these variants of the monologue "formalized" because they are shaped by the author into formal concomitant units of an ultimate whole. The whole is always multipersonal, each speaking voice being measurable by other voices speaking in their turn to confirm or elaborate the single message of the author, who speaks over and through the monologues by his formal structuring, his ordering of material, and his fashioning of rhetoric.

The formal structuring of rhetorical monologues can best be understood as a demonstration of that symbolic form described by Edmund Wilson in his book *Axel's Castle*. When Wilson discusses Joyce's *Ulysses*, he speaks of the author's seeking to "express directly in words states of mind which do not usually in reality make use of words at all." The use of unassociated metaphor to express what is customarily unverbalized is the hallmark of the Symbolist movement in poetry; it is also, however, a feature of much twentieth-century fiction other than that of James Joyce. Whenever a novelist seeks to transcend the conventional meanings of naturalistic literature he must engage, like the Symbolist poet, in the invention of special kinds of image-laden language. And when he further seeks to unify a complicated association of ideas and sensations in a variety of consciousnesses, then he needs to find a form which is itself a metaphor for those unique personal feelings which are, in the final analysis, his own. Symbolism can thus be seen to provide both substance and shape to the formalized monologue.

In the twentieth century, two of the greatest exponents of the formalized monologue have been Virginia Woolf and William Faulkner. We have already noted in *Mrs. Dalloway* some of the features I attribute to this kind of monologue. There is no doubt about the rhetorical nature of the monologues in *The Waves*.

This novel begins with an evocation of eternity, when Bernard sees "a ring" hanging above him in a loop of light,"[1] and ends with the defiance of Death, when the same Bernard hurls himself against the enemy (211). In the course of his summation in the last section

---

[1] Virginia Woolf, *The Waves* (London: Hogarth, 1943), p. 6. All page numbers in parenthesis are to this edition. Cf. the opening of Henry Vaughan's poem "The World": "I saw eternity the other night / Like a great ring of pure and endless light."

of the novel, Bernard states as his purpose the explanation of the meaning of his life (168), which — since he is not one but many people — is the meaning of life unqualified:

"I am not one person; I am many people; I do not altogether know who I am — Jinny, Susan, Neville, Rhoda, or Louis; or how to distinguish my life from theirs." (196)

Granted such scope, it is hardly surprising that the six voices whose monologues compose the novel, like the nature descriptions which provide an elemental background, should seem to enunciate a timeless unity. At every new reading of *The Waves* one is struck by the litany effect as each monologue follows each in a seamless rhythmic prose. The speeches seem to emanate from one voice, and as Guiguet has noted, "to define that voice is to solve the whole problem of *The Waves*."[2]

In the first sequence of speeches, when the six speakers, as children, express immediate sensations, the impression of litany is at once produced:

"The grey-shelled snail draws across the path and flattens the blades behind him," said Rhoda.
"And burning lights from the windowpanes flash in and out on the grasses," said Louis.
"Stones are cold to my feet," said Neville, "I feel each one, round or pointed, separately."
"The back of my hand burns," said Jinny, "but the palm is clammy and damp with dew."
"Now the cock crows like a spurt of hard, red water in the white tide," said Bernard.
"Birds are singing up and down and in and out all round us," said Susan. (7)

Of course this language is too well-ordered to be considered the language of children, whether spoken out loud as the quotation marks suggest, or formed inwardly in response to sensation. The six statements are divisible into three parallel pairs. In each pair, or couplet, the two "speakers" are complementary, male and female. The first couplet elaborates sight, the second temperature, and the third sound. Each line stems from its predecessor by association. Rhoda looks at the grass, Louis regards the same plane from a greater distance, seeing the effect of light on the grasses where Rhoda had bent close to watch a snail. Neville picks up the cue of "burning" to speak of the "cold" stones, and finds another antithesis

[2] *Virginia Woolf and Her Works* (London: Hogarth, 1965), p. 284.

61

in the smooth or the pointed surfaces which his foot feels. Jinny picks up both "burning" and "cold" to translate sensation from foot to hand. Bernard's reference to the cock's crow develops the idea of wetness in Jinny's description of her clammy, damp palm, and incorporates a new contrast between white and red. Susan builds on the sound of the cock, and refers to the singing of other birds.

Such associative patterns continue throughout. In a statement that precedes the quoted passage, Susan examines a caterpillar, prefacing Rhoda's examination of a snail, and Susan's reference to the sound of birds is followed by Louis's reference to the sound of a beast stamping In the entire continuum every transition from one associative sequence to another is signalled by the declaration "Look at ..." from one of the voices.

This is very artful composition. The speakers articulate an integrated response to sensory experience in an undifferentiated mode of expression. The most striking feature of the stylized statements is the patterning, which is present not only in the overlapping imagery and repetitive syntax of each linked sentence, but also in the rhythm of the sequence as a whole. Not only is each statement formalized into a balanced metrical unit, but the clauses naming the speaker also form a pattern: twice they occur at the end of the statement, twice in the middle, and twice again at the end. Thus their positioning reinforces the sustained irony of the whole. Whatever is being represented by the conventions of direct speech, it is not the spontaneous and consecutive dialogue of children, nor, indeed, of adults.

The rhythmic flow of this passage is maintained throughout the monologues, each "speaker" using consistent devices of repetition and parallelism:

[Louis:] "Here is Bernard. . . . He is composed; he is easy." (22)

[Susan:] "All here is false; all is meretricious." (23)

[Jinny:] "Here are my clean white stockings. Here are my new shoes." (30)

[Rhoda:] "My attitude is one of defiance. I am fearless. I shall conquer." (40)

[Bernard:] "One's mind is primed; one's lips are pursed." (42)

[Neville:] "We are about to part. . . . Here are the boxes, here are the cabs." (43)

These examples are drawn from the second section of the work, but any sequence provides similarly striking repetitions. The cumulative effect is one of poetry, so that someone listening to the monologues read aloud might construe the text as lines of verse. The insistent emphasis on rhythm is one which Virginia Woolf recorded in her Notebook as the controlling idea of the work: "The rhythm of the waves must be kept going all the time."

Susanne Langer defines rhythm through this same example of waves, and adds to it an interesting observation about the use of symbol in art:

> But the most impressive example of rhythm known to most people is the breaking of waves in a steady surf. Each new comber rolling in is shaped by the undertow flowing back, and in its turn actually hurries the recession of the previous wave by suction. There is no dividing line between the two events. Yet a breaking wave is as definite an event as one could wish to find — a true dynamic *Gestalt*.
>
> Such phenomena in the inanimate world are powerful *symbols* of living form, just because they are not life processes themselves. The contrast between the apparently vital behaviour and the obviously inorganic structure of ocean waves, for instance, emphasizes the pure semblance of life, and makes the first abstractions of its rhythm for our intellectual intuition. That is the prime function of symbols. Their second function is to allow us to manipulate the concepts we have achieved. This requires more than a recognition of what may be termed 'natural symbols', it demands the deliberate making of expressive forms that may be deployed in various ways to reveal new meanings. And such created *Gestalten*, that give us logical insight into feeling, vitality and emotional life, are works of art.[3]

Virginia Woolf might well agree that in writing *The Waves* she deliberately made "expressive forms" in order to reveal "new meanings," because her diary entries from 1928 to 1931, when the work was forming in her mind and on paper, repeatedly record her dissatisfaction with the old forms of fiction, indeed with fiction itself, and her desire to "saturate every atom":

> I mean to eliminate all waste, deadness, superfluity: to give the moment whole: whatever it includes. Say that the moment is a combination of thought; sensation; the voice of the sea. . . . Why admit anything to literature that is not poetry — by which I mean saturated?[4]

Furthermore, the new meaning which she strove to embody in words she seems to conceive in terms of a dichotomy of the kind Langer describes as being inherent in the simultaneous rolling in and flowing back of the breaking waves:

[3] *Feeling and Form* (Boston: Routledge and Kegan Paul, 1953), pp. 128-29.

[4] *A Writer's Diary*, p. 139. Cf. pp. 108, 159. All page numbers in parenthesis are to this edition.

Now is life very solid or very shifting? I am haunted by the two contradictions. This has gone on for ever; will last for ever; goes down to the bottom of the world — this moment I stand on. Also it is transitory, flying, diaphanous. I shall pass like a cloud on the waves. Perhaps it may be that though we change, one flying after another, so quick, so quick, yet we are somehow successive and continuous, we human beings, and show the light through.   (141)

Although we might notice, in this extract, the writer's own use of the repetition we have noted in the passages from the first section of *The Waves* ("so quick, so quick"), the more significant feature is the comment which follows: ". . . we are somehow successive and continuous we human beings, and show the light through."

The structure of *The Waves* demonstrates the simultaneously successive and continuous nature of the six human beings who speak its monologues. Communal passages like the one quoted earlier occur at intervals throughout the work, but they are separated by monologues from each of the six, in which present-tense declarations are made. The result, as David Daiches observes, is that "each character formalizes his impressions and attitudes into what for Virginia Woolf is quite a rigid piece of prose."[5] The rigidity relaxes only in the last long chapter, where Bernard's "summing-up" becomes more discursive and conversational. This uncharacteristic rigidity is in strong contrast to the fluid style we have noticed in *Mrs. Dalloway*. Virginia Woolf's own appellation of "statues" (157) seems singularly apposite to the effects produced by the rhetoric of *The Waves*.

This is not to say that physical immobility always prevails. The movement of the six is faithfully recorded in their musings; they walk together and apart; they enter rooms where the others are waiting; they travel in trains and buses, even in a foreign country, in Rhoda's case. Each occupies his own sphere. Here is Jinny at the ball:

"Now the car slides to a stop. A strip of pavement is lighted. The door is opening and shutting. People are arriving; they do not speak; they hasten in. There is the swishing sound of cloaks falling in the hall. This is the prelude, this is the beginning. I glance, I peep, I powder. All is exact, prepared. My hair is swept in one curve. My lips are precisely red. I am ready now to join men and women on the stairs, my peers. I pass them, exposed to their gaze, as they are to mine. Like lightning we look but do not soften or show signs of recognition. Our bodies communicate. This is my calling. This is my world. All is

---

[5] *Virginia Woolf* (Norfolk, Conn.: New Directions, 1942), p. 107.

decided and ready; the servants, standing here, and again here, take my name, my fresh, my unknown name, and toss it before me. I enter." (73)

This is Jinny's stasis, she is suspended in her world. We may note that her gaze encompasses the setting so as to depict it for us. All the signposts that are usually provided by an author are within the text of the monologue — the place, the time, the occasion, Jinny's appearance. This, however, is the poised moment before movement begins. In the paragraphs that follow, Jinny moves: "I tread naturally on thick carpets. I slide easily on smooth-polished floors, I now begin to unfurl." The unfurling becomes more and more dynamic as she says, "I flow," "I flutter," "I ripple," "I stream," "I fall." The prose gathers momentum; the rhythms of dance infuse it, Jinny's sensual undulations ripple through it. This is mimesis of a different kind; it is not so much a character as it is a mode of being that is expressed through such language.

There follows another mode of being as Rhoda enters. Is it the same room? We do not know at first. It seems to be a ballroom full of people, at night, but we share Rhoda's terror for two paragraphs before we are sure: "Jinny rides like a gull on the wave, dealing her looks adroitly here and there.... What then is the knowledge that Jinny has as she dances?" (76). While Jinny delights in the dance, Rhoda feels trapped; while Jinny invites — "O come!", Rhoda is seized; her partner is a threat; "a million arrows pierce" her:

"... I doubt; I tremble; I see the wild thorn tree shake its shadow in the desert.

"Now I will walk, as if I had an end in view, across the room, to the balcony under the awning. I see the sky, softly feathered with its sudden effulgence of moon. I also see the railings of the square, and two people without faces, leaning like statues against the sky. There is, then, a world immune from change." (77)

The remarkable contrast in mood is mirrored again in the prose. But always, behind the language, we hear the same voice. Similarly, we can trace this voice in the statements of the others:

[Neville:] "In a world which contains the present moment... why discriminate? Nothing should be named lest by so doing we change it. Let it exist, this bank, this beauty, and I, for one instant, steeped in pleasure. The sun is hot. I see the river.... A leaf falls, from joy. Oh, I am in love with life!... I do not know myself sometimes, or how to measure and name and count out the grains that make me what I am." (58-60)

65

[Susan:] "But who am I, who lean on this gate and watch my setter nose in a circle? I think sometimes (I am not twenty yet) I am not a woman, but the light that falls on this gate, on this ground. I am the seasons, I think sometimes, January, May, November; the mud, the mist, the dawn." (70-71)

[Louis:] "I have signed my name ... already twenty times. I, and again I, and again I. Clear, firm, unequivocal, there it stands, my name. Clear-cut and unequivocal am I too. Yet a vast inheritance of experience is packed in me. I have lived thousands of years. I am like a worm that has eaten its way through the wood of a very old oak beam. But now I am compact; now I am gathered together this fine morning." (118-19)

[Bernard:] "But it is only my body ... that is fixed irrevocably — so I desire to believe. I think more disinterestedly than I could when I was young and must dig furiously like a child rummaging in a bran-pie to discover myself." (153)

Common to all these utterances is the preoccupation with the mystery of self-hood, the declarative "I am." Though the six characters are differentiated in prevailing temperament, the fundamental character of their language is the same, immune from change. They draw on the same body of imagery, and traverse, as Bernard says, the same "sunless territory of non-identity" (83).

This is why many readers have solved Guiguet's problem of the voice in *The Waves* by declaring that the speaker throughout is Virginia Woolf. Hafley, for example, says that "one person is arranging and telling everything," and deduces that the one person is the author.[6] One can hardly quarrel with this. Nevertheless, the attempt to furnish a dramatic form in *The Waves* is surely significant. The reader is asked to accept the illusion that the characters are speaking for themselves. Perhaps the consistency of style and tone is intended to undergird the final equivalence of the six spokesmen. Perhaps the formal rhythms are deliberately designed to subjugate the representation of fully individualized personalities. Whatever the intention or design, the indisputable effect is that only the content serves to distinguish the monologuists each from one another, because the voice is the same throughout.

Certain generalizations can be made about the core content around which each character's ideas and images cluster. For Jinny it is a valiant, nerve-racked sexuality, the banner of the body. Her continual question, "Who will come if I signal?" (137), describes

---

6 James Hafley, *The Glass Roof: Virginia Woolf as Novelist* (Berkeley: University of California Press, 1954), p. 108.

the pattern of her life, and her statement, "My imagination is the body's" (156) is a summing-up of everything about her. For Susan, in some ways her counterpart, an equivalent sensuality derives from the principle of fecundity and the images of harvesting; earth-bound and complacent, Susan contemplates her cupboards, her garden, her children, and her husband with the same unwavering pride of possession. There is in her fierce maternal watchfulness a strain of the obsessive: "Sleep, I say, and feel within me uprush some wilder, darker violence, so that I would fell down with one blow any intruder, any snatcher, who should break into this room and wake the sleeper" (122). For Rhoda, in strong contrast to Susan, patterns of thought are mental rather than physical. She is haunted by fears of falling, and continually aware of the walls of the mind growing thin (159). She escapes the terrors of contact with the others by contemplating abstract shapes; she removes herself from the torture of "here and now" by imaginary journeys away from the real world (113, 146). In her, the death-wish which all six seem to share as they walk in the garden of Hampton Court (161-65) is most clearly enunciated. "Now I will relinquish; now I will let loose. Now I will at last free the checked, the jerked-back desire to be spent, to be consumed" (117).

The men are differentiated in similar terms. Neville has a more physical nature than his two male friends and is engrossed in personal relationships. His "Come closer" (142, 129) is the equivalent of Jinny's "Come." His life is organized around creature comforts and ephemeral liaisons; yet his true world is the world of poetry and roses, of Catullus and Shakespeare, in the quiet of the room which is his sanctuary (126-28, 140-42). Louis, like Rhoda, undertakes imaginary pilgrimages (144) and wrestles with feelings of anxiety and inadequacy (91). Though he becomes affluent, he keeps his attic room (121) because he prefers a view over chimney pots (156) which enables him to see life in terms of broken, soot-stained roofs (144). "Over broken tiles and splinters of glass I pick my way" (155). Bernard is, like Susan, strongly marked with a sense of community; he seems to initiate the reunions of the six, in part out of his dislike of solitude (154); and he alone reminisces at length in the company of a stranger (168-211). This is, however, typical of Bernard, since he is the acknowledged narrator of the group — the phrasemaker (110, 134, 154, 173, 194) who is best able to articulate the communal, deeply felt need to experience the "world seen without a self" (204).

Hermione Lee has discussed the individualization of the six speakers in a way I find helpful. She says:

Given a formal, undifferentiated style, distinctions can only be made on the basis of the images. This brings the novel dangerously close to a play of humours in which bits of the human personality are parcelled out among the different characters. Bernard's twisting of little toys, Neville's call to "one person," Rhoda's dreamland of swallows and pillars, Louis's vision of the Nile, Susan's screwed-up pocket-handkerchief and Jinny's yellow scarf seem at times like routine reminders of which "humour" is speaking. But there is a counterweight to this limiting technique of identification in the fact that many images are shared between the characters. . . . As they grow older, the voices become more distinct. But the narrative sustains their common consciousness through their participation in each other's private figures of speech. . . . [7]

We might add that the dominant image shared in this way is that of Percival, the beloved companion continually evoked, though never heard, who seems to be the symbol as well as the substance of their communion:

". . . without Percival there is no solidity. We are silhouettes, hollow phantoms moving mistily without a background." (87)

"It is Percival . . . who makes us aware that these attempts to say, 'I am this, I am that,' which we make, coming together like separated parts of one body and soul, are false." (98)

"Let us hold it for one moment . . . this globe whose walls are made of Percival, of youth and beauty, and something so deep sunk within us that we shall perhaps never make this moment out of one man again." (104)

It is out of such differences and such correspondences that the relationship of the speakers is created, the language endorsing the unity in diversity which is their constant spoken theme. Ralph Freedman has called the resultant fusion of voices the "lyrical I."[8] In treating the novel from the standpoint of lyric poetry, he maintains that in the speakers of the monologues "Je suis [becomes] Je est," and the result is a fusion of two aspects of being, the personal feeling self and the impersonal observer. This is the duality Bernard articulates:

". . . how incompletely we are merged in our own experience. On the outskirts of every agony sits some observant fellow who points; who

[7] *The Novels of Virginia Woolf* (London: Methuen, 1977), pp. 164-65.

[8] *The Lyrical Novel* (Princeton: Princeton University Press, 1963), p. 33.

whispers as he whispered to me that summer morning in the house where the corn comes up to the window, 'The willow grows on the turf by the river. The gardeners sweep with great brooms and the lady sits writing.' Thus he directed me to that which is beyond our predicament; to that which is symbolic, and thus perhaps permanent." (176)

But Bernard also articulates the fusion, "To be myself (I note) I need the illumination of other people's eyes, and therefore cannot be entirely sure what is myself" (83). "For this is not one life; nor do I always know if I am man or woman, Bernard or Neville, Louis, Susan, Jinny, or Rhoda — so strange is the contact of one with another" (199).

In Bernard's repeated identification of himself with the others we see a working out of the concept Virginia Woolf discussed in a letter to John Lehmann: "I wanted to . . . keep the elements of character; and yet that there should be many characters and only one; and also an infinity." This one character, or "lyrical I," is, I think, not so much the character of the author as it is a character she conceived as a possibility of perfect being. It may be true, as Guiguet has pointed out, that the six characters of *The Waves* present six aspects of Virginia Woolf, but ultimately they converge and blossom into a single entity, the six-sided flower (162). The result is that character is presented in the novel not in psychological, but in metaphysical terms, and the rhetoric provides a bridge which channels "these dancing impressions to one line, capable of linking all in one" (155).

The desire to "link all in one" is what is ultimately communicated through the monologues of *The Waves*, and it is the author's desire in creating the work. Virginia Woolf has sought to convey, through the form and content of the novel, her own concept of the timeless unity of all human experience. Therefore the monologues cannot be separated into a series of stylized quotations from the consciousness of six characters, for what is presented is in no way mimetic. In place of character we have what Blackstone calls "pure *being*: the hidden life"; in place of existence we have essence; in place of the ego we have the collective unconscious, which Jung tells us is "like an unceasing stream or perhaps an ocean of images and figures which drift into consciousness in our dreams or in abnormal states of mind." This is why Bernard, in summation, can become all six essences in one. When he does so, we recognize in his aesthetic assertions, in his confessed limitations, and in his defiance of death, a re-statement of those habitual concerns of Virginia Woolf herself.

More than this, we recognize in Bernard's repudiation of his life-long habit of story-telling and phrase-making Virginia Woolf's own distrust of words. "There are no words. Blue, red — even they distract, even they hide with thickness instead of letting the light through. How describe or say anything in articulate words again?" (204). And, in paradox, the fusion of Woolf with Bernard is endorsed by what follows, as Bernard "sees" the house and garden previously described only in the third-person interludes, and duplicates the decorative language of the interludes in depicting that scene (207). The "little language" he has sought (169) comes only with "the child's words of one syllable" (203) with which the third-person narrator closes the novel: "The waves broke on the shore" (211).

Whether the ending denotes victory or defeat has been debated. Guiguet asks the question, "Does this [ending] mean nothingness sanctioning the victory of time and space, our enemies and our defeat, or does it mean eternity sanctioning our victory over their vain and illusory opposition?" It seems to me that the answer, considering the paradoxical nature of the work as a whole, must be "Both." What I have called Virginia Woolf's metaphysical concern is precisely this — that the loss of self is of all things both most fearful and most desirable. She believes in an ultimate order of experience which is by its nature incommunicable and which can be known only by the individual at significant moments of being; yet the intensity of her desire to share that knowledge with others drove her to find, in *The Waves*, a unique expression of that very primacy of self which she sought to deny.

Faulkner's world is a very different one. There is considerable distance between Hampton Court and Yoknapatawpha County. Despite this, Faulkner was developing rhetorical monologues at the same time as Virginia Woolf, and with similar effect. And as in the development from *Mrs. Dalloway* to *The Waves*, so in the development from *The Sound and the Fury* to *As I Lay Dying* the monologue moves more and more from a psychological to a metaphysical frame of reference.

Perhaps *The Sound and the Fury* fits the category of monologue novel less readily than others, since the fourth of its four parts is a conventional narrative. The device of a culminating third-person narration is, however, essential to the meaning of the novel, since it provides in effect the key to the whole. Faulkner uses a shift in point of view as William Golding frequently does, to illuminate everything that has gone before. Only when the reader has reached the end can he read the monologues, and particularly the first one, with enlightenment.

In his artistic control of his material, Faulkner the artificer is always Faulkner the manipulator, shifting focus, shifting time, as if both were interlocking segments in a three-dimensional puzzle, each dimension provided by a distinctive speaker. The structure of *The Sound and the Fury* demonstrates the artifice. Part One occurs on April 7, 1928, as a monologue by the thirty-three-year-old idiot Benjy, and within two pages of it we are transported back in time to his childhood. By the associative principle of stream of consciousness we traverse with Benjy-Maury back and forth across the years, encountering Caddy and Jason and a Quentin who is mysteriously now male, now female, sharing sensations which alternately provoke the bellowing of grief and the quietening of comfort. The limitations of the mind in which we are imprisoned intrigue us at first, but soon we are engaged in a poetry which enables us to see everything as Benjy does, through "a mirror" provided by his distorted consciousness, and we are satisfied with the "smooth bright shapes," though as yet they have no form.[9]

Part Two takes us back to almost eighteen years before. Now it is the thought of the male Quentin that we share, in the formulations provided by a mind which is akin to that of Stephen Dedalus. At first the clear, formal rhetoric disarms us; time — the subject of the first three paragraphs — has rocked to a standstill and our reading can follow, temporarily, a linear path. Then come the italics signifying a shift, followed by an incoherence which will continue to flicker in and out of the reportage. We accompany a mature developed mind this time, a sensitive mind — but it soon shows itself to be as disordered, as non-sane in its own way, as poor Benjy's. And the question begins to tease us as we read: Which condition is more to be pitied? All we have learnt as the prose returns to a steady motivated flow at the end of Quentin's monologue is that he is "contemplating an apotheosis" as he dresses to walk across Harvard Square to the post office (195-97).

Part Three returns us to 1928, but to a day previous to Benjy's day. Here we are within the mean mind of Jason, and we find ourselves sharing reminiscences which offer no mystifying transitions. Far from being arrested, or sick, this is the mind of a man renowned

9 William Faulkner, *The Sound and the Fury* (New York: Random House, 1946), p. 94. All page numbers in parenthesis are to this edition.

in the town for his "smartness" (267). And what it exposes to us is more odious by far than idiocy or dementia. This monologue, furthermore, acts as a bridge to the narrative of Part Four, setting each character into a clearly defined place in the contemporary home. Like the others it has a clear unity of its own, being largely concerned with the girl Quentin and beginning and ending with reference to her, "Like I say, once a bitch always a bitch" (198, 280).

Jason's day was Good Friday. Benjy's day was Easter Eve. The culminating section of the novel takes place on Easter Day, and its focal point is Dilsey, who becomes an alter-ego for the reader. "I seed de beginnin, en now I seen de endin" (313). Conversely, once the reader has seen the ending, he can at last see the beginning, and begin to understand all that has come between.

Now a summary such as this does poor justice to the work, but it does raise some interesting questions. The monologues have seemed convincingly mimetic, but on completing each narrative unit we find that its apparent representation reveals itself to be a marvellous artifice. How can an idiot, who can hear only what he can smell (193), report so faithfully what he has heard, or know the words for what he remembers and feels? If he does know the words, how can he voice them, whose only sound is "the grave hopeless sound of all voiceless misery under the sun" (332)? And to whom does he voice them? Is not the monologue to which we listen the creation of someone who reports what Benjy might be speaking — to himself — if Benjy were able to express his voiceless misery in a style or register suited to his externally perceived limitations?

Reflection raises similar questions with regard to Quentin. To whom does he divulge his tormented thoughts immediately prior to his self-destruction? In a realistic novel the reader would be offered the suicide letter he wrote and it would serve the purpose of plot well enough. But in a realistic novel plot is of prior importance. Here the voice of Quentin is so much more important that the reader must himself piece a narrative sequence together from the apparently random disclosures that voice makes. And if the reader then seeks to justify Quentin's rhetoric as a mimetic interior monologue, he is obliged to accept that an imaginative observer, on the basis of an undisclosed suicide note, has conjectured and reconstructed the flow of Quentin's memories, perceptions and thoughts preceding his death.

The question of verisimilitude in the monologue generally is, of course, a vexed one. Although there are many mimetic monologues which are presented in unquestionably realistic terms as journals or memoirs, there are also many which end in the death of the speaking consciousness, and which require the reader to suspend retrospective disbelief in consequence.[10] What is to be questioned in *The Sound and the Fury* is not how much faith we can place in each separate monologuist as a dramatized consciousness, but rather how cunningly the monologues are formalized to fit together within a larger frame of reference than impersonation presupposes. Even in the case of Jason, whose monologue is readily acceptable as mimetic characterization from within, a consideration of the whole to which it belongs shows the extent to which it, too, is formalized to become concomitant with both the other monologues and the recapitulating narrative. Faulkner's unique treatment of eyewitness record through monologue is not to be described in customary mimetic terms. What is real in his representation of reality is neither psychological verisimilitude nor circumstantial context, but the truth of the moral world which is the author's *donnée*.

This is why there is no purpose served by examining Faulkner's characters as if they had life outside the novel. A psychologist is said to have proved that Benjy is not true to known mental retardation, and therefore is merely a literary figure. Perhaps it is just as well that Benjy is in a book, where he belongs. The same could be said of Quentin, or of Virginia Woolf's Septimus Smith in *Mrs. Dalloway*. What is interesting about these abnormal characters is not the accuracy of their representation, but the way each author has used their supposed aberrations to infuse into their monologues a poetic verbal pattern, matching super- or infra-consciousness with atypical rhetoric, and expressing a distortion of "normal" thought patterns in language which communicates at a level far above what the character may be supposed to be capable of achieving.

[10] Examples of written statements occur in such works as Mauriac's *Le noeud de vipères* (journal), Murdoch's *The Black Prince* (memoir), and Nabokov's *Despair* (film scenario), as well as in several of the monologues treated below. In the case of speaking monologuists such as Margaret Laurence's Hagar, Conrad's Marlow, or Cary's Gulley, an attempt is sometimes made to assist credibility by presenting the monologue as being dictated to a scribe, but more often the voice is presented dramatically, as in Browning's treatment of Guido in *The Ring and the Book*. The death of Guido, Gulley, or Hagar does not in itself vitiate the preceding monologue, since in the act of listening to it the reader has entered the dramatization in a continuous present.

Interesting examples of the fusion of the two methods occur in Margaret Drabble's *The Waterfall* and John Fowles's *The Collector*.

> I could hear the clock, and I could hear Caddy standing behind me, and I could hear the roof. It's still raining, Caddy said. I hate rain. I hate everything. And then her head came into my lap and she was crying, holding me, and I began to cry. Then I looked at the fire again and the bright, smooth shapes went again. I could hear the clock and the room and Caddy. (76)

> Versh set me down and we went into Mother's room. There was a fire. It was rising and falling on the walls. There was another fire in the mirror. I could smell the sickness. It was a cloth folded on Mother's head. Her hair was on the pillow. The fire didn't reach it, but it shone on her hand, where her rings were jumping. (80)

> She smelled like trees. In the corner it was dark, but I could see the window. I squatted there, holding the slipper. I couldn't see it, but my hands saw it, and I could hear it getting night, and my hands saw the slipper but I couldn't see myself, but my hands could see the slipper and I squatted there, hearing it get dark. (91)

These three excerpts from Benjy's monologue have been selected randomly. Almost any paragraph that does not recall dialogue would demonstrate the same characteristics. What is remarkable here is not so much the insistence upon the speaker's acuity of hearing and smell, as the hypnotic rhythms formed by the simple clauses. In the third example this is particularly noticeable. Faulkner could have conveyed Benjy's experience completely had he ended the paragraph with "night," but he repeats the motifs of "squatting," and of "hearing the approaching darkness." The "seeing" of the slipper with the hands, at the heart of the experience, is repeated twice, in two variant forms. As in *The Waves*, repetition is a hallmark of the rhetoric; it occurs not only within each statement, but from statement to statement, until it is formalized into the shape of the entire monologue, which ends:

> Father went to the door and looked at us again. Then the dark came back, and he stood black in the door, and then the door turned black again. Caddy held me and I could hear us all, and the darkness, and something I could smell. And there I could see the windows, where the trees were buzzing. Then the dark began to go in smooth, bright shapes, like it always does, even when Caddy says that I have been asleep. (94)

Benjy's sentences always follow the childish pattern, subject verb object, and they are always complete. A remarkable shift in compositional key confronts the reader as he enters the mental world of the second speaker. Quentin's sentences alternate between carefully formulated units of highly self-conscious prose, snatches of remembered dialogue, and fragmented stream of consciousness flow. Sometimes the punctuation is exact, sometimes it is perfunctory, and sometimes it is eliminated entirely. These three styles interweave with increasing complexity, and although transitions are sometimes signalled by the use of italics, frequently the reader has to make his own way unaided through the syntactic maze.

Some features of this maze bear analysis. Sometimes Quentin's sentences, though minimally punctuated, are models of subordination:

> From then on until he had you completely subjugated he was always in and out of your room, ubiquitous and garrulous, though his manner gradually moved northward as his raiment improved, until at last when he had bled you until you began to learn better he was calling you Quentin or whatever, and when you saw him next he'd be wearing a cast-off Brooks suit and a hat with a Princeton club I forget which band that someone had given him and which he was pleasantly and unshakeably convinced was a part of Abe Lincoln's military sash. (116)

And sometimes his description of what he sees is couched in the varied sentence rhythms of polished prose:

> The sound of the bees diminished, sustained yet, as though instead of sinking into silence, silence merely increased between us, as water rises. The road curved again and became a street between shady lawns with white houses.... The boy turned from the street. He climbed a picket fence without looking back and crossed the lawn to a tree and laid the pole down and climbed into the fork of the tree and sat there, his back to the road and the dappled sun motionless at last upon his white shirt.... His white shirt was motionless in the fork, in the flickering shade. The wheels were spidery. Beneath the sag of the buggy the hooves neatly rapid like the motions of a lady doing embroidery, diminishing without progress like a figure on a treadmill being drawn rapidly offstage. The street turned again. I could see the white cupola, the round stupid assertion of the clock. (142-43)

The effect of passages like these is double. We feel secure in the company of this articulate, intelligent consciousness, much as we do in the company of Stephen Dedalus, and we also enjoy sharing the perceptions of such a sensitive and imaginative recorder.

Sometimes, however the signposts of punctuation disappear entirely:

> ... I seemed to be lying neither asleep nor awake looking down a corridor of grey halflight where all stable things had become a shadowy paradoxical all I had done shadows all I had left suffered taking visible form antic and perverse mocking without relevance inherent themselves with the denial of the significance they should have affirmed thinking I was I was not who was not was not who. (188)

And sometimes Quentin's thoughts are as disjointed as any in the consciousness of Leopold Bloom:

Hats not unbleached and not hats. In three years I can not wear a hat. I could not. Was. Will there be hats then since I was not and not Harvard then. Where the best of thought Father said clings like dead ivy vines upon old dead brick. Not Harvard then. Not to me, anyway. Again. Sadder than was. Again. Saddest of all. Again.   (114)

These aberrations, however, are not the only shifting sands in Quentin's monologue. When in reverie he frequently reproduces the verbal patterns he has heard in childhood. Through his memory we hear the voice of his father, shaped by a noble intellect even when clouded by drink:

And Father said it's because you are a virgin: don't you see? Women are never virgins. Purity is a negative state and therefore contrary to nature. It's nature is hurting you not Caddy and I said That's just words and he said So is virginity and I said You don't know. You can't know and he said Yes. On the instant when we come to realize that tragedy is second-hand.   (135)

We hear also the voice of Herbert the blackguard, alternately threatening and cajoling as he smokes his cigar:

... look here Quentin we're about to do something we'll both regret I like you I liked you as soon as I saw you I says he must be a damn good fellow whoever he is or Candace wouldn't be so keen on him listen I've been out in the world now for ten years things don't matter so much then.   (128)

Interweaving throughout is the voice of Caddy:

Are you going to look after Benjy and Father. . . . Promise. . . . Promise I'm sick you'll have to promise. . . . Father will be dead in a year they say if he doesn't stop drinking and he wont stop he cant stop since I since last summer and then they'll send Benjy to Jackson I cant cry I cant even cry.   (125, 143)

And from time to time Quentin's memory duplicates the voice of his whining, self-righteous mother. This is the voice that is heard at greatest length, at times achieving the effect of a monologue itself, as in the extended passage which occurs when Quentin recalls his father's distinction between sin and morality, "your Mother is thinking of morality whether it be sin or not has not occurred to her":

Jason I must go away you keep the others I'll take Jason and go where nobody knows us so he'll have a chance to grow up and forget all this the others don't love me they never loved anything with that streak of Compson selfishness and false pride Jason was the only one

76

my heart went out to without dread . . . what have I done to have been given children like these Benjamin was punishment enough and now for her to have no more regard for me her own mother I've suffered for her dreamed and planned and sacrificed. (121)

The fragments of memories, the orts of immediate perception, interfuse with Quentin's obsessive death-wish until the tributaries form a single stream in which former thoughts all tumble together:

I could see the smoke stack. I turned my back to it, tramping my shadow into the dust. *There was something terrible in me sometimes at night I could see it grinning at me I could see it through their faces it's gone now and I'm sick*
Caddy
Don't touch me just promise
If you're sick you can't
Yes I can after that it'll be all right it won't matter don't let them send him to Jackson promise
I promise Caddy Caddy
Don't touch me don't touch me
What does it look like Caddy
What
That that grins at you that thing through them
I could still see the smoke stack. That's where the water would be, heading out to the sea and the peaceful grottoes. Tumbling peacefully they would, and when He said Rise only the flat irons. (131)

After the narrated incidents of the little Italian girl and the fight with Gerald ("Did you ever have a sister?") the stream gathers sound and fury:

Aren't you even going to open it Mr. and Mrs. Jason Richmond Compson announce the *Three times. Days. Aren't you even going to open it* marriage of their daughter Candace *that liquor teaches you to confuse the means with the end.* I am. Drink. I was not. Let us sell Benjy's pasture so that Quentin may go to Harvard and I may knock my bones together and together. I will be dead in was it one year Caddy said. Shreve has a bottle in his truck. Sir I will not need Shreve's I have sold Benjy's pasture and I can be dead in Harvard Caddy said in the caverns and the grottoes of the sea trembling peacefully to the wavering tides because Harvard is such a fine sound forty acres is no high price for a fine sound. A fine dead sound we will swap Benjy's pasture for a fine dead sound. It will last him a long time because he cannot hear it unless he can smell it. (192-93)

In what follows, "despair," "remorse," and "bereavement" (196) coalesce into "the saddest word of all" — "was," and the last paragraph resumes conventional sentence patterns as Quentin Compson resumes for the last time his conventional student self.

77

The second part of *The Sound and the Fury* defies the kind of analysis I have here tried to make. One of the frustrations of explication is that it can never replace a text such as this, in which the effect is deeply implicit. The monologue *is*. What its components are, and how they are fitted together, are in the end equally immaterial aspects of its being. All we can deduce from analysis is the artfulness of the author as he arranges his rhetoric. There is great satisfaction for the reader who eschews analysis and delivers himself into the hands of a writer who *knows*. "Tell us what you know, any way you will."

The third part of *The Sound and the Fury* represents an unaltered consciousness. As we read Jason's monologue we enter a perverted moral world in which, as Wayne Booth has pointed out, we "take delight in communion, even in deep collusion, with the author behind Jason's back." The consequence is blackly humorous. Here is a single episode, dramatized for us by the speaker, which shows both Jason's calculated malice and the long-suffering goodness of Dilsey:

"Ef I jus had a quarter," Luster says, "I could go to that show."
"En ef you had wings you could fly to heaven," Dilsey says. "I dont want to hear another word about dat show."
"That reminds me," I says, "I've got a couple of tickets they gave me." I took them out of my coat.
"You fixin to use um?" Luster says.
"Not me," I says. "I wouldn't go to it for ten dollars."
"Gimmie one of um, Mr. Jason," he says.
"I'll sell you one," I says. "How about it?"
"I aint got no money," he says.
"That's too bad," I says. I made to go out.
"Gimme one of um, Mr. Jason," he says. "You aint gwine need um bofe."
"Hush yo mouf," Dilsey says, "Dont you know he aint gwine give nothing away?"
"How much you want fer hit?" he says.
"Five cents," I says.
"I aint got dat much," he says.
"How much you got?" I says.
"I aint got nothing," he says
"All right," I says. I went on.
"Mr. Jason," he says.
"Whyn't you hush up?" Dilsey says. "He jes teasin you. He fixin to use dem tickets hisself. Go on, Jason, and let him lone."
"I dont want them," I says. I came back to the stove. "I came in here to burn them up. But if you want to buy one for a nickel?" I says, looking at him and opening the stove lid.

"I aint got dat much," he says.

"All right," I says. I dropped one of them in the stove.

"You, Jason," Dilsey says, "Ain't you shamed?"

"Mr. Jason," he says, "Please, suh. I'll fix dem tires ev'ry day fer a mont'."

"I need the cash," I says. "You can have it for a nickel."

"Hush, Luster," Dilsey says. She jerked him back. "Go on," she says, "Drop hit in. Go on. Git hit over with."

"You can have it for a nickel," I says.

"Go on," Dilsey says, "he aint got no nickel. Go on. Drop it in."

"All right," I says. I dropped it in and Dilsey shut the stove.

"A big growed man like you," she says. "Git outen my kitchen. Hush," she says to Luster, "Don't you git Benjy started. I'll git you a quarter from Frony tonight and you kin go tomorrow night. Hush up, now." (271-72)

Jason recounts this particular cat-and-mouse game with the same economy he shows throughout. There are no qualifiers, no elaborations, just the dramatic action stripped clean of nuance so that the reader must supply his own visualization. It is this laconic style which lends humour to Jason's monologue, as well as dramatic power. For Jason is master of the pithy, twisted retort.

Well, Jason likes work. I says no I never had university advantages because at Harvard they teach you how to go for a swim at night without knowing how to swim [so much for Quentin] and at Sewanee they don't even teach you what water is [so much for Father]. I says you might send me to the state University; maybe I'll learn how to stop my clock with a nose spray and then you can send Ben to the Navy I says or to the cavalry anyway, they use geldings in the cavalry. (213-14)

Jason's tone is consistently caustic, just as his character is consistently misanthropic, His monologue fits Humphrey's category of "direct interior monologue" as closely as does that of Molly Bloom. Why then do I view it as a rhetorical monologue?

The answer is to be found when the three consciousnesses of *The Sound and the Fury* are fitted together as part of the whole which Dilsey sees when she listens to the Easter Day sermon. It is a whole conceived in terms of the three-day sequence, of linear time. Quentin tries vainly to obliterate the "round stupid assertion of the clock," but he cannot conquer time by destroying his watch. In giving the ancestral timepiece to him, his father had bestowed on him "the mausoleum of all hope and desire," and had added, "I give it to you not that you may remember time, but that you might forget it now and then for a moment and not spend all your breath trying

79

to conquer it" (95). Quentin goes to his death because he cannot change the past, nor bear the reality of the present.

Jason, who seems admirably equipped to deal with the realities of the present in his totally self-interested way, spends all his breath keeping up with mechanical time. Leon Edel says of him, "His time-sense is as faulty as Quentin's, but at the opposite extreme. He knows only the inching present, as Quentin knew only an engulfing past."

Benjy is free of either extreme, because he is free from any concept of time. Arrested at the age of three, all he knows, as Faulkner explains in his Appendix, is loss (19). By a paradox he lost neither his beloved sister nor the pasture, because he remembered not them but only their loss. The same could be said of his manhood. In Benjy's world there is only sensation; to read his monologue is to enter that world and to cease to distinguish past from present. There is no sequence for Benjy, no time for healing, forgetting, adapting. There is only the sense of loss, a fluid continuum in which the family tragedy is always fresh, like a never-healing wound. Absence in the present is all Benjy knows.

As for Dilsey, she lives by a clock with one hand which is always three hours slow, and three times in the course of Easter Day she mentally adjusts the time as the clock strikes (290, 301, 316). In the fourth section of *The Sound and the Fury* the narrator carefully sets events contrapuntally in a linear tracing of time from dawn to afternoon. The sun measures time outside the house, and the clock, "the dry pulse of the decaying house" (301), measures it within. Mrs. Compson ignores both measurements; at noon she lies in her continual twilight (314). The church bells signal Dilsey and her family to worship (308) while simultaneously they remind Jason that time is running out as he savagely pursues his quarry (320, 321). At the moment that the bell ceases and the black worshippers enter their church, Jason bares his teeth at a church he passes, "And damn You, too," he said, "See if You can stop me..." (322). While the worshippers recollect the blood of the Lamb, Jason is striking a little old man on the head.

This counterpoint is one way in which the narrator confirms Dilsey's different relationship with time. As Waggoner has pointed out, Dilsey measures both past and present by eternity. Unlike Quentin and Jason, she neither repudiates the past nor struggles to keep abreast of the present. For Dilsey there is a world outside of time, an eternal world, which impinges, through Christ, on the timebound world of the Compsons. And this is powerfully portrayed in the sermon sequence. The Reverend Shegog does not retell the story of the Passion and the Resurrection as a scene from the past. He re-enacts it in the present, for a congregation to whom it is a continuing reality:

"Dey passed away in Egypt, de swinging chariots; de generations passed away. . . . I tells you, bredden, en I tells you, sistuhn, dey'll come a time. . . . I sees de whelmin flood roll between; I sees de darkness en de death everlastin upon de generations. Den, lo! Bredden! Yes, bredden! Whut I see? . . . I sees de resurrection en de light, sees de meek Jesus sayin Dey kilt Me dat ye shall live again; I died dat dem whut sees en believes shall never die. . . ."   (312)

This sermon, like a typical elegy, asserts the power of life in the face of death and despair. In the black church we watch a celebration of life in community; in the black people an integrity of feeling survives to transcend the fragmented story of the Compson decay. At the centre of this integrity sit Dilsey and Ben:

In the midst of the voices and the hands Ben sat, rapt in his sweet blue gaze. Dilsey sat bolt upright beside, [her hand on Ben's knee,] crying rigidly and quietly in the annealment and the blood of the remembered Lamb.
As they walked through the bright noon, up the sandy road with the dispersing congregation talking easily again group to group, she continued to weep. . . .
"Whyn't you quit dat, mammy?" Frony said. "wid all dese people lookin. We be passin white folks soon."
"I've seed de first en de last," Dilsey said. "Never you mind me."
"First en last whut?" Frony said.
"Never you mind," Dilsey said. "I seed de beginnin, en now I sees de endin."   (313)

In Dilsey we see not only the "endurance" which Faulkner attributed to her and her like in his Appendix (22), but also grace of the kind which redeems suffering and loss and grants a broader vision of life. At one level she provides the only disinterested love we see, so that her protection of Ben answers the question posited by Faulkner when he explains the genesis of *The Sound and the Fury*.

That began as a short story, it was a story without a plot, of some children being sent away from the house during the grandmother's funeral. They were too young to be told what was going on . . . the idea struck me to see how much more I could have got out of the idea of the blind self-centredness of innocence, typified by children, if one of these children had been truly innocent, that is, an idiot. So the idiot was born and then I became interested in the relationship of the idiot to the world that he was in but would never be able to cope with and just where could he get the tenderness, the help, to shield him from his innocence.[11]

The tenderness and help to shield him can come only from one who sees him as "de Lawd's chile" (333) and who rocks him on her lap like "Ma'y settin in de do wid Jesus on her lap, de little Jesus. Like dem chillen dar, de little Jesus" (312, 332).

But at another level too Dilsey's grace is sufficient. She affirms the ideal of wholeness against a splintered family and indeed against the fragmentation found in the white South as a whole. There have been attempts to portray the Compson brothers in Freudian terms as *id*, *ego*, and *super-ego*, with Caddy thrown in as *libido* for good measure, but Faulkner's own simpler reference to the three brothers as "idiot," "half-mad," and "perfectly sane, the first sane Compson for generations" differentiates them sufficiently for us to see in them symptoms of the disintegration and corruption (for Jason's sanity is monstrously corrupt) of their society. Southern idealism, rooted in a past which the Compsons have not outgrown, emphasizing honour, idealizing womanhood, and guilt-ridden about sex, has an inward and downward pull. The rhetoric of *The Sound and the Fury* expresses the conflict between two forces — one turning inward to self and downward to death, the other turning outward to others and upward to life. As the novel moves "from the completely closed and private world of the first section to the completely public world of the fourth,"[12] from subjectivity to objectivity, it moves into an arena of struggle between Jason and Dilsey, between the principle of destruction and the principle of sustaining integration. The hope for the future lies in Dilsey, and in men who, like her creator, can share her upward and outward look, for only such will endure.

This is why the novel is ultimately rhetorical, conceived and designed for its effect on an audience. The author is essentially a moralist, and though he speaks of the book as growing out of an image, which became a story without a plot, which became four versions of the same story, each of them a failure, none of his explanations of how it came to be account for the power with which the author speaks to us through the monologues and the narrative. "The result for the reader, if he is like myself, is an exaltation of faith in mankind. It is faith without, as yet, an argument; but it is the same faith

[11] Robert A. Jelliffe, ed., *Faulkner at Nagano* (Tokyo: Ken Kyusha, 1956), pp. 103-04.

[12] Olga W. Vickery, *The Novels of William Faulkner: A Critical Interpretation* (Baton Rouge: Louisiana State University Press, 1959), p. 30.

which has always lived in the most ultimate expression of the human spirit."[13]

The last quotation comes from a friend of Faulkner, a fellow poet and novelist who wrote a review the same year that *The Sound and the Fury* was published. There is some evidence that Faulkner may himself have collaborated in the essay; if he did, his essential voice changed little in thirty-five years. At West Point shortly before his death he was saying:

... the writer is simply trying to use the best method he possibly can find to tell you a true and moving and familiar old, old story of the human heart in conflict with itself for the old, old human verities and truth, which are love, hope, fear, compassion, greed, lust ... the eternal verities which haven't changed too much since man first found how to record them.

The old human verities occur again at the heart of *As I Lay Dying*. And once again, Faulkner's own account of the motive of this work is disarmingly ingenuous. "I simply imagined," he said, "a group of people and subjected them to the simple universal natural catastrophes which are flood and fire with a simple natural motive [the burial] to give direction to their progress." This statement solves no difficulty for the reader; the "simply imagined" situation is the easiest aspect of the work to discover, and might have been clearly set forth in a third-person narrative. But not so. Behind the simplicity of the situation is a complexity deriving from multiple points of view in richly suggestive monologues.

The fifty-nine monologues which compose *As I Lay Dying* issue from fifteen speakers. Unlike *The Sound and the Fury*, there is no disinterested narrative voice to provide objectivity, and no Dilsey to serve as a moral norm. The monologues offer some character mimesis, particularly in the case of the minor figures who speak only once, but in most of them the native idiom is superseded by a Faulknerian rhetoric. Furthermore, while many of them make explicit a circumstantial context, others operate from a void, or presuppose a clairvoyance or even an immortality on the part of the speaker. A reader who brings realistic expectations to the work will find difficulties like those we have noted in *The Sound and the Fury*. How can Darl describe the scene of his mother's dying when he is miles away from it? How can the dead Addie Bundren, not only dead but rotting in her coffin, "think" a monologue which alone substantiates

[13] Evelyn Scott, *On William Faulkner's* The Sound and the Fury (New York: Cape and Smith, 1929), p. 7.

the title of the work? Perhaps this objection could be removed if her monologue were to be relocated in the first fifth of the book, but why is it placed exactly two-thirds of the way through the sequence, after the flood and before the fire?

Some critics have considered the structure of *As I Lay Dying* in terms of "flashbacks," and noted four major "flashbacks" occurring in what seems to be a fairly linear chronology: the first monologue of Dewey Dell, through which we learn of her previous yielding to Lafe; Darl's last monologue before the disaster in the river, through which we learn of Jewel's labour of love to earn his horse; Cora Tull's reminiscences, placed after the river scene, in which we learn of Addie's prophecy that Jewel would save her "from the water and the fire"; and Addie's recollection of her married life, which Cora's memories preface. Pastor Whitfield's interior monologue about his abortive resolution to confess his adultery to Anse is chronologically displaced, but since it seems to be a record of inner thought, it could occur as a retrospective monologue; and since Whitfield is implicated in Addie's memories, there is a sequential logic for placing it after her last thoughts before death.

The positioning of Addie's monologue is crucial to the formalized structure of the text. There seem to be at least three reasons for its being found at the strategic centre of the work and thus, to paraphrase Darl, for its providing the rim around which the other monologues lie like spokes. It occurs in a pivotal context, between flood and fire, enabling the reader to discover additional significance in the narrative content thus far and to anticipate with fresh enlightenment the second tribulation. It serves to emphasize, retrospectively and prospectively, the power of Addie's will. Though dead, she continues to hold sway over the acts and the temperaments of her children. Finally, it reinforces the distinctive quality of Addie's voice by setting it off from the monologues on either side of it. This is particularly true of those immediately so juxtaposed, for in Cora and Whitfield we hear the same unmistakable cant, the self-righteous posturing of the practised sermonizer. Faulkner's orchestration of voices enables us to find in Addie's monologue a quality of raw, unadulterated truth from the heart of one who has learned "that words are no good; that words don't ever fit even what they are trying to say at."[14]

[14] William Faulkner, *As I Lay Dying* (New York: Random House, 1957), p. 163. All page numbers in parenthesis are to this edition.

Structure apart, however, the variant forms within the fifty-nine monologues, and the skilful modulation of the fifteen voices, create a formalized whole which has no counterpart in monologue novels. Unlike *The Sound and the Fury*, there is no easy distinction to be made between narrative and descriptive styles; unlike *The Waves*, the mode of expression is prevailingly determined by character. Although the author's voice is heard throughout, the characters through whom he speaks are individualized sharply enough to have an objective status; they can be visualized.

In discussing the "chameleonic, plural style" of this monologue novel, Bleikasten has attributed the vivid objective life of its characters to what he calls "Faulkner's prodigious gifts for verbal mimicry."[15] Certainly, as monologue follows monologue, we find ourselves listening to what is unmistakably oral communication: colloquial, pleonastic, and heavily larded with idiom and solecism. Every voice embodies the dialect, though it also embodies more:

[Anse:] I have heard men cuss their luck, and right, for they were sinful men. But I do not say it's a curse on me, because I have done no wrong to be cussed by. I am not religious, I reckon. But peace is my heart. I know it is. (37)

[Tull:] I be durn if it didn't give me the creeps. Now and then a fellow gets to thinking. About all the sorrow and afflictions in this world; how it's liable to strike anywhere, like lightning. I reckon it does take a powerful trust in the Lord to guard a fellow, though sometimes I think that Cora's a mite over-cautious. . . . (67)

[Samson:] A man can't tell nothing about them, I lived with the same one fifteen years and I be durn if I can. And I imagined a lot of things coming between, but I durn if I ever thought it would be a body four days dead and that a woman. (111)

[Armstid:] Trouble is, his quitting was just about to start our doing. He couldn't buy no team from nobody, let alone Snopes, withouten he had something to mortgage he didn't know would mortgage yet. (179)

[Cash:] So we set in the wagon, but the music wasn't playing now. I reckon it's a good thing we ain't got ere a one of them. I reckon I wouldn't never get no work done a-tall for listening to it. I don't know if a little music aint about the nicest thing a fellow can have. (247-48)

Bleikasten has analyzed this rough-edged spoken language to discover deformations peculiar to Southern pronunciation: double or

---

15 André Bleikaston, *Faulkner's* As I Lay Dying (Bloomington: Indiana University Press, 1977), p. 22. A linguistic analysis follows, pp. 23-24.

even triple negatives, parataxis, elliptical constructions, pseudo-causal subordination and anacoluthon. But we should note that the author's suppression or transposition of punctuation also serves to confuse syntactic relationships, and that the repetitions which seem to belong to the redundant character of spoken language are artfully designed to reinforce the ebb and flow of sensory or emotional experience. In short, the language is superficially mimetic, but it is also a vehicle for the author's rhetoric.

This is particularly true of those monologues in which narrative-reflection melts into stream of consciousness:

> [Dewey Dell:] The signboard comes in sight. It is looking out at the road now, because it can wait. New Hope. 3 mi. it will say. New Hope. 3 mi. New Hope. 3 mi. And then the road will begin, curving away into the trees, empty with waiting, saying New Hope three miles.
>
> I heard that my mother is dead. I wish I had time to let her die. I wish I had time to wish I had. It is because in the wild and outraged earth too soon too soon too soon. It's not that I wouldn't and will not it's that it is too soon too soon too soon. (114)

Although the immediate effect of this passage is one of atoms falling where they may, on close examination it yields an extraordinary number of rhetorical devices, as Robert Humphrey has observed:

> It is the piling up of [figures], the over-all use of *incrementum* that is unique and that, because it indicates a need for close reading and gives an enigmatic tone to the passage, serves to heighten the effect of the privacy of the materials.[16]

This same enigmatic tone, this same evinced need for close reading, prevails in many of the monologues of the child, Vardaman, whose affective logic — "My mother is a fish" (79) — produces mystifying ellipsis: "Pa shaves every day now because my mother is a fish" (95); "It was not her because it was laying right yonder in the dirt. And now it's all chopped up. I chopped it up. . . . Then it wasn't and she was, and now it is and she wasn't" (63).

It is in Vardaman's first monologue that a remarkable transition from verbal mimicry to an authorial literary style occurs. The boy's monologue narrates, in present tense, the events immediately subsequent to Addie's death. In his shocked grief he drives off Dr. Peabody's team of horses; like Benjy in *The Sound and the Fury*, he is helpless to control his own noise: ". . . I vomit the crying. As soon as

---

[16] *Stream of Consciousness in the Modern Novel*, pp. 72-73.

[the horse] gets through kicking I can and then I can cry, and crying can" (53). The sequel is expressed very differently:

It is dark. I can hear the wood, silence: I know them. But not living sounds, not even him. It is as though the dark were resolving him out of his integrity, into an unrelated scattering of components — scruffings and stampings; smells of cooling flesh and ammoniac hair; an illusion of a co-ordinated whole of splotched hide and strong bones within which, detached and secret and familiar, an *is* different from my *is*. (55)

This extraordinary change of register is, however, not the shock to the reader it might be had he not already heard the voice of Darl. From the first Darl's voice has been that of a self-conscious narrator:

The cotton house is of rough logs, from between which the chinking has long fallen. Square, with a broken roof set at a single pitch, it leans in empty and shimmering dilapidation in the sunlight, a single broad window in two opposite walls giving onto the approaches of the path. (3-4)

Although he occasionally makes use of dialect, most notably in dialogue, Darl speaks to his listener in an eminently lucid and expressive way. Therefore, when Vardaman's monologue incorporates language which the boy could not be expected to articulate, it is as if Darl has temporarily intervened — and since Darl shows himself capable of strange telepathic feats, becoming omnipresent in the consciousness of his brothers and sister, this is not impossible to accept.

When we come to consider the work in its entirety, as a formalized monologue, it is imperative to examine Darl's role as monologuist. Almost an exact third of the monologues belong to him. His voice opens the series, introducing the silent Jewel, with whom he runs a continuing verbal battle which is answered only by "Goddamn you." His goading of Jewel has all the fury of a Biblical elder brother. It implies the primal curse. In the first scene which Darl narrates, Jewel appropriately outstrips him, taking the nearest way. In the second, his clairvoyance operates for the first time. He describes Jewel's behaviour with his horse in the barn, as if he were there and not at the front of the house. Darl's voice is cool, however, in these early monologues, meditative and sensitive:

I used to lie on the pallet in the hall, waiting until I could hear them all asleep, so I could get up and go back to the bucket. It would be black, the shelf black, the still surface of the water a round orifice in nothingness, where before I stirred it awake with the dipper I could see maybe a star or two in the bucket, and maybe in the dipper a star or two before I drank. (10-11)

87

The limpid quality of this prose might perhaps be expected from a man like Darl, but before long a less ingenuous rhetoric appears, all the more startling in its contrast to the inner language of Jewel. Jewel has noticed his mother's hands "laying on the quilt like two of them roots dug up and tried to wash and you couldn't get them clean" (15). Darl, describing his mother, now a corpse, uses these words:

She looks down at the face. It is like a casting of fading bronze upon the pillow, the hands alone still with any semblance of life: a curled, gnarled inertness; a spent yet alert quality from which weariness, exhaustion, travail has not yet departed, as though they doubted even yet the actuality of rest, guarding with horned and penurious alertness the cessation which they know cannot last. (50)

Nor can the change be accounted for by the mystical circumstances — Darl seeing the scene in the bedroom while he and Jewel struggle to lift a load of lumber from where a broken wheel has tilted it in a ditch. The same lofty rhetoric operates in the "here and now" description of the menacing river:

Before us the thick dark current runs. It talks up to us in a murmur become ceaseless and myriad, the yellow surface dimpled monstrously into fading swirls travelling along the surface for an instant, silent, impermanent and profoundly significant, as though just beneath the surface something huge and alive waked for a moment of lazy alertness out of and into light slumber again. (134)

Darl is entrusted with most of the expository scenes. He movingly describes the water and fire episodes. His love-hate for Jewel enables him to conceive the centaur-figure of Jewel on his horse as a powerful emblem of pure will (12). Darl even portrays himself riding to the Jackson asylum, alternately talking to himself and reporting in the third person. "Darl has gone to Jackson. They put him on the train, laughing. . . . 'What are you laughing at?' I said. Yes yes yes yes" (243). And he is able to see into the secret thoughts of others, to know their concealed motives and their subconscious fears. Tull, the only major monologuist whose inner language never deviates from the vernacular, expresses the effect of Darl's strange eyes this way. "I always say it ain't never been what he done so much as how he looks at you. It's like he had got into the inside of you, someway. Like somehow you was looking at yourself and your doings outen his eyes" (119). Darl and Dewey Dell communicate without words (26) so that her knowledge of his knowledge fans her fear into hatred (115) and causes her to turn against him in the end (227).

He discovers the truth of Jewel's bastardy in the same intuitive way
(129) and communicates the truth to Jewel (202). There are readers who find him the most sympathetically presented character of
all, and who identify him with the author because of this and because of his god-like powers of observation. But pitiable as Darl is,
when he weeps on the coffin (215) or finds himself rejected even by
Cash (228), there is in him a bitterness which is more demonic than
angelic. Not for nothing do neighbours speak of him as "queer"
(119), and the view that would render him loving and deserving of
love comes from the least reliable source in the book (23, 159).
Cash is finally right, "This world is not his world; this life his life"
(250).

The warmest fraternal relationship in the family seems to be verbalized between Darl and Vardaman. It lends a special poignancy
to the boy's bewildered recognition of loss (239-42). Darl's only kind
words, and even here the kindness is equivocal, are to his youngest
brother about his own obsession with questions of identity (95).
One result of the closeness of these two is that we see in Vardaman
the possibility of a continuance of Darl's sensitivity. The brooding of
Darl upon questions of space, time, and existence (76) has its childish counterpart in Vardaman's conception of life in the horse (53,
55), and Darl's poetic evocations of water and fire are incipient in
Vardaman's phrases:

> The barn was still red, but it wasn't a barn now. It was sunk down,
> and the red went swirling up. The barn went swirling up in little red
> pieces, against the sky and the stars so that the stars moved backward.
> ... The barn is still red. It used to be redder than this. Then it went
> swirling, making the stars run backwards without falling. It hurt my
> head like the train did.   (213, 215)

But the authorial consciousness is not conveyed only by Darl and
Vardaman. Peabody voices it:

> That's the one trouble with this country: everything, weather, all,
> hangs on too long. Like our rivers, our land; opaque, slow, violent;
> shaping and creating the life of man in its implacable and brooding
> image.   (44)

Dewey Dell speaks in its language:

> The cow breathes upon my hips and back, her breath warm, sweet,
> stertorous, moaning. The sky lies flat down the slope, upon the secret
> clumps. Beyond the hill sheet-lightning stains upward and fades. The
> dead air shapes the dead earth in the dead darkness, further away

than seeing shapes the dead earth. . . . I feel like a wet seed wild in the hot blind earth. (61)

And imprisoned as he is in a native idiom and a slow consciousness, Cash is able to say:

But I aint so sho that ere a man has the right to say what is crazy and what aint. It's like there was a fellow in every man that's done a-past the sanity or the insanity, that watches the sane and the insane doings of that man with the same horror and the same astonishment. (228)

The last passage reminds us of Bernard, in *The Waves*, noting the existence, outside every agony, of "an observant fellow who points," it is perhaps the only way that the voice behind the rhetorical monologue can define itself. But Cash's insight also illustrates the struggle any speaker has with words as a defining medium. Even Cash finds words easier than Jewel. And Darl, to whom words used to be easy, disintegrates to the point where the only word distinguishable from maniac laughter is "Yes"; whereas Jewel explodes into a fiery deed which makes him the true protagonist, substituting action for words in a final justification of Addie's faith. For Jewel does "not love in word, neither in tongue; but in deed and truth" (1 John 3:18). In Faulkner's art the "simple," "universal," and "natural" themes seem to be inseparable from Biblical ones.

This is the reason for the metaphysical tenor of *As I Lay Dying*. Eventually, after the epical struggle of the Bundren family has been described, full explication of the text must revert to those concerns for sin and salvation that are voiced in the pivotal retrospective monologue referred to earlier. For as Jewel's baptism of fire is a triumph of deed over word, so Addie's dying thoughts have played on the difference between the two, ". . . because people to whom sin is just a matter of words, to them salvation is just words too" (168). Addie's entire meditation vitiates the efficacy of words:

That was when I learned that words are no good; that words don't ever fit even what they are trying to say at. When he [Cash] was born I knew that motherhood was invented by someone who had to have a word for it because the ones that had the children didn't care whether there was a word for it or not. I knew that fear was invented by someone that had never had the fear; pride, who never had the pride. I knew that it had been, not that they had dirty noses, but that we had to use one another by words like spiders dangling by their mouths from a beam, swinging and twisting and never touching. . . . And so when Cora Tull would tell me I was not a true mother, I would think how words go straight up in a thin line, quick and harmless, and how terribly doing goes along the earth, clinging to it, so that after a while *the two lines are too far apart for the same person to straddle from one to the other*; and that sin and love and fear are just sounds that people who never sinned nor loved have for what they never had and cannot have until they forget the words.   (163-66; my italics)

Addie repudiates the word of Anse, "love" (164), letting him be the shape and echo of it — "I would be I" (166). She tells Cora, substituting doing for speaking, "My daily life is an acknowledgement and expiation of my sin" (159), and as she gets ready to "stay dead" she thinks in terms of "cleaning up the house afterward" (168). The promise she extracts from Anse to bury her in Jefferson when she dies is a revenge for the trickery of words (164), but it is also the last cleansing rite in the cleaning of her house. All of this seems to be understood in an elemental way by the one son who is hers alone. From the start of her dying he has dreamed of carrying her off to where it would be "just . . . me and her on a high hill and me rolling the rocks down the hill at their faces, picking them up and throwing them down the hill faces and teeth and all by God until she was quiet . . ." (15). Jewel does not need Darl to tell him in words that his mother is a horse and his father is unknown (202).

The theme of alienation embodied in Addie is expressed through the failure of words. Yet the paradox exists; it is the "word" extracted from Anse by Addie — the promise to bury her with her own people — that controls events, and it is the word, as it must be, that tells this story.

Throughout the formalized monologue as a whole, the reader confronts antithesis: life and death, water and fire, success and failure, loneliness and solidarity, occurring and recurring in rhythmic patterns through the central consciousnesses. As a result, the little world of the Bundrens becomes a paradigm of human struggle everywhere, and the wordless love that bears the son through the water and the fire triumphant is the true and only power of salvation. If Jewel explicitly symbolizes the child born in sin, as does Pearl in *The Scarlet Letter*, then implicitly he symbolizes mankind, and his heroism is the human capability, to which Faulkner repeatedly referred, to prevail. "I believe that man will not merely endure: he will prevail. He is immortal, not because he alone among creatures has an inexhaustible voice, but because he has a soul, a spirit capable of compassion and sacrifice and endurance."[17] This statement is readily

[17] William Faulkner, *Essays, Speeches and Public Letters*, James B. Meriwether, ed. (New York: Random House, 1965), p. 120.

recognizable as an expression of Faulkner's native rhetoric. My contention is that it is also recognizable as a compressed expression of the rhetoric infusing and linking all the monologues of *As I Lay Dying*.

As we have already noted, Robert Humphrey describes the technique of *The Waves* as "soliloquy." He uses the same term for the technique of *As I Lay Dying*. "Soliloquies," he says, "present the psychic content and processes of a character directly from character to reader without the presence of an author but with an audience tacitly assumed." In discussing these two novels, he adds that in them we find ". . . an arrangement of thought units as they would originate in a character's consciousness rather than as they would be deliberately expressed" (*Stream of Consciousness in the Modern Novel*, pp. 36 and 54).

Though "soliloquy" is a term Virginia Woolf herself used of *The Waves*, I have given reason for rejecting it as a description of the monologues in the novels discussed in this study, and it is the reason supported by Humphrey's own definition — namely, that "the presence of an audience is tacitly assumed." This tacit assumption is the hallmark of the monologue, for a soliloquy occurs only when a speaker believes himself to be alone. Furthermore, it seems to me untenable that the monologues contained in *The Waves, The Sound and the Fury*, and *As I Lay Dying* present a psychic content to the reader "without the presence of an author," or that they formulate thought units "as they would arise in a character's consciousness rather than as they would be deliberately expressed." On the contrary, in all three of these novels the author can be discerned at work selecting, arranging, and formulating these thought units as very deliberate expressions of what the spokesmen might say if they were conscious of a design beyond the circumstances of time and place in which they find themselves "speaking." What we have in these formalized monologues is exactly what we have seen Langbaum describe as the generic characteristic of the dramatic monologue, ". . . a consciousness . . . beyond what the speaker can lay claim to, . . . [in which] we find . . . the counterpart of our own consciousness."

Beyond this essential claim upon the listener, however, there are other notable similarities in these three monologue novels. Each has a schema for division which is not chronological in the usual linear way. *The Sound and the Fury* and *The Waves* can both be construed as proceeding from childhood to maturity, but in each, as also in *As I Lay Dying*, the emphasis on internal time produces dislocation and persistent cross-reference within the progression. Each novel signals its structure in a distinctive way: *The Sound and the Fury* by means of a date for each of its four divisions, *The Waves* by means of its system of italicized interludes tracing a metaphoric day from dawn to nightfall, and *As I Lay Dying* by chapter headings naming, quite simply, that character who seems to be speaking the monologue. All have been accorded a place in the literature of stream of consciousness, regardless of whether the term is understood as naming a genre or a technique, because critics find they all explore regions of consciousness below the rational level. All three are examples of symbolic form. Death and dementia occur in them all; evocative images undergird them all; paradox weaves through them all. The striking elaboration of sensory impression found in all of them results in rich descriptive passages. Each author makes use of ingenious hidden devices to assist the reader in discovering the context in which the monologues occur, withholding total enlightenment until the component multi-personal monologues have been integrated into a formalized whole. And, finally, each author ironically undergirds his own rhetoric with statements disputing the efficacy of words to express his transcendent concerns. Bernard repudiates his phrases; Addie finds that words obscure or even falsify experience, and Benjy's wail, which is nothing but sound, is nevertheless "all time and injustice and sorrow become vocal for an instant by a conjunction of planets" (304).

In these novels, then, language is both technique and theme. The monologues they contain are infused with the distinctive voice of an author who invites his reader to collaborate in making meaning from what is, after all, an imperfect medium of communication for "the eternal verities," but which is the only one we have.

At the outset of this chapter we noted that formalized, or rhetorical monologues are shaped by an author through multiple voices to reach an audience, and to convey metaphysical rather than psychological meaning. This is a function I find undertaken alike by Faulkner and Virginia Woolf, in their very different ways. Both have used the monologue as a symbolic form to enshrine a personal view of life; to contemplate the evils of despair, loneliness, and death; and to fathom mysteries of time, perception, and personality. In *The Sound and the Fury*, *As I Lay Dying*, and *The Waves* we have the result, novels of vision. They are novels that demand a great deal of the reader, and that invite repeated re-reading — but one might add, for these very reasons, "They endure."

93

CHAPTER FOUR

Autobiographical Monologues

Each mortal thing does one thing and the same:
Deals out that being indoors each one dwells;
Selves — goes itself; *myself* it speaks and spells;
Crying *what I do is me: for that I came.*

GERARD MANLEY HOPKINS,
"As Kingfishers Catch Fire"

An account may earn the appellation "autobiographical" for one of three reasons. It may be acknowledged by the author as autobiography, and recounted in the third, or, more usually, the first person. It may be concealed autobiography, in which case the reader discovers extrinsically the personal relationship between the "I" narrator, or the protagonist of the work, and the author; David Copperfield, Jane Eyre, Philip Carey, and Paul Morel are only a few figures in the gallery of such heroes. Or it may be fictive autobiography, in which case the author invents a character who then addresses the reader with every appearance of recording his own history. Another way of designating these three forms would be to speak of the first as "true autobiography," and the second as "autobiography disguised as fiction," and the third as "fiction disguised as autobiography."

It is important to notice that in the first two forms the same shaping principle is at work. Northrop Frye has pointed out that true autobiography merges with the novel "by a series of insensible gradations." He adds, "Most autobiographies are inspired by a creative, and therefore fictional, impulse to select only those events and experiences in the writer's life that go to build up an integrated pattern."[1] In the final analysis of any novel, it matters little whether

---

[1] *Anatomy of Criticism* (Princeton: Princeton University Press, 1957), p. 307.

the novelist has "invented" his narrator and his material or whether he has drawn them directly from his own experience. What matters is the way he has transformed them into fiction by the art of building up an "integrated pattern." All autobiography, true and invented, may, if it is to become a work of art, be shaped by its author into the unified whole which is the finished account.

In considering autobiographical monologues our major concern is with the third form noted here, the fiction disguised as autobiography, and with the speaker of the monologue as a fictive being. However, since the most memorable autobiographical monologue of the twentieth century is the one provided by Marcel Proust in *Remembrance of Things Past*, I will preface my examination of other novels with a brief comment on the integrated pattern found there.

In writing the "Book of Himself" Proust's process was memory — the recapture of his own personal experience:

This book, the most difficult of all to discover, is also the only one dictated to us by reality, the only one the "imprinting" of which on our consciousness was done by reality itself. No matter what idea life may have implanted within us, its material representation, the outline of the impression it has made upon us, is always the guarantee of its indispensable truth.[2]

From the outset, the emphasis is upon remembered, even ritualized acts. The famous sentence beginning, "For a long time I used to go to bed early" (I, 3), continues in the imperfect tense, "my eyes would close so quickly . . . the thought that it was time to go to sleep would awaken me; I would try to put away the book." The experience of recapturing memories is both the subject and the essential mode of this narration.

When the reader approaches this work he is at first aware of only two figures operating within a double framework of time. An I-narrator recalls his childhood. Marcel old remembers Marcel young. Both Marcels appear to be identifiable with the author of the work, Marcel Proust. It is later that the reader discovers a third, hovering figure, when the narrator begins to tell of the thoughts and actions of people surrounding Marcel, thoughts and actions which Marcel himself could not possibly have known. Much later he reaches the long disquisition in which Marcel discovers the ultimate truth about

[2] *Remembrance of Things Past*, 2 vols., trans. C. K. Scott Moncrieff and Frederick A. Blossom (New York: Random House, 1932), II, 1001. All page numbers in parenthesis are to this edition.

life and art (II, 990-1028) and proclaims the power of imagination, as well as memory, in the re-creation of time past:

It is quite possible that, to produce a literary work, imagination and sensibility are interchangeable qualities and that the latter can, without much disadvantage, be substituted for the former. . . . A man born sensitive to impressions but without imagination, might nevertheless write admirable novels. (II, 1017)

"Might," only. "Imagination and reflexion" (II, 1022) are the twin resources of the writer. *Remembrance of Things Past* in its entirety works towards Marcel's assertion of the extraordinary creative power of those twin faculties. And the assertion serves a double purpose. It endorses the autobiographical mode of the fiction, because despite our knowledge of the differences that exist between the narrator's life and personality and the life and personality of the Marcel Proust who gave us that narrator, the poetics proclaimed by the narrator are indisputably those of the author. It also justifies the procedure of omniscience within what appears to be eyewitness, and therefore limited, narration. Just as important as the famous "Madeleine" account, and its illustration of the function of sensory impressions as a means of emotional recall, is the implicit assumption that an imaginative eyewitness need not be limited by constraints of space and time. We are all makers, in Proust's aesthetic, creating our lives as we recall them. Therefore, there is no incompatibility between the narrator as witness and the narrator as creator.

This, it seems to me, is Proust's great gift to succeeding novelists. When the story of Marcel's life is complete, Marcel is ready to write the novel we have just finished reading. As readers we have been involved in the process of creation together with the writer; with him we have discovered that truth is to be found not in empirical fact but in the act of creation itself. Art, not reality, furnishes truth. This is the premise upon which all fictive autobiography is based.

When a novelist sets out to achieve fiction in the guise of autobiography his essential starting point is the creation of the "I" who will speak to the reader. Out of the many such monologuists in twentieth-century fiction I have chosen three: Thomas Mann's Felix Krull, Joyce Cary's Gully Jimson, and Margaret Laurence's Hagar Shipley. These characters are very different from one another; indeed they have little in common apart from their being fictive speakers who offer retrospective life-histories. All are far more distanced from their creators than is Marcel from Proust; but, like Marcel, they each strive to recapture the past by exercising memory and imagination. And in this shared function we see an essential difference in artistic methods. Proust began with memory, his own memory, and exercised imagination upon it. Mann, Cary, and Laurence all began with imagination, and having imagined their monologuist in fulness of detail, they invent through his voice the memories he might be expected to have. On the one hand there is "memory-founded imagination";[3] on the other imagination-founded memory.

In 1936, Thomas Mann wrote an introduction to the Knopf edititon of his *Stories of Three Decades* in which he spoke of the first book of the *Confessions of Felix Krull* thus:

> *Felix Krull*, like *Royal Highness*, is in essence the story of an artist; in it the element of the unreal and illusional passes frankly over into the criminal. The idea of the book was suggested to me by the memoirs of a Romanian adventurer named Manolescu. I was fascinated by the novel stylistic problem of direct autobiographical presentation on the model of my somewhat coarse-grained original; and still more by the grotesque idea of linking such a theme with another, traditional and beloved: *Dichtung und Wahrheit*, the aristocratic, confessional self-portrait of the artist. The conception had in it the germ of truly great humour; and I wrote the existing fragment of *Felix Krull* with such zest that I was not surprised to have many excellent judges pronounce it the best and happiest thing I had done.

This is Mann at sixty remembering the zest with which he had begun his only autobiographical monologue twenty-five years before. He left off writing it at the end of the "Childhood" section to seek variety (for he "could not hold the note for too long at a time without relief") and proceeded to develop *Death in Venice* and *The Magic Mountain*. In due course came *Mario and the Magician* and *Joseph and His Brethren*. Eight years after he wrote the Preface quoted above, he was deliberating whether to take up Krull again or to develop the not unrelated Faustus theme; then in the eighth decade of his life he returned to his "happiest" — if not his "best" — thing, and wrote a continuation which was still not to be a conclusion.

We shall never know whether Mann had anything further in store for his monologuist. Erika Mann tells us that not one word more of the confessions was written after the third part; the work came to a complete halt. Perhaps one so incomprehensibly and winningly successful (*der Erwählte*) could not be coerced out of his dream of

---

[3] This is the happy formulation of Barbara Hardy. It occurs in her discussion of Proust's treatment of memory in *Tellers and Listeners* (London: Athlone, 1975), pp. 84-98.

self-transformation to become the native son returned to his homeland,[4] much less to become the exposed criminal placed under "first arrest" (58) — and how many others? The future adumbrated for Krull is never realized. We do not follow him every step of the way into complete retirement (3) but leave him at the climax of his masquerade, when Kuckuck's noble view of man — "disposed to universal sympathy" (277) — is unerringly born out by his guest's complaisance to both daughter and mother.

In the opening sentences of chapter one, Felix discloses himself and his purpose: ". . . I take up my pen to commit my confessions to this patient paper in my own neat and attractive handwriting" (3). The note of self-approval is at once sounded, and the proof of his eligibility as memoirist follows in the same complacent tone. It resides in his "upper class though somewhat dissolute family," his intimacy with a godfather who was a "greatly admired artist," and his "natural instinct for good form" (3-4). Furthermore, the tenor of the memoirs is revealed in the next breath — it is to be a "whole career of fraud," and the writer will expend upon it "the utmost frankness. . . . For what moral value or significance can attach to confessions written from any point of view except that of truthfulness?" (4). So in a single paragraph, with aplomb matched by economy, Felix Krull, confidence man, introduces himself. If we remember that the distinguishing mark of the confidence man is that, unlike other criminals, he requires the consent of his victim, we can see what a masterly introduction of himself Krull achieves here, requiring the reader's consent to his story before he begins telling it.

The remainder of the first chapter is devoted to the environment into which Felix was born — the Rhine Valley, the gentle father, the observant godfather Schimmelpreester,[5] and the rococo villa. What is noticeable about this idyllic passage is its ambience of petty fraud. The *Loreley extra cuvée* is, for all its elaborate gilded packaging, a trashy wine — but it becomes an emblem for Felix, who later labels himself *"extra cuvée"* (34) and passes himself off for what he is not. The "charming little estate" abounds in bric-à-brac which is seldom what it seems, and includes in the garden "a mirrored glass sphere,

---

4 Thomas Mann, *Confessions of Felix Krull, Confidence Man*, trans. Denver Lindley (New York: Knopf, 1955), p. 71. All page numbers in parenthesis are to this edition.

5 This is the name given in the 1954 revision of Part One, and defined by Schimmelpreester himself as the "high priest of the mould" (8). In 1911 he was named Maggotson — a less ingenious embodiment of the same idea.

which distorted faces most comically" (6). The mode of the memoirs is comic.

Such was the home, announces Felix, into which he was born a Sunday child (8). From the moment when he begins a chronological record, Felix displays the narcissism which is his *modus vivendi*. Not content with earliest memories themselves, he augments them with reports elicited from parents and nurses, and discourses upon the significance of his behaviour from birth through early childhood in the fashion of one who finds himself of consuming interest. Krull connects his reluctance to exchange the darkness of the womb at birth for the light of day with his extraordinary enjoyment of sleep; significantly, Freud connects sleep with narcissism. He connects his given name of Felix — the fortunate or happy one — with his physical fineness and attractiveness. "Yes, I have always believed myself favoured of fortune and of Heaven, and I may say that, on the whole, experience has borne me out" (9). He connects his unusually active imagination, which enables him to fantasize himself into Kaiser or Prince, with a secret inborn superiority to coarse-grained school fellows. "I could not conceal from myself that I was made . . . of finer clay, and I do not shrink from the charge of self-compla-cency. . . . I should have to be a fool or a hypocrite to pretend that I am of common stuff, and it is therefore in obedience to truth that I repeat that I am of the finest clay" (11).

Note the subtle gradation here, from the "finer clay" of popular idiom to "the finest clay." Felix is not repeating himself, but improv-ing on the estimation others might make. By this point in the mem-oirs, without as yet a single corroborating voice, we are under the spell of a charm which seems entirely compatible with its possessor's superb sense of his own excellence.

In fashioning his Felix, Mann has devoted the utmost care to the communicative mode he makes him adopt. He has him compile his memoirs lovingly as for posterity, and for a larger public than he has seemed at first to envisage. It is as if his first audience of one — himself — is so impressed by his skills of composition that he cannot conceive of this approbation's not being shared:

These papers have lain for a long time under lock and key; for at least a year now indifference toward the enterprise and doubt of my success have kept me from continuing my confessions, piling page on page in faithful sequence. For although I have often maintained that I am setting down these reminiscences principally for my own occupa-tion and amusement, I will now honour truth in this respect, too, and admit freely that I have in secret and as it were out of the corner of my eye given some heed to the reading public as well; indeed, without the encouraging hope of their interest and approval I should hardly have had the perseverance to continue my work even this far. . . .

Today . . . once more and not without emotion I ran through the [earlier composed] chronicle of my childhood and early youth; aroused, I continued to spin my reminiscences in imagination; and as certain striking moments of my career appeared vividly before me, *I was quite unable to believe that incidents which exercised so enlivening an effect on me could fail to entertain the reading public as well.* (57-58; my italics)

The first phase of the communicative act, therefore, is intra-personal — "I continued to spin out my reminiscences in imagination" — and the reminiscences thence become carefully processed for an imagined audience in a manner familiar to most readers. In the secret lives of all of us there is a fantasizing "I" who rehearses for his own ears a self-justifying account of past behaviour. The aggrandizement we achieve for ourselves in our daydreams is a means of salvaging our self-image, and in most of us these private fantasies remain private. But our awareness of them, even if they belonged only to our childhood, may account for a shiver of recognition when we meet their counterpart in Krull's monologue. There are, however, two extraordinary features of Krull's expressive technique to be noted. One is his developed narcissism, which so far exceeds customary intra-personal rationalization as to regard its subject of the self as the lovable object "he":

Now observe this youth in ragged clothes, alone, friendless, and lost in the crowd, wandering through this bright and alien world. He has no money with which to take any real part in the joys of civilization. . . . But his senses are lively, his mind attentive and alert; he sees, he enjoys, he assimilates; and if at first the rush of noise and faces confuses this son of a sleepy country town, bewilders him, frightens him indeed, nevertheless he possesses mother wit and strength of mind enough slowly to become master of his inner turmoil. (75-76)

. . . the lonely youth descended into this tumult from his refuge for third-class members of society. Observed by no one, his small suitcase in his hand, he departed from the noisy, rather unattractive hall. (123)

This is the way a Narcissus contemplates himself, as an image quite separate from his observing self.

The other extraordinary feature of the monologue is the sustained quality of this self-absorption. Nothing is recounted in which the monologuist does not occupy the centre, showing himself more interested in the fineness of his perceptions than in the people, objects, and situations he perceives. Indeed the state of awareness Felix describes when recording his cab ride with Rozsa serves admirably as an exemplification of the pervasive mode of the confessions:

> I scruple to set [our conversation] down, for I am sensible enough to see that its freedom lies beyond the compass of my voluble and chatty pen. It was without introduction, this conversation, it was without polite conventions of any sort; from the very beginning it had the free, exalted irresponsibility that is usually a characteristic only of dreams, where our "I" associates with shadows that have no independent life, with creations of its own, in a way that is after all impossible in waking life where one flesh-and-blood being exists in actual separation from another. (113)

Felix's "I" habitually associates with shadows that have a life only in relation to his own avid ego, and in the hands of a clumsier writer the continual self-dramatizatiton would quickly become tedious.

Mann himself found problems of surfeit; the note of unclouded self-approval, as we have seen, he could not hold for long without relief. In creating a narrator whose voice is altogether foreign to his own, Mann has submitted to a detachment of the most complete kind, and to the particular constraints imposed by impersonation. In his essay, "Variations on Picaresque (*Felix Krull*)," Robert B. Heilman has discerned some elements of self-portraiture in the work by enumerating parallels between the Mann story in *A Sketch of My Life* and the Felix story, and has found what he calls "oblique self-revelation" in several correspondences.[6] But granted such correspondences in family circumstances and biographical ordering that might be found, granted even the gifts of rational analysis and creative imagination transferred from Mann's mind to that of his created narrator, the sustained expression of so different an ego remains a *tour de force*. The brilliant masterstroke in Mann's conception is that he uses impersonation in order to develop and define a theme of impersonation, so that the final effect is that of a masquerade within a masquerade. This seems a perfect working out, through art, of the theme of the impersonator and his pretensions.

There can be no masquerade without spectators, however, and no impersonation without an audience. Felix's awareness of the effect he is making in his memoirs is continually exemplified as he for-

---

[6] *Thomas Mann: A Collection of Critical Essays,* ed. Henry Hatfield (New Jersey: Prentice Hall, 1964), pp. 142-44.

mulates his monologue. Having decided upon a "reading public," he addresses himself to satisfying the requirements of such an audience zealously: "Writing is not a conversation with oneself. Orderly development, self-possession, and an unhurried approach to the subject are indispensable" (369). His acknowledgement of his reader continues to find expression intermittently even as far as the penultimate page of his narrative: "Who of you who peruse these lines will not envy me such sweet instants?" (382). His tone, in these periodic asides to the reader, is an interesting blend of rationalization and unctuous flattery. The reader is "kind" (257); he is "earnest" (116); he is "sympathetic" (253); in summation, he is a "reader of sensibility," because it is "for such readers alone that I am setting down my confessions" (278). The reader's patience is commended (130); his continued alertness is implored (185); his intense interest in the affairs of the writer is taken for granted (186). The ultimate flattery, however, is that of providing this superior reader with sustained implicit analogies which he can work out for himself, thus becoming a collaborator with the monologuist in seeking out all the implications of that speaker's experiences.

The implicit analogies embodied in the person and the record of Felix Krull are at least three in number. They are the rogue biography (inspired by the memoirs of George Manolescu), the mythopoeic dimension which links Felix to Joseph through the figure of Hermes, and the *"Bildungsroman"* aspect of the monologue which links it to *The Magic Mountain*.

An early example of rogue biography occurs in Defoe's *Moll Flanders*. Moll emerges from her autobiographical monologue as a lovable rogue, moving essentially unassailable through the episodes of her colourful career, and lacking, even in retrospect, all but the most superficial of moral concerns. She is a typical *picaro*, and Heilman's aforementioned essay deals ample justice to every aspect of the "picaresque" in fiction.

However, in Felix we have the "finer clay," not coarse-grained like the insouciante Moll or the model Manolescu. For illustration of the difference we might compare Moll's account of her first act of theft with Felix's. Moll is careful to depict the extremity to which poverty has reduced her. "Poverty presses, the Soul is made Desperate by Distress, and what can be done?"[7] She describes herself, at "the last gasp," dressing herself up without any conscious design in

---

[7] Defoe, *Moll Flanders* (London: Oxford University Press, 1971), p. 191. All page numbers in parenthesis are to this edition.

her head, and wandering forth, the pawn of the Devil. Her steps lead her to an apothecary's shop where a little bundle lies unattended on a stool; the promptings of the Devil "like a Voice spoken to me over my shoulder" impel her to snatch up the bundle and make off with it unnoticed. Her subsequent guilty terrors are graphically described, though they do not seem to diminish the satisfaction with which she catalogues the loot in the safety of her lodging, and she is able to rationalize her theft sufficiently to try her luck again — and again, and again.

Compare with this the young Felix on his way to school. He has money in his pocket, and the shop he frequents is a haunt of sensory delight. He describes the splendid sights and tantalizing smells of the delicatessen with the relish of a gourmet. It is joy, not terror, that seizes him when he realizes the opportunity afforded by the absence of the proprietor (42). He has the presence of mind to cloak his purpose by pretending to call for service. He grabs a fistful of chocolate creams, and later gloats over his "dream treasure" in the privacy of his room (44). The pattern is now established. Infrequent forays into the tempting array of food continue — always at noon, when the shop is unattended, always carried out with cunning circumspection, always accompanied by an "incomparable expansion of my whole being" (44). There is no acknowledgement of guilt, however spurious. In its place we read:

No doubt I shall be accused of common theft. I will not deny the accusation, I will simply withdraw and refuse to contradict anyone who chooses to mouth this paltry word. But the word — the poor, cheap, shopworn word, which does violence to all the finer meanings of life — is one thing, and the primeval absolute deed forever shining with newness and originality is quite another. . . . Whenever an act is in question, it is not the what or the why that matters (though the second is the more important), but simply and solely the who. Whatever I have done or committed, it has always been first of all *my* deed, not Tom's or Dick's or Harry's, and though I have had to accept being labelled, especially by the law, with the same name as ten thousand others, I have alway rebelled against such an unnatural identification in the unshakable belief that I am a favourite of the powers that be and actually composed of finer flesh and blood.   (43)

The emotions with which the two rogues recall their first act of theft are decidedly different, but the essential difference in character is embodied also in the narrative technique each employs. Moll tells her story in her customary breathless style, piling detail upon detail in careful chronological order, and pausing in her prattle only to offer the rationalization of the imperfect Penitent:

... I think I may truly say I was Distracted and Raving, when prompted by I know not what Spirit, and as it were, doing I did not know what, or why. (191)

... two or three times I fell upon my Knees, praying to God, as well as I could, for Deliverance; but I cannot but say my prayers had no hope in them. (193)

... I had an Evil Counsellor within, and he was continually prompting me to relieve my self by the worst means; so one Evening he tempted me again by the same wicked Impulse that had said, *take that Bundle,* to go out again and seek for what might happen. (193)

These rationalizations are accompanied by qualifications expressive of doubt ("as it were," "as well as I could," "what might happen"); they depend heavily upon the doctrine of the personal devil; and they revolve around those same unresolved questions of "what and why" which Felix dismisses as of no importance in his case. The emphasis in Moll's account, once all self-justification is stripped away, is upon sequence and quantification, every hour of the evening in question, every step of the journey made, and every last content of the stolen bundle, being precisely accounted for. The record is that of a tabulating mind intent upon the scrupulous fixing of every practical and material detail.

Felix's account, on the other hand, is almost entirely impressionistic. His description of the opulent treasures of the delicatessen store is lovingly designed to convey the richness and profusion of the sensory delights it still offers his memory. An artist could readily translate Moll's description of the interior of the apothecary's shop into a sketch, because the few details given are graphic indeed — the little white bundle on a stool in front of the counter, the maid with her back to it, and the apprentice standing on the counter with a candle, searching something on the upper shelf. A few strokes, in paint as in words, and it is done. But an artist attempting an exact picture of the interior of Felix's paradise would find his task difficult indeed. Analysis of the prose shows the artistry of the word-picture, the catalogue of treasures unified by the repeated construction "There were...," the re-enactment of the experience unified by images of fairy-land, enchantment, and the dream. And unlike Moll, Felix attempts no interweaving rationalization, nor colours his remembered "dreamlike foray" with any imputation of guilt. Instead, as we have seen, he reminds his reader ("if I ever have one") that what he recalls is not an act of theft but a "Primeval absolute deed" which — like the "Great Joy" of the sexual act (46, 48) — produces "an incomparable expansion of my whole being" (44). His entire account is permeated with joy, the joy of feasting in secret — in memory now as in reality then — and the joy of owning himself to be, yet again, "the darling of the gods." Thus Moll's question to herself after her first crime, "Lord, what am I now? A thief!" (192) has as its counterpart in the reflections of Felix: "I am I, the darling of the gods, I am not subject to the appellations accorded to the Toms, Dicks and Harrys of this world" (43). Whatever one finds in Felix of the "picaresque" — guile, shrewdness, dissimulation, hedonism, chicanery — all these are transcended by the autistic voice of a magnificent ego. Mann may have imitated other fictions in endowing his rogue with a love of the world, a cinematic instinct for the episode, and an ability to gratify those whom he uses, but he invented the voice. The voice is able to justify not only theft, but venery and procurance also:

Whoever thinks that actions make people equal may go ahead and take refuge in this simple procedure [of applying a short, ugly word to my way of life at that time]. For my own part, I am in agreement with folk wisdom which holds that when two persons do the same thing it is no longer the same; yes, I go further and maintain that labels such as "drunkard", "gambler", or even "wastrel" not only do not embrace and define the actual living case, but in some instances do not even touch it.   (116)

In other words, Felix the equivocator is able to disarm his listener, whenever he describes one of his past escapades, by pointing out that he is, at least, being completely honest, "I am making [this confidence] of my own free will and could easily have passed over it in silence" (116) — and by adding the practised reminder that he is not to be classified with those lesser mortals who might be considered deserving of censure.

By exercising twin skills, elegant reportage which glosses over the act itself and wily circumvention of any imputation of guilt, Felix prevents any association his reader-listener might be tempted to make between his behaviour and that of the "rogue" of tradition. But disclaimers are only one part of his presentation of himself. Along with them are two subtle claims which reside in positive analogies. The first is an artfully pursued comparison which links him, "darling of the gods," to Hermes. The second is an implicit identification of himself with the artist.

Hermes first enters the account at the end of Part Two when Madame Houpflé, alias Diane Philibert, makes the likeness explicit. She begins with a generalization: Armand is a Hermes on account of his beautiful legs, ". . . the divine, the masterpiece of creation, the model of beauty, that's you, you young, very young man with Hermes legs" (175). Immediately she undertakes his education in mythology, and momentarily disconcerts Felix by her definition of Hermes as "the suave god of thieves." When she discovers that this boy who does not know "*le dieu voleur*" is himself the thief of her jewels, she responds in a transport of joy — "*C'est une humiliation merveilleuse . . .*" — to the degradation of being coupled with "a common, ordinary thief" (179). The generalization now becomes particular. "Oh, how much more precious to me is the thief than what he took! Hermes! He does not know who it is — and it is he! Hermes, Hermes!" And to complete the ritual she phonetically blends and associates the name "Armand," by which Felix is currently known, with the French form "Hermes."

Now this, to be sure, is the first time in his life that Felix comes upon an identification with this particular deity. But it is by no means the first time a deistic association has been made. In speaking of his godfather's questionable painting, Felix early recalls being used as "a natural costume boy" (22). Among the many poses, in many costumes, that he remembers, is one which served Shimmelpreester several times: ". . . I posed in the nude for a large picture out of Greek mythology that was to adorn the dining-room of a wine dealer in Mainz. When I did this my godfather was lavish in his praises; and indeed I was a little like a young god, slender, graceful, yet powerful in build, with a golden skin and flawless proportions" (21). Harmony, symmetry, and dimorphism are all suggested in Felix's description of his god-like young self. Furthermore the sexual ambiguity associated with Greek sculpture is matched, in an earlier descriptive passage, with an ambiguity of colouring: ". . . my hair was silken soft, as it seldom is in the male sex, and it was fair; like my blue-gray eyes, it provided a fascinating contrast to the golden brown of my skin, so that I hovered on the borderline between blond and dark and might have been considered either" (11) — an ambiguity which so fascinates Diane: "With your blue eyes and blond hair, where do you get this colouring, this tint of light bronze?" (177).

This hovering "on the borderline" suggests two things. Between blond and dark implies bronze statuary — the famous sixth-century statue of Hermes is bronze; the blond-dark combination may also be equated with the gold and ivory of Phidias' statue of Zeus in the significant anecdote of Schimmelpreester about artists (21). Between male and female — the silken soft hair, the stature at once powerful and delicate — implies those hermaphroditic or androgynous propensities which are borne out in Felix's relationships. He complacently refers to exciting homosexual impulses in Monsieur Stürzli, the hotel owner (143-44), certain vagrant enthusiasts who seek neither woman nor man, but some extraordinary creature in between (108), and in Lord Strathbogie (212-20). In the latter case, the parallel and interwoven account of the infatuation of poor Miss Twentyman underwrites the sexual ambiguity of the beloved boy. The androgyny registers also in the well-modulated voice, pleasing alike to the lustful woman (168) and the elegant priest (60), and in the gift for mimicry which encompasses both masculine and feminine styles of language (146-57). Finally, Felix draws attention to the extraordinary delicacy of his skin, "so very sensitive that, even when I had no money, I was obliged to provide myself with soft, fine soaps, for if I used the common, cheap varieties, even for a short time, they chafed it raw" (63).

All of this helps to explain why Felix, despite the undoubted masculinity attested by his sexual prowess, is, before he is invested with a fully masculine identity by the Marquis de Venosta, a peculiarly feminine love-object. For in addition to rejected suitors like Miss Twentyman and Lord Strathbogie, the sexual partners of his formative years, Genovefa, Rozsa, and Diane, all actively sought him out; he co-operated with extreme grace, yet he appears to have played a peculiarly passive role in the courtship. It seems the Marquis is right: before the masquerade it is his function to be loved rather than to love (237). And when he discourses on love, conceiving ideas and images that will be recapitulated in his conquest of Zouzou (362), his emphasis on the gaze, the glance, the *eye*, has its own mythological symbolism also, the eye being equated in myth with the female sexual organs (83, 107).[8]

A counterpart to Felix's androgyny is found in Andromache, *La fille de l'aire* (191), in whom he recognizes an alter ego. This amaz-

---

[8] We should note in this regard the "shimmering" eyes of Rozsa (112) and the "swimming" gaze of Diane (169), who has a trick of continually "widening" (151, 167) the golden-brown eyes which Felix finds so pleasing (151). Of interest also is the little interruptive discourse in which he considers the importance of the eye (83).

ing and intrepid trapeze artist has a Grecian profile and the body and hands of a boy. Felix worships her, wonders if she is human, and finally ascribes to her a proximity to the angels (192-96). We may find in Felix's descriptiton of Andromache marked affinities with Hermes; like the god she is a creature of the air, she flies, she even wears little sprouting wings as part of her costume. She is "neither man nor woman," but she is demonstrably statuesque, fulfilling all the criteria of Greek art: "Her breasts were meagre, her hips narrow, the muscles of her arms ... developed ... and her amazing hands, though not so big as a man's, were nevertheless not so small as to rule out the question whether she might not, Heaven forbid, be a boy in disguise. No, the female conformation of her breasts was unmistakable, and so too, despite her slimness, was the form of her thighs" (192). This is an image which, like others we shall notice, activates in Felix a longing for unity; an archetypal, suprapersonal image which coincides with his stint as elevator boy. And the coincidental rising and falling through the air of two kindred spirits endorses another aspect of Hermes, whose function it was to escort such figures as Persephone up to the presence of Zeus, or down to Hades.[9]

Many other mythological parallels occur. Hermes was a trickster whose tricks brought joy to the victims of his pranks; Felix serves and continually pleases those whom he robs or seduces. Hermes was known as a magician, suddenly and magically present when least expected; Louis de Venosta, delighted with Felix's ubiquity, calls him "a magician" (233). Hermes, patron of servants, was adroit in all manner of technical skills; Felix seems to be peerless in every aspect of hotel service entrusted to him. Hermes was cup-bearer to Zeus; Felix exercises a ministerial function at the court of Dom Carlos (331-38). Hermes, patron of thieves, was adroit at removing possessions secretly; Felix's appropriation of Madame Houpflé's jewel case "was an occurrence rather than an action, and it happened quite secretly" (122). Hermes was identified with travel; Felix, in love with the world, is offered a means of extensive voyaging. The "Herm" (head and phallus of the god) was raised on the door posts of Greek dwellings to secure fertility and good luck; Felix is to some extent the "protector of the home" for Louis and Zaza — he is fertile at least in the metaphoric sense — and his assurance of his own good fortune has already been noted. Finally,

9 Hermes appears in this guise in *Death in Venice*, where he guides Asenbach's soul on its journey to the underworld.

Hermes was credited with the invention of the lyre, which he graciously offered to Apollo; Felix, "a fanatical lover of music," perpetrated his earliest fraud as an infant prodigy of the violin, being rewarded by the gift of a lyre-shaped diamond brooch from an aged Russian princess (17-19).

Many of these correspondences might be construed as evidence of the design of the creator rather than the conscious identification of his created monologuist. But Felix himself voices his recognized kinship to Hermes in a distinctive and definitive way when he challenges Kuckuck's account of the origin of man (269), and complacently accepts the professor's wry comment as descriptive of himself: "Highly ingenious, your Hermes must have been. . . . The fabric of cells in his brain, if one may speak of such a thing in connection with a god, must have assumed especially artful forms" (270). Kuckuck goes on to speculate on the nature of a Hermes pictured in flesh and blood instead of in marble or plaster or ambrosia, and the reader recognizes, along with Felix, that this is the nature expressing itself throughout the monologue.

The same transfer of imaginative energy from speaker to listener occurs in relation to the Felix-artist equation. Explicitly, Felix claims a facility with the pencil in the same narcissistic way as he describes his unlooked-for prowess at tennis (342). Sinse he is impersonating an artist (256) it is important that he develop a flair for appearing to sketch with ease, and ultimately it is his appropriation of Louis's drawings which enables him to break through Zouzou's sturdy defences (381). But these are the direct intimations of artistry, and of a highly derivative and pseudo artistry at that. The more subtle instances of Felix's artistic propensity are, like the pattern of Hermetic allusion, woven into the monologue in such a way as to elicit the recognition of the reader-listener, who must once again collaborate with the writer-speaker in the making of meaning.

The documentation of Felix as artist-figure can be quickly surveyed. His delight in fantasy and costuming; his imaginative reconstruction of his experiences; his sensitivity to music, display, and form; his ever-present sense of an audience, his essential solitariness; his ability to gratify the senses of others; and his awareness of the gulf between the illusion and the reality — all testify to his "artistic" nature. But these are all phenomena. The *numen* in Felix which makes of him an exemplar of the artist is the longing for unity, paradoxically, in duality. Only in the double, in a combination of complementary or antithetical elements, can Felix conceive of meaning or beauty. This is the motif which fuses the episodes of his life together, and which pervades his dreams, which are "self-created and self-sufficient, dependent, that is, only on imagination" (221).

The two "artists" of Felix's boyhood both introduce to him the concept of duality, Schimmelpreester explicitly in the story of Phidias (21) and Müller-Rosé implicitly by the shocking contrast of his stage appearance, in which "He seemed indeed, not to belong to this world. . . . [He] dispensed the joy of life — if that phrase can be used to describe the precious and painful feeling, compounded of envy, yearning, hope, and love, that the sight of beauty and lighthearted perfection kindles in the souls of men" (24-26), and the disgusting sight of his real self in the dressing room. Not only is the divested performer ugly and dirty, but his exposed flesh is covered with pustules "red-rimmed, suppurating, some of them even bleeding" (28). The theme of discrepancy between the artist as artist and the artist as person, all unknown to Felix, is embodied in himself. His quest for "The Great Joy" (48) is a creative quest for which he is well endowed in perception and imagination, and he has the talent he ascribes to Müller-Rosé, a "devotion and drive of his heart" towards satisfying the yearning of others and becoming their darling. But with the talent for joy he has also what his godfather describes as "other oddities . . . associated with it, and perhaps essential to it" (21). As artist Felix seeks to create and perpetuate joy; as person he plans and perpetrates fraud. And the instrument of both the desire and the activity is himself, for his frauds are works of art derived not from words or music or paint but from his own person.

Neither "the artist as picaro," nor "the picaro as artist" is really the denigration of art that some readers protest. Love is the condition of art, and whether it is love of self, or of the world, or of ideas, or a compendium of them all, matters little — the concerns of art are less moral than they are universal. For this reason a continual thread in Felix's thinking is provided by his insistent groping towards unity in diversity. He conceives this first in a "double image" which is linked with his own bisexual propensity. Wandering through the streets of Frankfurt, feasting his eyes on shop-windows ("O scenes of the beautiful world!"), he comes upon an unexpected vision. A beautiful young couple, apparently brother and sister if not twins, appear momentarily on a balcony. They excite Felix's imagination in a new and wondrous way:

Dreams of love, dreams of delight and longing for union — I cannot name them otherwise, though they concerned not a single image but a double creature, a pair fleetingly but profoundly glimpsed, a brother and sister — a representative of my sex and of the other, the fair one. But the beauty here lay in the duality, in the charming doubleness. ... Dreams of love, dreams that I loved precisely because — I firmly believe — they were of primal indivisibility and indeterminateness, double; which really means that only then is there a significant whole blessedly embracing what is beguilingly human in both sexes. (81)

This "charming doubleness" is what Felix sees again in the single figure of Andromache, but later still the idea of a double creature moves away from the androgynous into the fusion of mother and daughter. In one of the coincidences that proliferate in the later part of his memoirs, Felix meets the wife and daughter of his new friend Kuckuck in a tea-shop, where they sit with a man who does not appear to be related to them:

I glanced surreptitiously at the trio. My curiosity and lively interest centred on mother and daughter — for such I considered them — and their disparate charms blended in my mind into an enchanting image of that relationship. This has been a characteristic of my emotional life. Earlier in this book, I reported the feelings with which, as a young sidewalk idler, I had drunk in the glimpse of a lovely brother and sister. ... The connoisseur of humanity will be interested in the way my penchant for two-fold enthusiasms, for being enchanted by the double-but-dissimilar, was called into play in this case by mother-and-daughter instead of brother-and-sister. (287)

Later, when his intuitive grasp of the women's identity is confirmed and Felix (now Louis) becomes a guest in their home, he begins to incorporate his awareness of doubleness into a wooing of both. He says to the mother, "My advantage is that I can behold beauty in a double image, as childlike blossom and as regal maturity" (320). He says to the daughter, "It delights me to hear you say 'we', 'we two', of yourself and your mother. But after I have enjoyed the combination, I divide you again and proceed to admire you separately" (360). And he is careful to divide his favours judiciously:

At this I kissed her hand, smiling at the same time at Zouzou. That is what I always did. It was dictated by the double image. When I paid the daughter a compliment, I looked at the mother, and vice versa. The starry-eyed man of the house, sitting at the head of the small table, observed this byplay with vague benevolence, a testimony to the stellar distances from which he gazed. The reverence I felt for him was not one jot diminished by the realization that in my courtship of the double image, consideration for him was wholly superfluous. (353)

It is small wonder that eventually both prickly daughter and stormy mother throw themselves into the ready arms of the Marquis de Venosta. But "the starry-eyed man of the house" Kuckuck (cuckold?) is not without his part to play in Felix's attempts to find wholeness. Through Kuckuck's lectures, Felix's esemplastic imagination discovers unifying analogies in the vast reaches of natural history. He quotes with tacit approval the paleontologist's benison, "All's well when Being and Well-Being are in some measure reconciled" (277). Kuckuck's exposition of life on our planet produces in Felix the sense of a significant whole, a symbolic continuity of experience:

... I was extremely excited, thanks to a feeling of expansion that almost burst the limits of my nature and was the result of my companion's conversation about Being, Life, and Man. Strange as it may sound, this vast expansiveness was closely related to, or rather was identical with, what as a child or half a child I had described in the dreamlike phrase "The Great Joy," a secret formula of my innocence used at first to denote something special, not otherwise nameable, but soon endowed with an intoxicating breadth of significance. (276)

Here Felix's habitual mode of perception, which is dualistic, expands to embrace the universal and he experiences a marvellous release from separateness. As Heilman notes:

The artist as artist does many things, but universality is his need and unity his obsession. Such is the oneness ironically concealed behind the narrative disunity of the picaresque, the acquisitive and amatory episodes of the mobile rogue; these are the wonderfully original design for that part of the old *ars poetica* traditionally assigned to the *poeta*.[10]

In Felix Krull, Thomas Mann has created an artist who works with the materials of his own person and whose object is fusion with others. The apotheosis of this aim is found in his long hymn to love, with which he seeks to break down Zouzou's resistance to his advances. "What is the digression on Nature's part that, to the astonishment of the universe, wipes out the division between one person and another, between the me and the you? It is love" (362). The treatment here, as elsewhere, is in the comic mode. Felix harangues his love-object with a carefully prepared and oratorically delivered

10 *Thomas Mann: A Collection of Critical Essays*, p. 151.

speech, but the theme is the serious theme of the work as a whole. If the "denial of the aversion of stranger for stranger" is indeed "a secret sign of omnipresent love" (365), and if the artist, as I have suggested, celebrates omnipresent love, then in the ability of Felix Krull to identify wholly with others — not merely as counterfeiter but as one who completely assumes a protean identity — we see realized the role of the artist:

> ... intricate and varied paradoxes are the motive force of Krull's whole existence; in fact they are the very substance of his improbable existence, in which dream and reality, truth and deception, all but merge. Here the very truth is elusive mutability, transformation of identity, olympian manipulation of identity. In this graceful, deceptively easy book Thomas Mann has once more given us a picture of the artist, this time of an artist who works with his own flesh and blood.[11]

There is a similarity of purpose to be noted in Joyce Cary's portrayal of Gulley Jimson, but the similarity is limited to the fact that Gulley is an artist in the most restricted sense of the term. He is a painter, and he sees the world in terms of shapes and colours, but beyond that aspect of an artist's vision he is no more like Felix Krull than William Blake is like Nietzsche.

To provide fitting perspective for Gulley we must briefly consider Cary's total design. In his own words, this was a design which would make "all the characters and incidents form parts of one coherent experience for the judgement, and at the same time give it the vitality of a narrative from actual life." In speaking of "all" here, Cary is considering the trilogy of which *The Horse's Mouth* is the last part. Thus in his preface to the Carfax edition of *Herself Surprised*, Cary explains:

> [*Herself Surprised*] is the first book of a trilogy which was designed to show three characters, not only in themselves but as seen by each other. The object was to get a three-dimensional depth and force of character. One character was to speak in each book and describe the other two as seen by that person. ... The centre of the plan was character, the character of my three leading persons in relation to, or in conflict with, other characters and the character of their times.[12]

It follows from this description that Gulley was not originally meant to be isolated from Sara and Wilcher, but I have no com-

[11] Erich Kahler, *The Orbit of Thomas Mann*, trans. Krishna and Richard Winston (Princeton: Princeton University Press, 1969), p. 63.

[12] *Herself Surprised* (London: Michael Joseph, 1941), p. 7. All page numbers in parenthesis are to this edition.

punction in so isolating him because critics and readers commonly do so, and because Cary himself acknowledged that his design failed, in practice, as a result of the intractability of his characters (7). The Gulley of *The Horse's Mouth* is considerably older than the Gulley of Sara's narrative, and too much occupied with his obsessive need to paint a last masterpiece to waste much breath on describing the companions of his younger days. Rather he is in quest of a final clean canvas:

> I love starting, Nosy. . . . But I don't like going on. The trouble with me is that I hate work, that's why I'm an artist. I could never stand work. But you can't get away from it in this fallen world. The curse of Adam. . . . You want to start clear, with a clean canvas, and a bright shining vision of whatever you call the thing. A sort of coloured music in the mind.[13]

Gulley tells the story of his last few months through a "sort of coloured music" in his mind. In those months he has three new shining visions, and begins work accordingly on three paintings: *The Fall*,[14] *The Raising of Lazarus*, and *The Creation*. He is not destined to finish any of them, and the account ends when he suffers a stroke coincidentally with the demolition of the last paintable surface he has been able to appropriate. His monologue is in essence a running commentary on the theme of inspiration, and expatiation upon his three creative ideas and his abortive attempts at their execution. Whatever else is told, of the past or of immediate circumstance, is subordinate to the Blakean metaphysic: "Energy is Eternal Delight."

> Yes, I thought, here's Billy again. Handing me the truth. Even when I wouldn't take it. That's what he was saying all his life. A tear is an intellectual thing. And a joy. It's wisdom in vision. It's the prophetic eye in the loins. The passion of intelligence. Yes, by Gee and Jay, I thought. The everlasting creation of delight. The joy that is always new and fresh because it is created. The revelation ever renewed, in every fall. (98)

In Gulley's pursuit of this "joy" there is a single-mindedness reminiscent of Felix Krull. But in all else the two hedonists are poles apart. Where Felix was equivocal, Gulley is embarrassingly direct. Where Felix cultivated arts of dissimulation, striving to conquer

---

[13] Joyce Cary, *The Horse's Mouth* (London: Michael Joseph, 1944), p. 164. All page numbers in parenthesis are to this edition.

[14] This painting on the wall of his boathouse had already been started before his prison sentence; nevertheless he approaches it with a new vision — each new start, as he explains to Nosy in the continuation of the cited paragraph, is a fresh creative act.

others by his spurious but winning "sincerity," Gulley delights in playful sarcasm, cultivating the ear of Nosy, and therefore of the reader-listener, by means of self-denigrating badinage:

"Who told you Mr. Jimson was an artist?" I said. . . . "Look here, I'll tell you a secret. Jimson never was an artist. He's only one of the poor beggars who thought he was clever. Why, you know what the critics said about his pictures in 1908 — that's thirty years ago. They said he was a nasty young man who didn't even know what art was . . . and since then he's gone off a lot. As he's got older, he's got younger." (19)

Most of all, as this quotation shows, Gulley's salient characteristic is his sense of humour. Perhaps it need hardly be added that a sense of humour is as alien to Felix Krull as is a sense of humility.

The form of Gulley's monologue is strikingly different from Krull's confessions also. We have seen how Felix laboured to produce his memoirs in belletristic form spasmodically and over a long period of time, and frequently declared himself charmed with his own expertise. Gulley, on the other hand, rattles off his story without pause or any but the slightest comment on what he is about. He notes in passing that he is dictating his memoir to his "honorary secretary, who has got the afternoon off from the cheese counter" (54), and presumably he is doing so from a hospital bed, since the account ends with his being told he is "seriously ill" (291). Apart from this there is little to suggest that the monologue is addressed to an audience, and certainly nothing to indicate that Gulley is his own admiring audience, as Felix is. Indeed, the flow of narrative seems to be autobiographical by accident rather than design, and, perhaps because this is the third book of the trilogy, Gulley seems to address a reader already familiar with his life story. Scenes from his past life appear in reminiscence only when they are evoked by his present condition, and we learn that he is sixty-seven, and in poor health, as we learn of his former life with his parents, his sister, and his three women, all incidentally. Even when these pieces of the puzzle are fitted together, the picture of Gulley's life is far from complete. His memory is not subject to ordering any more than his syntax is subject to refinement. And the sequence which threads together the fragmented memories — a narrative comprising the few months of Gulley's existence between prison and stroke — frequently melts into present tense reflection which effectively removes the distance established by the past tense framework:

... And I shoved him out and banged the door. And got back to the fishes for a hour or six.

Then I had a disinterested look at them and they were not at all what I expected. Nothing ever is. But after a little reflection, I waked up about half past two in the morning and perceived that their noses were not big enough and too near together. Water too bright. And soft. Had to be harder to get the plane flat.

The middle of the night is a good time for a man to study his picture because he can't see it then; and the new scheme worked out well. On Saturday morning it looked so good that I began to like it. . . . When all at once I had visitors. Mr. Plant and two other preachers. . . .

Plantie is a very strong Protestant, that is to say, he's against all churches, especially the Protestant. (39-40)

This particular digression about religion continues for four paragraphs until Plantie expresses admiration for the painting and the narrative continues once more in the past tense. The present tense verbs in the entire sequence outnumber the past tense verbs by fifty-six to thirty-one, and but for Gulley's habitual ellipsis the ratio of present to past would be even higher. The total effect is of immediacy, of being in the presence of a lively raconteur who is in the act of recounting an anecdote but whose personality is far more engaging than the little history itself.

The "raconteur" style of Gulley's monologue is clearly attributable to its origin as speech rather than as writing. Throughout his spate of narrative, description, and exposition, his unedited flow of talk is punctuated by "I said," or "I said to myself," so that the reader feels himself to be constantly in the role of witness to, or participant in, a running dialogue. That Gulley's dialogue is frequently with himself intensifies the reader's impression of a life process at work, as he listens to another human being orientating himself to his world, or even creating his world, as he speaks. In his exposition of the phenomenology of verbal communication, Merleau-Ponty has said:

What I [as listener] communicate with primarily is not "representations" of thought, but with a speaking subject, with a certain style of being and with the "world" at which he directs his aim. . . . What then does language express, if it does not express thoughts? It presents or rather *is* the subject's taking up of a position in the world of his meanings. . . . The spoken word is a gesture, and its meaning, a world.[15]

It seems a singularly appropriate description of Gulley that he is a "speaking subject with a certain style of being and with a 'world'

15 Maurice Merleau-Ponty, *Phenomonology of Perception*, trans. Colin Smith (London: Routledge and Kegan Paul, 1962), pp. 183-93.

at which he directs his aim." As a speaking subject, his style of being is ejaculatory. He adds statement to statement so that sentence after sentence begins with "and" or "but" (40, 23); frequently he augments his initial statement with an afterthought formulated as a separate subordinate clause (57, 182, 264); frequently a single word or phrase becomes an elliptical summation of a preceding flow of thought (90, 182, 288). Almost any excerpt will demonstrate these peculiarities of expression, or "gestures":

> I wanted to grieve for Papa. That man suffered a lot. Even more than my poor mother who had to watch him suffer. For she had seven children to worry about as well, and children are a duty. Whereas a broken-hearted man with a grievance is only a liability, a nuisance. And he knows it too. . . . Cold morning. My legs a bit stiff. Didn't look at Adam and Eve in case it hadn't come back. But went straight out. . . . Old Renoir painting his red girls with the bushes strapped to his wrists. Best things he ever did. Monuments. (21)

Furthermore, these stylistic quirks are consistent throughout, marking Gulley's style of address to himself, to his various acquaintances (regardless of their status) and to the silent listener whom the reader has become.

In his address to the reader, as in his address to Nosy or Coker or the Beeders, Gulley assumes an understanding of, if not an agreement with, everything he says. An example of this occurs when he gives an account of how he came to be an artist, an account which he begins by addressing the reader directly:

> If . . . I may make a personal explanation, which won't be published anyhow; I never meant to be an artist. You say, who does. (54)

Frequently during the subsequent "explanation," Gulley claims the assent of his listener with a characteristic "of course." More importantly, however, he threads into his narrative ten quotations from Blake, with no kind of indication of what they are doing there. The implication is clear. "Of course" the silent listener will be able to understand. It is Gulley's superb sense of meaningfulness in his every verbal gesture which leads him to claim as his unquestioned right the collaboration of his listener.

Gulley's self-assurance never deserts him, and shows itself in his mode of speech as much as in his actions. His consciousness of himself as artist leads him to contemplate himself in the third person in much the same way as Felix Krull does (106, 190, 221, 235, 264), and his awareness of Gulley Jimson extends even to his favourite oath, "By Gee [for Gulley] and by Jay [for Jimson]!" (20, 56, 98). Gulley's "world" is himself, and his awareness of himself, whether as "a genius. God damn it, of course I am" (105) or as a disreputable con-artist giving his fans "the famous Gulley Jimson smile" (268)becomes, inevitably, the reader's also. The consequent immediacy of personality continues throughout the monologue to the final catastrophic event:

Nosy and Jorky were fighting three councillors and two policemen. And I remonstrated with them. "Don't go on like that, boys. You'll end by creating a disturbance in your tempers, you'll spoil your appetites, which in children takes the place of a rational power. Besides," I said, but speaking in a quiet voice, to save my breath, because nobody was listening to me, "it's unnecessary to make all this fuss. . . . If they killed me, I could run them in for damages. I've had some before, and I've never paid any attention. It's what you call the pischological attack. Everybody goes in for pischology these days. It started in Genesis, and it reached the government about 1930. But when anyone gives you pischology, you can always give it 'em back. Pay no attention. Look at me, here I am, and here I sit." (288-89)

"Here I am, and here I sit" might be a fitting epigram for the monologue as a whole. However, the above paragraph is unusually connected and complete. More frequently Gulley's mode of speech is laconic and elliptical; his verbal style is at once staccato and colourful, like the spurting of paint onto a canvas:

An evening by Randypole Billy. Green lily sky, orange flames over the West. Long flat clouds like copper angels with brass hair floating on the curls of the fire. River mint green and blood orange. Old man lying along the water with a green beard, one arm under head, face twisted up — vision of Thames among the pot-houses. . . . Yes, yes, just what I wanted. But not a cloud. Don't want solid cloud. How then. A dead branch. A rhino's horn. A gorilla's finger. Stump of a leg. (237)

And so it continues, a spate of analogies expressive at once of the painter's imagination and the vision molded by the arch-exemplar, William Blake. But because Gulley is a conscious humorist, every soaring inspiration is accompanied by deliberate bathos. In this passage his ruminations are interrupted by a hastily gulped meal of sausage and mash; at the Beeders a similar rhapsody to the feet he has painted on the studio wall ends in a series of puns — ". . . the soul of a great baby. In milk and dill water. Pour soul, it's a flat life. One flatness on another. Flattery to flats" (191) — in which the allusions and verbal tricks are clever as well as comic. A typical example of Gulley's characteristic juxtaposition of the poetic and the prosaic occurs at the end of chapter forty-two:

As I slipped out, something like a fiery comet whizzed past my left ear and I saw old Snow land in the light in front of me; all four feet at once. And then with one spring, in every joyful lovely muscle, ascend into Heaven; or the garden wall. (282)

The fusion of sublime and ridiculous found in Gulley's voice is a source of continual humour. He becomes increasingly lovable, a person the reader would like to believe exists for much the same reason that the child believes Puss-in-Boots or leprechauns exist. Such a figure is not likely to exist in real life, but he exists most persuasively in fantasy. The charm of *The Horse's Mouth* is the charm of the folk-tale, in which order is achieved in a disordered universe by means of a hero who is gloriously out of step with the army of trudging mankind.

Much criticism of the character of Gulley Jimson slides into one of two errors. Either he is measured by the norms of the socially extensive novel, in which case Cary is labelled with Fielding as a moralist who had no conception of the irrational,[16] or he is seen as a pathetic victim, in which case Cary is charged with sentimentalism.[17] Neither view, however, sufficiently accounts for the authority with which Gulley speaks. For he is the horse of the significant title; he may be toothless, rather than long in the tooth, but he speaks assertively whenever he opens his mouth:

I was still scraping at the fish and Nosy was looking at me with eyes like another fish. "What are you doing, Mr. J-Jimson, you're spoiling it." "These fish stink. And what are you doing here, young man? How long have you been interrupting me?" . . . "But Mr. Jimson, you're not going to take them all out?" "All of 'em." "Why?" "They're dead. They don't swim — they don't speak, they don't click, they don't work, they don't do anything at all." "But why don't they?" "God knows. But he won't go into details. The truth it, THE OLD HORSE DOESN'T SPEAK ONLY HORSE. And I can't speak only Greenbank." "Horse," said Nosy, with his eye revolving in different directions. "Here," I said,

16 See, for example, Frederick Karl, whose argument in *A Reader's Guide to the Contemporary Novel* (New York: Noonday, 1967), p. 130, is that Gulley is a Rousseauistic natural man who retains his vision only by dissociating from the corrupt structure of institutions and academies.

17 Andrew Wright, *Joyce Cary: A Preface to his Novels* (London: Chatto and Windus, 1958), pp. 124-37, and Kenneth Hamilton, "Boon or Thorn? Joyce Cary and Samuel Beckett on Human Life," *The Dalhousie Review*, XXXVIII Winter 1959), 435. "The comedy of Gulley's story lies in the resourcefulness and pugnacity of a little man willing to take on all comers."

"what are you talking about? You're doing it on purpose. Go away."
... "But I like the fish, Mr. Jimson. Are you s-sure they're wrong?"
"No, I'm not shushure of anything except that if you don't go away
and shut up I'll have the stroke." "What stroke, Mr. J-Jimson?" "THE
STROKE! Nosy, the finisher, the cut-off. What you'll get some day with
the hatchet." (44)

The authority here, cloaked as usual with quip and word play (to
say nothing of horse play, Gulley accompanying his repartee with
blows and feints like a pint-size boxer), extends to prophecy. Gulley
knows he is living on borrowed time, and quite without self-pity, he
means to go on living, which for him means painting, until he dies.
He submits to the indignities of penury, hunger, vagrancy, and physical abuse without complaint. In one of the finest comic scenes in
the novel, he even submits to being put to bed like a dangerous baby
by his aggressive protector Coker (85-86). And come what may he
pursues his creative function with an inveterate single-mindedness
which makes him impatient to the point of fury with those who frus-
trate it. Nosy, Coker, Plant and his coterie of preachers, Sara (in
retrospect), and, in the *dénouement*, the combined forces of councillors, policemen, and demolition squad, all provoke his ire when they
offer to impede him. On the other hand, he can tolerate any amount
of confusion about him — as when he shares his appropriated Beeder
studio with a noisy sculptor (192) — when he is allowed to pursue
his function unimpeded. Gulley knows what he must do, and though
it change with the changing stimuli of sky and river and chance
human forms, it is the artistic vision which obsesses him and which,
denigrate it as he may, he must eternally pursue. Therefore his
monologue ends, as it begins, with reference to Blake who is "the
real horse meat" for a dying old "horse" to offer. And when he
speaks finally to the vigilant nun, it is to predict that he will die —
if such a hero can indeed die — laughing, and praying ("little creature born of joy and mirth"), because it is the same thing. The
dichotomous states of innocence and experience postulated by Blake
can become one. This is what Gulley's monologue is all about to the
collaborating listener.

As a creation, then, Gulley Jimson is no more "realistic" than
Felix Krull. Neither character can be judged by the standards of
common humanity. They exist only in the monologues they speak,
for — as Forster says of Fielding's Amelia and Jane Austen's Emma
— "The barrier of art divides them from us. They are real not be-

cause they are like ourselves . . . but because they are convincing."[18]
For this reason we turn now to a character who is much more like
ourselves than they; Margaret Laurence's Hagar Shipley is not easily
separated from the world in which modern Canadian readers live;
she is an undoubted example of Frye's fourth category of heroes in
fiction, the low mimetic mode. We find in her experience the prob-
ability we find in our own.[19]

Yet, as a monologue, Hagar's disclosures in *The Stone Angel*
present severe problems of credibility. Both Mann and Cary provide
a *locus standi* from which their creatures can speak — Felix writing
his memoirs and Gulley dictating his. Laurence makes no attempt to
provide a memoir frame. Hagar speaks from the present, to no
named listener, alternately recording the immediate scene and recalling the past as present impressions evoke it, and in both mental
activities we share her thoughts at first hand, living her life with her
up to the moment of her death. And whereas we may question
Gulley's ability to dictate so comprehensive and colourful an account of his life while he is dying after his "final stroke," in Hagar's
case there is no room for even this kind of doubt. The last thoughts
of Hagar in the novel are the last thoughts of Hagar in life. Dying,
she wrestles with a nurse for possession of a glass. "I'll not counte-
nance anyone else's holding it for me."[20] Successful, she holds it in
her own hands, the symbol of a lifetime of independence. "There.
There." Two words follow in a separate paragraph. "And then
—." The rest is silence.

It is only upon reflection, however, that the reader questions the
validity of the private thoughts and memories he has shared. The
vivid reality of character in Hagar suspends any question of authenticity in much the same way as does the fulness of life in Molly
Bloom, whose monologue in *Ulysses* is similarly accepted for its psychological, rather than its empirical, truth. Like Molly, Hagar seems
to be speaking to herself, and the reader overhears a voice which is
consistently true to the self-perpetuating ego it embodies. Unlike
Molly, Hagar works out her associations in complete and consecutive statements, consciously keeping her memories in step with the
events of her last few weeks of life, and struggling to understand
her extensive past in an attempt to come to terms with her ever-

[18] *Aspects of the Novel*, p. 61.

[19] *Anatomy of Criticism*, pp. 103-05.

[20] *The Stone Angel* (Toronto: McClelland & Stewart, 1968), p. 308. All page
numbers in parenthesis are to this edition.

diminishing present. The art of her creator is shown in the interweaving of memory and perception, and in the controlling imagery and allusion which create a unity from the alternating strands.

Hagar's monologue begins with a retrospective description of the stone angel of the title, standing sightless in a cemetery above the prairie town of Manawaka where she, the only Currie girl, was born at the cost of her mother's life. She recalls the cemetery and her walks there as a child; she recalls the planted peonies and the tough wild cowslips; she associates the blind statue with the pride of her father and the feeble ghost of her mother. She becomes, she says, "rampant with memory" (5), as, in extreme old age, she grieves for her lost men.

What follows is an unfolding of the past as she remembers each lost man in turn. The order of her memories, deceptively random, is in fact both consecutive and climactic. The first lost man, her brother Daniel, is linked in his life with the despised frailty of Mrs. Currie and in his death with Hagar's own intransigence. Though she knows it would ease his passing, the young Hagar is unable to "bend enough" to play the part of his mother. Her pride never will permit her to dissimulate, or even respond to any acknowledgement of dependence. So it is the other brother, Matt, who sits at the bedside wearing his mother's shawl (25).

Later it is Matt's death she remembers, with a savage anger that he too had slipped quietly into death. "Why hadn't he writhed, cursed, at least grappled with the thing?" (60). When Jason, her estranged father, dies, her memories of his former strength and possessiveness are marked with her own lack of responsiveness (44), and her regret at his repudiation of her marriage leads her to feel alienation from her firstborn, Marvin, and chagrin that Jason died before he "saw my second son or knew at all that the sort of boy he'd wanted had waited a generation to appear" (64).

Jason Currie was lost to Hagar before he died, and so was her husband Bram Shipley. She remembers occasions when she was as stonelike in the face of his need as she had been with her father. The tenderness she feels in retrospect she was never able to voice; the nearest she ever came to it — an expression of sympathy at the loss of his cherished horse — she remembers with pain, such was the surprise in his face at her gentle tone (87). Her memories of Bram are infused with shame, even with disgust, yet the sight of an old man at dusk is enough to deceive her into a momentary fantasy:

So familiar is he that I cannot move or speak nor breathe. How has he come here, by what mystery? Or have I come to the place he went before? This is a strange place, surely, shadowed and luminous, the trees enfolding us like arms in the sheltering dark. If I speak to him, slowly, so as not to startle, will he turn to me with such a look of recognition that I hardly dare hope for it, and speak my name? (106)

The old man in the summer house is a reminder of the broken Bram to whom Hagar returned as his death seemed imminent. But before she recalls his dying, memories of John, her best beloved, intervene. And as her memories of father and husband show her to resemble the angel in stoniness, so her memories of her two sons show her to resemble the angel in blindness. She cannot see, as the reader sees, the devotion and worth of the elder, nor the weakness and obduracy of the younger. After twenty-five years with Bram, she abandons him to devote her remaining years to John, and in one of the many ironies of her history John returns to Manitoba and to the Shipley place to live out *his* remaining years.

Thus it is that the two dearest lost men come together in the last third of Hagar's monologue. John "nurses" his father to death, easing his last days with the home-brew he himself drinks too freely. Hagar still fails to see that John is Bram's son, as Marvin is hers. When Bram is dead, and she returns again for a summer visit, she fails to see that John has become Arlene Summers's man as he was never hers. But in their terrible end Arlene dies, mercifully, first; it is Hagar who sits beside his deathbed. The words she recalls then, "words that must have spun, unspoken, through me at that moment" (241), are the words of her Biblical counterpart, Hagar of the desert. *If he should die, let me not see it. Let me not see the death of my son.*

Biblical allusions and analogies thread through Hagar's musings explicitly and implicitly, often providing a level of meaning deeper than what she herself descries. Marvin is notably missing from her gallery of lost men, not only because he was never lost, but also because he was never loved. But as she reaches her own end both stoniness and blindness are mitigated in Hagar. John's insight, "You always bet on the wrong horse. . . . Marv was your boy, but you never saw that, did you?" (237) becomes her own. There had been a time when she had wanted to see John as Jacob wrestling with the angel, as, in a very tangible way, he struggled to raise the fallen monument over the joint Currie-Shipley grave. But no, he sweated and grunted and swore, looking for no blessing (179). Now Marvin, sitting beside her hospital bed, unexpectedly clasps her hand:

> Now it seems to me he is truly Jacob, gripping with all his strength, and bargaining. *I will not let thee go, except thou bless me.* And I see I am thus strangely cast, and perhaps have been so from the beginning, and can only release myself by releasing him. (304)

In an inversion of the earliest deathbed scene, Hagar is able to dissimulate. She blesses him in her own gruff way, speaking her only lie, and he lets her go. Thus before her death she learns that a blessing is reciprocal:

> As he goes out, I hear the nurse speaking to him in the corridor.
> "She's got an amazing constitution, your mother. One of those hearts that just keeps on working, whatever else is gone."
> A pause, and then Marvin replies.
> "She's a holy terror," he says.
> Listening, I feel like it is more than I could now reasonably have expected out of life, for he has spoken with such anger and such tenderness. (304-05)

"A holy terror" is a fitting description of Hagar Shipley. Throughout her voicing of memories the present has intruded its reminders of mortality and drawn from her a magnificent "rage against the dying of the light." Throughout her dialogue with others the same characteristics of belligerence and obduracy appear. Forgetfulness, grim humour, enraged helplessness, and always the intractable pride, are alike consistently conveyed:

> I have lived with Marvin and Doris — or they have lived in my house, whichever way one cares to phrase it — for seventeen years. Seventeen — it weighs like centuries. How have I borne it? How have they?
> "I always swore I'd never be a burden —"
> Now I perceive, too late, how laden with self-pity my voice sounds, and how filled with reproach. But they rise like fish to the bait.
> "No — don't think that. We never said that, did we?"
> "Marv only meant — I only meant —"
> How ashamed I am, to play that worn old tune. And yet — I am not like Marvin. I do not have his urge to keep the peace. I am reconciled to this question of the house, my house, mine. . . .
> "I'm going to the evening service, Mother. Care to come along? You've not been for some time now."
> Doris is very religious. She says it is a comfort. Her minister is plump and pink, and if he met John the Baptist in tatters in the desert, stuffing dead locusts into that parched mouth for food, and blazing the New Kingdom out of those terrible eyesockets, he would faint. But so would I, likely.

"Not tonight, thanks. Next week, perhaps."

"I was going to ask him to call on you. The minister, I mean, Mr. Troy." . . .

Tact comes the hardest of all to me now. How to say that pearly Mr. Troy would be wasting his time in offering me his murmured words? Doris believes that age increases natural piety, like a kind of insurance policy falling due. I couldn't explain. Who would understand, even if I strained to speak? I am past ninety, and this figure seems somehow arbitrary and impossible, for when I look in my mirror and beyond the changing shell that houses me, I see the eyes of Hagar Currie, the same dark eyes as when I first began to remember and to notice myself. (37-38)

On the way home, the bus in packed. A teenage girl in a white and green striped dress, a girl green and tender as new Swiss chard, rises and gives me her seat. How very kind of her. I can scarcely nod my thanks, fearing she'll see my unseemly tears. And once again it seems an oddity, that I should have remained unweeping over my dead men and now possess two deep salt springs in my face over such a triviality as this. . . .

After supper they baggage me into the car and off we go. I ride in the back seat alone. Bundled around with a packing of puffy pillows, I am held securely like an egg in a crate. . . .

All would be lovely, all would be calm, except for Doris's voice squeaking like a breathless mouse. She has to explain the sights. Perhaps she believes me blind.

"My, doesn't everything look green?" she says, as though it were a marvel that the fields were not scarlet and the alders aquamarine. Marvin says nothing. Nor do I. Who could make a sensible reply?

"The crops look good don't they? . . . Oh look at the blackberries all along the ditch. . . . We should come out when they're ripe, Marv, and get some for jam."

"The seeds will get under your plate." I can't resist saying it. She has false teeth, whereas I, through some miracle, still possess my own. (92-94)

It is easy to share the anger and tenderness Hagar inspires in Marvin. She is as indomitable and pugnacious as Gulley, but unlike him she has lapses of self-pity, and she is painfully aware of the embarrassment she causes by her loud voice and her incapacity to control her bodily functions. She is continually exercising her caustic tongue, and alternately feeling shame and delight at its effects. But though she accounts herself "unchangeable, unregenerate" (293), we know better. She rises to the stature of a tragic figure through her recognition of herself and an understanding of her lifelong isolation — the state which Frye has called the "centre of tragedy." For when the "pearly" Mr. Troy visits her for the last time, he is persuaded — and his courage raises him highly in the old woman's estimation — to replace his "murmuring" with singing, and he sings the old hundredth with assurance.

> I would have wished it. This knowing comes upon me so forcefully, so shatteringly, and with such bitterness as I have never felt before. I must always, always, have wanted that — simply to rejoice. How is it I never could? I know, I know. How long have I known? Or have I always known, in some far crevice of my heart, some cave too deeply buried, too concealed? Every good joy I might have held, in my man or any child of mine or even the plain light of morning, of walking the earth, all were forced to a standstill by some brake of proper appearances — oh, proper to whom? When did I ever speak the heart's truth?
> Pride was my wilderness, and the demon that led me there was fear. I was alone, never anything else, and never free, for I carried my chains within me, and they spread out from me and shackled all I touched. Oh, my two, my dead. Dead by your own hands or by mine? Nothing can take away those years. (292)

The dramatic intensity of these lines demands access through the ear as poetry does, and it is not surprising that actresses have achieved renown by reciting them. The insight which prepares Hagar for her death breaks through the mimetic mode of the monologue in a cry from the heart. But it is not in her epiphany only that Hagar proves unforgettable. Before her end she returns once more to the cussed, querulous old woman whose voice we have come to recognize as unique:

> How I hate the sound of a person crying. She moans, snuffles wetly, moans again. She won't stop. She'll go on all night like this, more than likely. It's insufferable. I wish she'd make some effort to be quiet. She has no self-control, that creature, none. I could almost wish she'd die, or at least faint, so I wouldn't have to lie here hour after hour and hear this caterwauling. (299)

In this, too, she is unforgettable.

In her use of language, Hagar Shipley draws upon several registers, so that her speaking voice sometimes resembles that of Felix, and sometimes that of Gulley. When she contemplates her past or attempts to describe her pain, her language is frequently rhetorical and rich in imagery:

> Here were crates and cartons, tea chests with torn tin stripping, the unrecognizable effluvia of our lives, burned and blackened by the fire that seasonally cauterized the festering place. Here were the wrecks of cutters and buggies, the rusty springs and gashed seats, the skeletons of conveyances purchased in fine fettle by the town fathers and grown

as racked and ruined as the old gents, but not afforded a decent concealment in earth. Here were the leavings from tables, gnawed bones, rot-softened rinds of pumpkin and marrow, peelings and cores, pits of plum, broken jars of preserves that had fermented and been chucked reluctantly away rather than risk ptomaine. It was a sulphurous place, where even the weeds appeared to grow more gross and noxious than elsewhere, as though they could not help but show the stain and stench of their improper nourishment.   (26)

Up flames the pain now, and I am speared once more, the blade driving under my ribs, the heavy larded flesh is no shield against it, for it attacks craftily, from the inside. Breath goes. I cannot breathe. I am held, fixed and fluttering, like an earthworm impaled by children on the ferociously unsharp hook of a safety pin. I am unable to draw breath at all, and my quick panic is apart from me and almost seen, like the masks that leer out of the dark on Hallowe'en, stopping the young in their tracks and freezing their mouths in the "O" of a soundless wail.   (54)

In the first passage we notice chiefly the literary devices of parallelism, repetition, balance, skilful subordination, and even alliteration. In the second we notice chiefly the weaving of metaphor and simile into a speech made rhythmic by its variety of sentence structure. In both, despite the concession to a low demotic style found in such expressions as "in fine fettle," "the old gents," and "chucked away," structure, syntax, and vocabulary intimate that this is a secondary and not a primary mode of expression, formulated for the pen.

At other times, in her present-tense record of immediate sensation, Hagar's voice recalls the verbal spurts of Gulley:

I'm confused. It was nice of him, that man, to leave his coat. Not one in a hundred would have done that. If only I had a drink of water. I think he'll come back. . . . It had better be soon. I'm thirsty. I'm feeling faint. If I ate something, I might be all right. Perhaps he'll bring oranges. An orange would go down well right now. Or-no. I don't believe I could eat, after all. A glass of water is really all I want.   (250)

Most of her monologue, however, is couched in a middle register which shows the traces of both styles, so that we listen to a racy commentary by a speaker whose colloquialisms are informed by apt analogies and shaped into appropriate structures:

Lottie was podgy as a puffball. She looked as though she'd either burst or bounce if you tapped her. The Driesers always ran to fat. I didn't remember her mother very well, who'd died so conveniently young with a bare left hand, but the dressmaker aunt who reared Lottie used to waddle like a goose force-fed for Christmas.

Lottie wore navy blue that day, a tailored silk, probably thinking that dark colour would reduce her girth. What a hope. And of course she hadn't been able to resist looping her neck with a dozen dangling strands of artificial pearls. I wasn't very slim myself, it's true, but I was solid — never that flabby fat that seems to quiver and tremble by itself, unbidden. I wore the dusky rose silk suit I'd bought on sale that spring, and a hat to match. (209-10)

Here we see at work another device linking Hagar to Felix and Gulley. Like them, she enables her listener to visualize her as she speaks. But her self-description is always oblique; she does not regard or present herself in the third person as they do. She incorporates into her monologue a subtle self-reference which evokes in the listener that response which has been described by Alex Comfort, as we have noted earlier, as "active participation in the illusion, the process of composition, and the acceptance of the result." A clear example of this occurs towards the end of her ordeal, when she sits alone in the old cannery:

I have everything I need. An overturned box is my table, and another is my chair. I spread my supper and eat. When I've done, the light still holds and in one shell lying on the floor at my feet I see half a dozen June bugs have been caught. I prod them with a finger-nail. They're not alive. Death hasn't tarnished them, however. Their backs are green and luminous, with a sharp metallic line down the centre, and their bellies shimmer with pure copper. If I've unearthed jewels, the least I can do is wear them. Why not, since no-one's here to inform me I'm a fool? I take off my hat — it's hardly suitable for here, anyway, a prim domestic hat sprouting cultivated flowers. Then with considerable care I arrange the jade and copper pieces in my hair. I glance into my purse mirror. The effect is pleasing. They liven my gray, transform me. I sit quite still and straight, my hands spread languidly on my knees, queen of moth-millers, empress of earwigs. (216)

The picture of Hagar at this moment is one which the reader has to make for himself. She has, with the utmost economy, shown herself through her monologue, and the listener must supply for himself those additional details of composition which allow the scene to unfold before him, and which make the result — a visualized empress of earwigs — an unforgettable imprint of his imagination.

It is this quality of being unforgettable which characterizes all the monologuists of fictive autobiography at its best. The autobiographical monologue is memorable not for its content, but for its voice. Could we ever fail to recognize these speakers, once we had listened to them?

128

I refrain from pronouncing moral judgment on a craving which, when I was the object of it, seemed not incomprehensible.

*   *   *

But I knew that Hickson was dead. I knew it just as a man knows when he's had his leg shot off, though he can still feel his corns. And it upset me. I felt as if the ground had given a yawn under my feet. I felt like that little dog in the story who ran out of Lombard Street to do his morning pee against the Bank of England and found it gone. Gone to nothing. Not even a hole in the ground. But nothing at all. Nothing even to bark at. What would be the good of a bark at nothing. Nothing. Because it would be nothing itself as soon as it went over the edge. I refuse to believe it, I said. But then I gave a great sigh and found that I was crying. This cheered me up a little. Yes, real tears. I can't be so old, I said, if I can still cry. There's sap in the old trunk yet. And I got up and hobbled home.

*   *   *

They can dump me in a ten-acre field, for all I care, and not waste a single cent on a box of flowers, nor a single breath on prayers to ferry my soul, for I'll be dead as a mackerel. Hard to imagine a world and I not in it. Will everything stop when I do? Stupid old baggage, who do you think you are? . . . There's no one like me in this world.

"There's no one like me in this world" is true of all three speakers. Lubbock has aptly noted of the novel generally, that we cannot retain it entire. "As quickly as we read, it melts and shifts in the memory; even at the moment when the last page is turned, a great part of the book, its finer detail, is already vague and doubtful." But the imprint made by the persons of Felix Krull, Gulley Jimson, and Hagar Shipley, different as they are, is lasting. They live in the mind, unsusceptible, as our real life intimates are, to change; and if we turn to their accounts again it is to renew acquaintance with old friends, secure in the knowledge that they will engage us once more in the delights of their inimitable voices.

CHAPTER FIVE

Eyewitness Monologues

. . . all impression is twofold, half-sheathed in the object, prolonged in ourselves by another half which we alone can know. — PROUST, *Remembrance of Things Past, Time Regained*, ch. 3

In considering the autobiographical monologue, we have responded subjectively to subjective disclosures. If a Hagar or a Gulley, or even a Felix, is reporting his own story, we accept it as a means to the end of knowing him. Though the way he sees himself may not always be the way we see him, it is the self that occupies us rather than the story he tells, because he is, after all, his own subject, and his words are, in the terms of phenomenology, "gestures" by which he expresses the world of his meanings.

A different situation exists when a monologuist presents a narrative as an eyewitness of events befalling others. At once susceptibility to error, misinterpretation, or exaggeration becomes not only possible, but likely. In place of an unforgettable speaker as the terminal, if essentially egoistic, object of our attention, we have a recorder whose experience of others is our major focus, as it is his. His egoism may or may not fascinate, but his overt purpose is not self-disclosure. Instead he struggles towards an understanding of people he has known and events he has witnessed. This struggle towards understanding — a more or less disinterested pursuit of objective truth — is a constant feature of eyewitness monologues, and to the extent that we learn to trust the speaker we either collaborate with him in the making of meaning or separate ourselves from his reconstruction of events to contemplate both him and his story with a similar degree of ironic detachment.

In view of several critical discussions of "reliable" and "unreliable" narrators, it should perhaps be noted that this ironic detachment is frequently the objective of the creator of an eyewitness narrator, and in itself this objective may determine the compositional key of the work. Booth and others have quarrelled with the reliability of such narrators as I shall discuss without always recognizing that their limitations of judgement or temperament serve designedly to make the operations of their minds the true fascination of their monologues. Eyewitness narrators may, in short, be totally reliable in their unreliability. In choosing to examine the testimony of Marlow, in Conrad's *Heart of Darkness*; Dowell, in Ford Madox Ford's *The Good Soldier*; and the governess in James's *The Turn of the Screw*, I find myself with three witnesses who are as interesting, as tellers, as are the tales they tell. Each intervenes between us and the subject matter of his story so as to persuade us to evaluate his testimony through him, and thus to estimate his veracity as we frequently estimate that of an interlocutor in life. Cognizance of bias and lapsing credibility may augment our delight in the telling of any tale, since it renders us, fallible listeners that we are, aware of our complicity and convinced that the teller is human as we.

For this reason it seems useful to signal the ambiguity in the term "reliable" by enclosing it in quotation marks, and to order the discussion in this chapter from the apparently most "reliable" to the apparently least "reliable" of the three witnesses. We begin therefore with Marlow, who seems to evince at least a similarity in background with his creator, and to be, in some particulars, his considered spokesman.

It is well known that Conrad, distrusting his own capacity for inventiveness, drew upon his personal experiences, diverse and rich as they were, for all his novels, and modelled his protagonists upon men of his acquaintance. His "Author's Notes" to the first collected edition of his work show his abiding concern with "the effect of actuality" and it is this concern which he professes to have persuaded him to choose an eyewitness narrator for *Under Western Eyes*. The "personal contacts and origins" of persons in other tales have been fully explored; Marlow remains a singularly enigmatic figure. As an eyewitness narrator he has many affinities with his creator, in that the experiences he has as a seaman, from youth to age, are experiences similar to those we know Conrad to have had. But Conrad's artistic purpose, always concerned with the truth that lies beyond impressions, yet required an ironic control of his spokesman, particularly when that spokesman was a yarnspinner. In other words,

Conrad always knows what Marlow knows, but he also knows much more.

Marlow belongs to the earlier period of Conrad's work, and enters four of his fictions as narrator. In "Youth" (1898) he retrospectively relates his own voyage of discovery to the land of the golden fleece. In *Chance* (1913) his swan song is a chivalric romance of disenchantment. In both these tales, he might be termed a narrator *"tout simple."* But in the greater works *Lord Jim* (1900) and *Heart of Darkness* (1898?) Marlow's function as eyewitness is more cunningly integrated into the tale he tells. In both, like the Ancient Mariner, he chooses his audience and his occasion with an implicit motive of mission and seems to be driven by inner compulsion. In the case of *Lord Jim* he sits on the veranda of an hotel at twilight before an audience of Eastern tradesmen; the tale he tells is at once a reconstruction of remembered fragments and an exorcism. He seems unable to terminate his episodic account until he has reviewed the little he knows of Jim's behaviour in every possible light, by every possible standard. Accordingly, Jim's tragic story has a double meaning to the audience — to whom the reader voluntarily belongs. It has its own intrinsic enigma and pathos, and it has Marlow's probing, synthesizing attempt to discover the truth for himself by discovering it to others. It is to the second meaning that the testimonies of the lieutenant, Brierly, and Stein belong. They are important not as characters in Jim's story, but as a means of perspective for Marlow, helping him to understand Lord Jim and the truth of existence. In attaining that truth Marlow accomplishes what Conrad has accomplished in creating him — Conrad being, as it were, the secret sharer of Marlow's quest.

In *Heart of Darkness*, Marlow's compulsive selection of an audience is not, however, prefaced by a careful circumstantial introduction of his eligibility to narrate. His sudden opening remark is greeted as the typical allocution of an old friend, whom the anonymous frame-narrator briefly introduces as a "wandering" seaman with a propensity for spinning yarns. The story Marlow has to tell has no prefigurement, as has Lord Jim's, through third-person narrative. The layered structure of the work, wherein a frame-narrator reports how the crew of the *Nellie* silently submits at nightfall to another yarn while awaiting the turn of the tide, suggests its own hidden centre to substantiate the title. The Buddha-like pose of Marlow as he begins his yarn suggests the darkness of the *Via Negativa*. But the double use of monologue in *Heart of Darkness* has a further

132

significance to interest us. Of the two I's speaking, which, if either, is Conrad's "double"?

The significance of the frame for Marlow's monologue has been variously estimated. Robert Evans, comparing Marlow's story to Virgil's *Aeneid* and Dante's *Inferno*, dismisses the audience as "incapable of understanding" the account, which he sees as being addressed to an audience outside the work. William Stein, investigating the Buddhist imagery in the frame, recognizes moral and thematic significance in the "*tableaux*" which punctuate the recital, but also contends that the story itself falls upon the spiritually deaf ears of "the four auditors who cannot possibly understand the significance of a subtle spiritual voyage." In the Conrad criticism of the fifties, only Seymour Gross sees the anonymous narrator of the frame as a significant auditor. He points out that the three taciturn listeners — the lawyer, the accountant, and the Director of Companies — have their counterparts within Marlow's story in "the corrupt pilgrims, the fantastic Russian, and the company officials, none of whom is able to grasp the hidden truth of the moral abysm into which they have descended."[1] These listeners comment on Marlow's story once only, when one of them interjects "Absurd!" and receives an angry rejoinder from the raconteur: "Absurd! . . . This is the worst of trying to tell. . . . Here you all are . . . normal — you hear — normal from year's end to year's end. And you say, Absurd! Absurd be — exploded."[2]

Having agreed that three of the four listeners are imperceptive and of little interest, Gross goes on to demonstrate that the fourth, the anonymous narrator, stands in the same relationship to Marlow as Marlow stood to Kurtz in the actual experience. His early remark, "We knew we were fated . . . to hear about one of Marlow's inconclusive experiences," Gross notes as a superficial comment illustrative of his judgment before he has lived through Marlow's tale, corresponding to Marlow's "silly little bird" (6) judgment

1 Evans, "Conrad's Underworld," *Modern Fiction Studies*, II (May 1956), 56-62; Stein, "The Lotus Posture and 'The Heart of Darkness'," *Modern Fiction Studies*, II, 4 (Winter 1956-57), 235-37; Gross, "A Further Note on the Function of the Frame in 'Heart of Darkness'," *Modern Fiction Studies*, III, 2 (Summer 1957), 167-70.

2 Conrad, *Heart of Darkness* (New Jersey: Prentice-Hall, 1960), p. 40. All page numbers in parenthesis are to this edition. The exposition here is as Gross presents it. Actually there has been another interrupting sound (30) and one explicit previous interjection ("Try to be civil, Marlow!" [128]), and the sound which provokes Marlow's irritation at this point is no more than a "sigh" which he construes as scoffing.

before he has met Kurtz in Africa, and deduces that both Marlow and the anonymous narrator, metaphorically speaking, "start at the same place, take the same trip, and arrive at the same destination." Thus Marlow's experience of Kurtz as "A voice. He was very little more than a voice" (40), has its counterpart in the narrator's experience of Marlow as "no more . . . than a voice . . . a narrative that seemed to shape itself without human lips in the heavy night air of the river" (22); Marlow's experience of Kurtz's benighted condition, "His was an impenetrable darkness" (58), has its counterpart in the changed vision of the narrator, who becomes able to see, in place of "the benign immensity of unstained light" (2), a path into "the heart of an immense darkness" (65). Gross sees the anonymous narrator as a latter-day Wedding Guest, who will now, like the mariner who has captured him, be "set apart from all those who do not know the truth." The reflective function of the frame he sees as an endorsement of Conrad's faith in the moral efficacy of experience through literature, the anonymous narrator achieving enlightenment at second-hand as Marlow has achieved it at first-hand, and his presence justifying the telling of the tale. This is an interesting theory because of its implication. If the anonymous narrator is to be understood as Marlow's double, then he will share Marlow's abomination of lies, and the truth of the story will thus be vindicated — perhaps. Marlow's massive lie remains to be understood, and this theory does not accommodate it.

A more recent explication seeks to account for Marlow's lie by interpreting it as the epitome of meaning in a tale about the failure of language to communicate truth. Wasserman sees in Marlow not only a character and a narrator, but the visual focus of the novel, in whom the ineffectual nature of words is concretized:

> Sitting before his audience and trying to recount his experience through words, Marlow himself embodies his experience. His physical presence both compensates for the limitations of language and helps explain them. Only by seeing Marlow can his auditors ever hope to understand. . . . The form of Marlow's tale embodies not only his own experiences but Kurtz's as well, and in a sense the potential experiences of his audience, whose reactions confirm his meaning. Thus the style is the theme, in coherent and concrete form.[3]

In discussing the function of the frame, Wasserman deduces that at the end of the yarn all four listeners continue "in the dark." Though

---

[3] Jerry Wasserman, "Narrative Presence: The Illusion of Language in *Heart of Darkness*," *Studies in the Novel*, 6 (1974), 328.

the frame-narrator is strangely enough affected by the tale to retell it, he remains safely sheltered behind the very illusions Marlow has tried to expose, and therefore speaks of perceiving what only "seems" to be an immense darkness (65). The puzzling lie Wasserman interprets as a final demonstration of the illusion that is civilization, and as an ironic anticipation of the outcome of the tale, for Marlow's audience will hear what it wants to hear, as the Intended does, rather than understand what Marlow shows in his telling.

This reading is highly suggestive. Unlike the fictive audience, as listeners to the monologue we "see" Marlow only by the power of our imagination to interpret the visual signs incorporated into the anonymous narrator's account. We are engaged in a paradox, cast in the role of listeners to a verbal eloquence designed to convince us that language is not to be trusted. In this sense we become a necessary part of the whole experience, because if, to Marlow, "the meaning of an episode was not inside like a kernel but outside, enveloping the tale which brought it out only as a glow brings out a haze" (3), then we, outside the episode, contribute to the meaning as the glow brings out the haze. Furthermore, Marlow requires his listeners, as the frame-narrator reports, to "see the story" (22), and to see him in the way he first saw Kurtz, as a disembodied voice in the darkness and the silence (23).

However we interpret the responses of the fictive audience, there can be no doubt that as sharers in the monologue readers have to become temporary denizens of the *Nellie*. Some of us may react as three of the four listeners react — restive, uninterested, or protesting with sighs ("Absurd?"), while fewer of us may respond like the frame-narrator with a glimmer of understanding. But which of us, I wonder, would willingly undergo Marlow's experiences of the darkness to test our own likeness to Kurtz, or our own ability to emerge into and blend with the "civilized" world again after knowing him?

Let us look briefly at the characteristics of Marlow as Conrad has created him and as the anonymous narrator perceives him. He is, we quickly find, a man who has passed through a test which still haunts him as he seeks to evaluate it, and also to evaluate himself through his behaviour during it. He appears to value "restraint" above all else, except perhaps truthfulness, and his intelligence and moral sensibility equip him to model in his conduct those codes of behaviour to be expected from the upright European. Such, at least, was the exemplary character of our man of action before his ordeal.

We accept as modesty his explanation that the good reports made of him were due solely to his aunt's indulgence (20). But we note also his implicit assumption that imperialistic profit-motives could be acceptable (9), and that the "idea" of world conquest could be ennobling (5). These qualities and attitudes, accompanied by undoubted courage (6) and a boyish enthusiasm for a glamorous line on a map (5), befit him for his voyage into the unknown.

From the moment his journey begins, Marlow discloses his gradual education. Event and impression crowd his narrative, each encounter and each observation contributing to his dawning awareness of unexpected horrors, ". . . the general sense of vague and oppressive wonder grew upon me. It was like a weary pilgrimage among hints for nightmares" (11). His discovery of bestial cruelty towards "unhappy savages" shakes him in spite of his disclaimer, "You know I am not particularly tender" (12); his experience of the death grove leaves him "horror-struck" (14); the trek upcountry, littered with corpses and abandoned villages, resonates with ominous sounds of far-off drums (16). Throughout this early account of his pilgrimage, however, Marlow maintains his sense of humour and is sustained by the routine task that faces him — "Camp, cook, sleep, strike camp, march" (16), just as later he is sustained by work.

Marlow's limitations of judgement, self-confessed, first appear when he discovers that his steamer is at the bottom of the river. "I did not see the real significance of that wreck at once. I fancy I see it now, but I am not sure — not at all. Certainly the affair was too stupid — when I think of it — to be altogether natural" (17). And later, when he has met the odious manager, he reports him as saying, "Well, let us say three months before we can make a start. Yes. That ought to do the affair" (18). Immediately following, Marlow remarks with apparent unawareness of its significance, that later he was startled to discover "with what extreme nicety he [the manager] had estimated the time requisite for 'the affair'."

This observation occurs when Marlow has just received his first description of Kurtz, through the same devious manager's comments. And it is from this point on that the salient aspect of Marlow's education becomes a quest for meaning.[4] As he proceeds upriver he

---

[4] Marlow is intrigued to learn from the first agent (the "brick maker") of the Central Station that the enigmatic painting of the blindfolded woman (Justice?) is attributed to Kurtz (20), and comments that, thus far, the man is "just a word" for him. "I did not see the man in the name any more than you do" (22).

soon discovers that none of the names associated with Africa bear any relation to reality. Everything associated with the native people mystifies him, from a thread of white muslin to a lavender-coloured chunk of food. He has particular difficulty in relating the term "cannibal" to the manifest "restraint" of that "savage" when he is starving (34). He seems at times unaware of the peculiar irony of some of the names he uses (the rapacious colonials are "civilized," the company-men are "pilgrims," the band of pirates bent on tearing treasure out of the bowels of the land is the "Eldorado Exploring Expedition," a half-caste who has behaved with courage and grace is "that scoundrel"). He believes the notes made in the margin of the Lowser (Lowson) book are in cipher (31) and is surprised to find later they are in Russian. At all events, perusal of comments he cannot read gives Marlow the "delicious sensation of having come upon something unmistakably real" (31) in the midst of muddled meanings that are becoming increasingly nightmarish. He seems to be approaching ever nearer the verges of sanity, and again and again his sense of unreality threatens to overwhelm him. And the worst confusion of familiar meaning comes when he remembers "the incomprehensible frenzy" of whirling black limbs on the shore and acknowledges that "prehistoric man," "monstrous," "inhuman," as he is variously called, is not after all far removed from his "civilized" conqueror.

They howled and leaped, and spun, and made horrid faces, but what thrilled you was just the thought of their humanity — like yours — the thought of your remote kinship with this wild and passionate uproar. Ugly. Yes, it was ugly enough; but if you were man enough you would admit to yourself that there was in you just the faintest trace of a response to the terrible frankness of that noise, a dim suspicion of there being a meaning in it which you — you so remote from the night of first ages — could comprehend. (29-30)

Thus prepared for the recognition to come, and saved from anticipation of it only by his labour to keep the steamboat chugging along "by hook or by crook," Marlow approaches the final reach of river leading to Kurtz. When Kurtz's natives first cry out, unseen, one of the pilgrims stammers, "Good God! What is the meaning —," and, as if in answer, the shutter of white fog descends again (33). The thick fog is the correlative for the disorientation Marlow now feels, sensing that he is floundering towards a realm where his former sense of direction will be futile. His "dream-sensation" quickens. Consequently, when the attack begins and arrow and spear fall at his feet he cannot find names for them; the arrow is a "stick," the spear clutched by his dying helmsman appears as a "long cane" (37, 38).

Marlow's problem with names, his continuing inability to match appearance to reality, cannot be accidental. It seems to be connected to his passionate desire to hear Kurtz speak, and to measure *his* "gift of expression." In confessing his desire he breaks the chronology of his narrative to assure his own listeners that the time did come when he had heard enough — "heard more than enough . . . the memory of that time itself lingers around me, impalpable, like a dying vibration of one immense jabber, silly, atrocious, sordid, savage, or simply mean, *without any kind of sense*. Voices, voices — even the girl herself — now —" (40, my italics). The digression continues with his first explicit reference to the lie he later told, and with his own first retrospective description of Kurtz: of Kurtz's grandiloquent report for the International Society for the Suppression of Savage Customs (another ironic name); of his scrawled postscript, later expunged, "Exterminate all the brutes!" (42).

Then he recalls his hasty disposal of his helmsman's body and his regret at the loss of a partner to whom, despite that partner's "lack of restraint," he had been bonded by "a claim of distant kinship" (42). Interestingly enough he fleetingly compares the helmsman to Kurtz, "no restraint" in either case, which implies his "distant kinship" with the "universal genius." Then the next things Marlow sees, and again wrongly names, are the "round carved balls" of the stockade, which are later known to be human heads. Finally, after another delaying digression describing the Russian disciple, he describes meeting Kurtz at last, and in this climactic moment Marlow makes two striking observations. The first is that Kurtz is seen to belie his name: "Kurtz — that means short in German — don't it? Well, the name was as true as everything else in his life — and death. He looked at least seven feet long" (50). The second is that despite debilitation Kurtz is talking with vigour. "I saw him open his mouth wide — it gave him a weirdly voracious aspect, as though he wanted to swallow all the air, all the earth, all the men before him" (50). Again the inefficacy of names, and the speech of Kurtz, come together.

Marlow is never so clear-sighted and articulate as in his account of his pursuit and capture of Kurtz within thirty yards of the "unspeakable rites" on the hillside. For once, he is able to recount proudly that he said the right thing (55). He is helped in his verbal struggle by the knowledge he has already received of the "heavy, mute spell of the wilderness . . . the awakening of forgotten and brutal instincts, . . . the memory of gratified and monstrous passions" (55); he is helped too by his realization that he must, like "the niggers," in speaking to Kurtz, "invoke him — himself — his own exalted and incredible degradation" (56).

The departure of the steamer is accompanied by a "satanic litany" on the part of the bereft natives. "Do you understand this?" Marlow asks Kurtz. "Do I not?" he replies slowly. At last Marlow seems to be on the brink of elucidation. At last he can listen at first-hand to the discourse of Kurtz, the voice he has sought, expecting to find some definitive meaning. But the words of Kurtz are cliché-ridden or unspeakably childish; there is no *logos* for Marlow, whose own grasp of reality now seems to revive as Kurtz's weakness grows. When the dying whisper finally comes, heralded by a convulsion of Kurtz's face, what, after all, does it mean? "The horror! The horror!" has no fixed meaning. Everything in Marlow's monologue has led to this moment by showing how Marlow's experience and developed perspective have conditioned him to interpret it. He accepts it as Kurtz's articulation of his own judgement, his naming, unequivocal and unambiguous, of what he has done and been, and he consigns Kurtz to the damnation that he would feel he deserved in his place. And this consignment is not without admiration, since the hollow man has also pronounced his own emptiness, and at last, as Marlow sees it, spoken truth.

This, I think, is the legacy in Marlow's consciousness which leads to his final episode, the account of the celebrated lie to the Intended. The motif of naming and meaning which is discernible throughout Marlow's monologue reaches its ironic fulfilment when the grieving woman demands that he repeat to her Kurtz's last words. In spite of his former protestations about his inability to lie (22), Marlow equivocates throughout the interview. He does not correct the lies with which the Intended completes his sentences. He permits her to misconstrue his meaning. He even admits, as he tells of her delight in receiving the bundle of letters, that he has privately wondered whether it was indeed the packet intended for her (63), and if not, what disclosures might it hold for her after he left? "His words will remain," Marlow declares, and he himself has seen to it that some of them have been destroyed (64). After all of this, the lie of commission seems very pale. And surely there is irony even in it. For we never know the woman's name. It is nowhere mentioned. For Kurtz, she is always "My Intended." That is his name for her. Therefore when Marlow says, "The last word he pronounced was — your name," he is saying, "The last word he pronounced was — My Intended." And "the horror" is, indeed, as Marlow has seen it, Kurtz's "Intended." So Marlow's vaunted act of chivalry, or cowardice, or what you will, is yet another act of ambiguity, or of misnaming reality by using an approximation to the truth. Pilate's question is at the heart of darkness. Only Kurtz has answered it, and the meaning of his answer remains unknown.

Any single approach to *Heart of Darkness* is doomed to be superficial, since the work is myth as well as fiction. In concentrating upon its semantic aspect I have done poor justice to Conrad's mighty wrestling with the giants of abomination.[5] But my purpose has been to show that Marlow has involved his listeners in a quest for meaning beyond any which language is able to reveal. The dream content of his narrative forms itself around distortion, displacement, and disparity — and this leaves us aboard the *Nellie* where we began, gazing into any centre of human habitation to discern — perhaps — an immense darkness at its heart. It leaves us, in fact, in the position of the anonymous narrator. How would we retell this story?

Writing of *Lord Jim*, Guerard identifies it as Conrad's "first great impressionistic novel," and defines impressionism in fiction as "a form bent on involving the reader in a psycho-moral drama which has no easy solution, and bent on engaging his sensibilities more strenuously and more uncomfortably than ever before." He adds that such a form compels the reader to collaborate with the author and refers to Ford's statement that the aim of impressionism is to experience life as the sensitive observer does:

The digressive method does indeed convey the "feel" of life. But the impressionist aim is to achieve a fuller truth than realism can, if necessary by "cheating," and to create in the reader an intricate play of emotion and a rich conflict of sympathy and judgement, a provisional bafflement in the face of experience which turns out to be more complicated than we ever would have dreamed. (*Conrad the Novelist*, pp. 126-27)

As this is true of the effect of *Lord Jim*, so it is true of *Heart of Darkness*, in which Conrad appears to be working out a further

---

[5] This I find fully dealt with by Albert J. Guerard in *Conrad the Novelist* (Cambridge: Harvard University Press, 1958), pp. 33-48. All page numbers in parenthesis are to this edition.

theory he had discussed with Ford. "We used to say . . . that a subject must be seized by the throat until the last drop of dramatic possibility was squeezed out of it. . . . From this the novel got its unity. No doubt it might have its caesura — or even several; but these must be brought about by temporal pauses, markings of time when the treatment called for them."[6] The *caesurae* in Marlow's tale aboard the *Nellie* mark time in a way which is matched by the desultory flow of Dowell's monologue in *The Good Soldier*.

The history of collaboration between the two writers is of course well known, but even without it the similarity of method in *Heart of Darkness* and *The Good Soldier* would testify to a shared aesthetic. We can find in the conjectural, probing nature of Marlow's reconstructive narrative, with its back-trackings and leaps in time, considerable affinity with John Dowell's alinear treatment of his "saddest story." The affinity may be accounted for by what Ford retrospectively names as a mutual desire to draw the reader into the monologue. "We wanted the readers to forget the writers, to forget that he was reading [sic]. We wished him to be hypnotized into thinking that he was living what he read — or, at least, into the conviction that he was listening to a simple and in no way brilliant narrator who was telling — not writing — a true story."

"The simple and in no way brilliant narrator" of *The Good Soldier*, however, despite affinities with Marlow, has a markedly different way of addressing himself to his audience. The "you" of Marlow's narrative comprises the four listeners we have discussed, and in particular the anonymous narrator who may become the "double" of the reader. The "you" of Dowell's narrative is the reader without intermediary, and the relationship of the "you" to the "I" is not only immediate but also suggestively intimate. Ford himself described the difference in tone thus: "As for me, I went on working beside Conrad, trying . . . to evolve for myself a vernacular of extreme quietness that would suggest some one of refinement talking in a low voice near the ear of someone he liked a good deal."[7]

Translated into the art of *The Good Soldier*, this theory finds articulation at once in Dowell's frequent confidential references to "you." Eighteen times in Part One of his discourse, in as many

[6] Ford Madox Ford, *Return to Yesterday* (New York: Horace Liveright, 1932), p. 203.

[7] *Mightier than the Sword* (London: Allen and Unwin, 1938), p. 378.

paragraphs, he addresses his reader as if he knows, and likes, him a good deal:

> Paris, you see, was our home. . . . You will gather from this statement that one of us had, as the saying is, a "heart." . . . You will perceive . . . that our friendship has been a young-middle-aged affair. . . . They were descended, as you will probably expect, from the Ashburnham who accompanied Charles I to the scaffold, and, as you must also expect with this class of English people, you would never have noticed it. . . . Florence was a Hurlbird of Stamford, Connecticut, where, as you know, they are more old-fashioned than even the inhabitants of Cranford, England, could have been. . . . You may well ask why I write.[8]

Dowell's confidences continue in this familiar vein until by the end of his opening remarks he involves his reader in a state of complicity which can be signalized as "we":

> I don't know. And there is nothing to guide us. And if everything is so nebulous about a matter so elementary as the morals of sex, what is there to guide us in the more subtle morality of all other personal contacts, associations and activities? Or are we meant to act on impulse alone? It is all a darkness. (12)

And by the beginning of chapter two, Dowell is ready to make the implicit explicit:

> I don't know how it is best to put this thing down — whether it would be better to try and tell the story from the beginning, as if it were a story; or whether to tell it from this distance of time, as it reached me from the lips of Leonora or from those of Edward himself.
> So I shall just imagine myself for a fortnight or so at one side of the fireplace of a country cottage, *with a sympathetic soul opposite me.* And I shall go on talking, *in a low voice* while the sea sounds in the distance and overhead the great black flood of wind polishes the bright stars. *From time to time we shall get up and go to the door and look out at the great moon.* (12)

I have italicized the terms which embody Ford's theories as we have noted them, the low tone, the attributed congeniality, and the interruptive *caesurae.* We may note too that Dowell discloses himself to be a man of "some refinement" who is at the same time "simple, in no way brilliant." Though he is a Dowell of Philadelphia with title-deeds to inherited property in his pocket, and though he asserts his unsullied reputation: "For I solemnly avow that not only have I

8 Ford Madox Ford, *The Good Soldier* (New York: Random House, 1957), pp. 4-5. All page numbers in parenthesis are to this edition.

never so much as hinted at an impropriety in my conversation in the whole of my days; and more than that, I will vouch for the cleanness of my thoughts and the absolute chastity of my life" (11-12), he approaches his self-imposed task of setting down what he has witnessed with a pathetic confession of bewilderment:

I know nothing — nothing in the world — of the hearts of men. I only know that I am alone — horribly alone. No hearthstone will ever again witness, for me, friendly intercourse. No smokingroom will ever be other than peopled with incalculable simulacra amidst smoke wreaths. Yet, in the name of God, what should I know if I don't know the life of the hearth and of the smokingroom, since my whole life has been passed in those places?   (7-8)

This last quotation is doubly significant. It ironically undergirds Dowell's imaginary act of telling the saddest story he has ever heard to the only sympathetic hearthside listener left to him — a phantom; and it brings together the characteristics of refinement and simplicity. The limited knowledge and understanding of this narrator exist not so much in spite of his refinement as because of it.

In the opening paragraphs of *The Good Soldier*, then, through the striking effects of his narrator's self-consciousness, Ford accomplishes what he has elsewhere given to be his aim, that of realizing his central figure by "getting him in with a strong impression," so that he can proceed by working "backwards and forwards over his past."[9] And the question immediately arises, who is the central figure? Dowell or Ashburnham? From the aspect of narrative substance, the central figure is undoubtedly Ashburnham, the "good soldier" of the wry second-choice title. He is the narrator's own hero, and the tale is of Ashburnham's passion in the double sense of that term. But when the work is discussed as the story of Dowell telling his story, it is Dowell who becomes the central concern of the reader, not Ashburnham. The critical debate that has formed about the novel has focused upon Dowell's reliability and integrity, and to a lesser, consequential degree upon the genre of the work. Where Dowell is despised or at least discounted, the story is seen largely in comic terms. Where Dowell is esteemed or at least accepted, the story is seen largely in tragic terms. Dowell's own appellation of "sad" is, of course, ambiguous.

[9] *Joseph Conrad: A Personal Remembrance* (Boston: Little and Brown, 1924), p. 137. For a critique of this kind of realism as the sole desirable kind see Booth, *The Rhetoric of Fiction*, pp. 40-41.

Mark Schorer's argument is probably the most influential one, both for its cogency and for its placement as Preface to the current paperback edition of the novel.[10] Schorer regards Dowell as a comic, even a grotesque character. He contends that "the book's controlling irony lies in the fact that passionate situations are related by a narrator incapable of passion, sexual and moral alike," and that this narrator's mind is "not quite in balance." He correctly notes Dowell's moral indecisiveness, his determined attempts to exonerate and sanctify Edward, and his fatuous, "self-infatuated" attempts to see himself as Edward's double. He taxes Dowell with *accidie*, and with absurdities which extend to his "simple-minded" and "grotesquely-comic" images and figures of speech. Thus Schorer arrives at the description of the novel's genre as "a comedy of humour, and the humour is phlegm."

Many readers have followed Schorer's "Interpretation," modifying or extending it perhaps, but substantially agreeing with its view of Dowell. But others have been more inclined to follow the lead of Theodore Dreiser, who, reviewing the novel in 1951, held its theme to be "tragic in the best sense that the Greeks knew tragedy, that tragedy for which there is no solution."[11] Thus Robie Macauley saw in *The Good Soldier* that "the saddest story is the perpetual story of love between man and woman, love that can never quite arrive at understanding and decays," and found in Dowell a narrator who is the disinterested, if short-sighted, purveyor of that story.[12] Departing strongly from Schorer's view, John A. Meixner makes the strongest case for viewing the novel as tragedy, while acknowledging that "around this awful core, and without diminishing its power," Ford has placed a context of comic irony. Meixner sees Dowell as a Prufrock before Prufrock, a "creature of pure pathos . . . an alienated being," a spiritual invalid. In this entirely charitable view of Dowell, his sensitivity and poetic propensity are enlarged upon; he is seen as a conscious and consummate imagist, and he is accorded sympathy on account of his "damaged spirit," a con-

---

10 I.e., the Vintage Book edition cited above and throughout this study. Revised after its first appearance in *The Princeton University Library Chronicle* in 1948 and its second in *Horizon* in 1949, the essay, entitled "*The Good Soldier*: An Interpretation," has appeared unaltered in several studies of Ford in the past fifteen years.

11 "The Saddest Story," *New Republic*, III (June 12, 1915), 156. In seeing Dowell merely as the author's own mouthpiece, Dreiser seems unaware of Ford's self-description as "a sentimental Tory and a Roman Catholic."

12 "The Good Ford," *Kenyon Review*, XI (1949), 271, 277.

sciousness receptive to "the ache in the universe."[13] A notable and less polarized judgement has come from Samuel Hynes, who sees the novel as a work "which raises uncertainty about the nature of truth and reality to the level of a structural principle." Hynes is careful to show that Dowell's moral indecisiveness is shared by all the main characters he reports upon, that despite his inadequacies as a narrator he has positive qualities of forgiveness and compassion, and that he performs the only two unselfish acts in the account — both of them errands of mercy. Consequently, Hynes accepts as a serious and sincere gesture the act of identification by which Dowell invests himself with the person, as well as the former possessions, of the late Edward Ashburnham.[14]

Almost half way through his monologue, Dowell remarks with his accustomed naïveté, "I don't know that analysis of my own psychology matters at all to this story" (103). But the foregoing summary shows that to many perceptive readers it has mattered a great deal. If asked to state whose view of Dowell was right, or even most right, many readers would have to say, with Dowell at so many points in his reconstruction, "I don't know; I don't know. Who knows?" Ford's accomplishment seems to be this, that every reader has to respond individually, according to his own observation and experience, and perhaps also his temperament, to Dowell's injunction, "I leave it all to you."

One significant feature of the novel — its onomatology — has to be attributed chiefly to the implied author rather than to the monologuist. Nevertheless, it should be reviewed as a source of powerful impressions upon the reader. Meixner has shown the eponymous nature of most of the names in *The Good Soldier*, from Dowell ("a piece of wood driven into a wall, so that other pieces may be nailed to it" — to which might be added the *Oxford Dictionary* definition of "a headless pin, peg, or bolt"), to Rufford (a name in which he sees evidence of the author's partiality, containing as it does the double "f" of Hueffer and the whole of Ford's last name). To his exposition might be added the suggestion of feline predator in "Leonora," and the strange reverberatiton from "Bagshawe" to "Bran-

13 "The Saddest Story," in *Ford Madox Ford: Modern Judgements*, ed. Richard A. Cassell (New York: Macmillan, 1972), pp. 70-78. First appeared in *Ford Madox Ford's Novels* (Minneapolis: University of Minnesota Press, 1962).

14 "The Epistemology of *The Good Soldier*," in *Ford Madox Ford: Modern Judgements*, pp. 98-104. First appeared in *Sewanee Review*, LXIX (Spring 1961), 225-35.

shaw (Teleragh)." In view of the similarity of two major scenes of the novel, in both of which a very young woman enters the bedroom of a man to whom she is constrained to offer herself ("as a present?"), it is notable that the names associated with the homes where the two encounters occur sound alike. Although one name refers to the owner of a house, and the other to a house itself, the echo in Dowell's mind reinforces the link between the promiscuous Florence and the (heretofore) adulterous Edward. The "affairs" of Dowell's narrative, we hardly need note, are the triangles set up in the first instance between Florence, Edward, and Leonora, and in second between Nancy, Edward, and Leonora; in each case Dowell is himself an involved but impotent observer. A similar underwriting occurs when Dowell uses names which are connected to his view of Edward Ashburnham. Apart from the reference to the Ashburnham ancestor's loyalty to Charles I, Dowell attributes to "Teddy"[15] a desire to be "looked upon as a sort of Lohengrin" (157); he tells Leonora that her husband "must really be Lohengrin and the Cid in one body" (96); he recalls that Nancy used to make him out "like a cross between Lohengrin and the Chevalier Bayard" (95-96). These names, together with the extraordinary story of Peire Vidal (16-17) which resonates throughout the reflections, cloak Edward Ashburnham in the archetypal vestments of a medieval knight; they justify his acts of feudal protection of subservients, and give to his passionate search for the "ultimately satisfying woman" the appearance of a quest. The conventions of "courtly love," Humility, Courtesy, Adultery, and the Religion of Love, all find expression in this knight errant's intrigues with enchantresses, chatelaines, and damsels in distress.

Similarly, Dowell's imagery produces highly suggestive nuances of tone. The language in which he describes and recreates events and impressions is remarkably evocative; it has an almost Shakespearean range of diction and allusion from the first metaphor on:

15 Dowell frequently uses the pet name for Edward which Leonora once used publicly at the beginning of the Dowell-Ashburnham acquaintance. It may remind us of the Royal family's pet name for Edward VII, referred to in Dowell's account as "a pleasant, affable sort of royalty" (35). Socio-political readings of the novel have noted the significance of the date of August 4, and the way in which Dowell's recognition of the collapse of codes and conventions prefigures that social and moral overthrow which erupted with the Great War. No one appears to have noted similarities between Edward Ashburnham, model son, soldier, "landlord and father of his people," and the womanizing Edward VII, King of Great Britain and Ireland, Emperor of India, and man of the turf.

You may well ask why I write. And yet my reasons are quite many. For it is not unusual in human beings who have witnessed the sack of a city or the falling to pieces of a people to desire to set down what they have witnessed for the benefit of unknown heirs or of generations infinitely remote; or, if you please, just to get the sight out of their heads.

Someone has said that the death of a mouse from cancer is the whole sack of Rome by the Goths, and I swear to you that the breaking up of our little four-square coterie was such another unthinkable event. ... We were an extraordinarily safe castle. We were, if you will, one of those tall ships with the white sails upon a blue sea, one of those things that seem the proudest and safest of all the beautiful things. (5-6)

In the next paragraph the relationship is described as a "minuet de la cour" which cannot be destroyed though the Trianon fall; in the next this falsehood is denied, "It wasn't a minuet that we stepped; it was a prison — a prison full of screaming hysterics." Finally, calm descends again, the narrator swears that it was true — "true sunshine, the true music." Dowell compares his recent discoveries to finding that what he possessed for nine years as a goodly apple was rotten at the core, and asks if that denies that for nine years he possessed a goodly apple. And the architectural metaphor of the castle is revived as he admits that the physical rottenness of at least two pillars of the four-square house never seemed to present a menace to its security (7).

Now this circuitous pattern is a paradigm of the whole story. The images seem too rich, too diverse, too seemingly incongruous with each other and with the story Dowell has begun to tell. The reference to screaming hysterics "tied down so that they might not outsound the rolling of our carriage wheels as we went along the shaded avenues of the Taunus Wald" (7) intrudes with particular violence upon what has been a quiet introduction of four characters, all of them middle-aged, and "quite good people." Yet there is a logic of association connecting each metaphor with the next, and the movement from the solid and safe through the ephemeral and anguished back to resigned acceptance of a diminished thing adumbrates the path, stumbling and also circuitous, the story will take. Furthermore, many of these images will appear again. Animal imagery will abound.[16] The figure of four, now square, now round, will

---

[16] For an exhaustive treatment of this, see Jo-ann Baernstein, "Image, Identity and Insight in *The Good Soldier*," *Critique*, IX (1966).

reverberate; metaphors of pain will recur; Nancy will be seen at the "sail of a ship, so white and definite in her movements" (128).

Just as Dowell's narrative takes him now backward, now forward, over the same ground, so his mental pictures recur in different contexts. His image for Florence is "dancing" (cf. the minuet) and "bright," "like a gay tremulous beam, reflected from water upon a ceiling" (15), "radiant as the track of sunlight along the sea" (30); she is, quite simply, "electric" (43). When her corpse is described for the second time Dowell says, ". . . there she lay. Oh, extremely charming and clear-cut — looking with a puzzled expression at the electric-light bulb that hung from the ceiling, or perhaps through it, to the stars above" (120).

In a key scene, Florence's brightness has been matched by the light she insists be admitted to the room where Luther is thought to have slept. She points "at a piece of paper," declares it is the Protest, and twice affirms the importance of "that piece of paper" (44). The image that occurs to Dowell when he later sees Florence, all black and white, in a state of shock, is paper: "It was like that — Florence running with a face whiter than paper and her hand on the black stuff over her heart" (102). Immediately after the second description of her death he says, "She just went completely out of existence, like yesterday's paper" (120), and adds later, "I . . . had realized long before that Florence was a personality of paper. . . . I should have run up sooner to her room. . . . But I just couldn't do it; it would have been like chasing a scrap of paper" (121).

Dowell's image for bondage to Florence is a knapsack, so that he can describe his relief at her death thus:

It was a feeling so tranquil. It was as if an immensely heavy — an unbearably heavy knapsack, supported upon my shoulders by straps, had fallen off and had left my shoulders themselves, that the straps had cut into, numb and without sensation of life. (120)

This is in extraordinary contrast to the image with which he described his feelings at the beginning of his career as male nurse: "She became for me a rare and fragile object, something burdensome, but very frail. Why, it was as if I had been given a thin-shelled pullet's egg to carry on my palm from Equatorial Africa to Hoboken" (91). But the measure of Dowell's changed perception, from Florence as fragile egg to Florence as unbearable weight, is suggested earlier when he uses the same "knapsack" image to denote a different kind of freedom:

148

And yet I do believe that for every man there comes at last a woman
— or, no, that is the wrong way of formulating it. For every man there
comes at last a time of life when the woman who then sets her seal
upon his imagination has set her seal for good. He will travel over no
more horizons; he will never again set the knapsack over his shoulders;
he will retire from those scenes.   (115)

This observation is made of Edward and his final love for Nancy.
But it is significant that the last woman of Edward's preliminary
passions, and therefore the last knapsack, was Florence.

One last example of an interwoven image occurs towards the end
of the narrative. Immediately before her announcement that Florence, too, committed suicide, Leonora has said, "Edward has been
dead only ten days and yet there are rabbits on the lawn" (105).
Dowell has been noticing "a couple of rabbits on the extreme edge
of the lawn." He dazedly notes that rabbits do a great deal of harm
to the short grass in England. Then the shock of the disclosure drives
everything else from his mind. Much later in his narrative, but quite
soon in the world's time, Leonora marries Rodney Bayham, who
reminds Dowell of a rabbit (238-39), and settles down "to have her
good time" awaiting the birth of a child who is to be raised a Ro-
manist (255). "Yes, society must go on; it must breed, like rabbits"
(254).

As with illustration and analogy, so with reportage. Dowell's process is one of vision and re-vision, impression and query, probe and
counter-probe. As Dowell re-interprets, in the light of new knowledge, scenes he has recounted earlier, trying to show his own growth
in enlightenment and, paradoxically, bewilderment also, the reader
is called upon to re-evaluate with him and to reconsider his earlier
responses to both narrative and narrator. Our task, in fact, mirrors
the education and the reversals that Dowell himself has experienced.
Furthermore, though it is obfuscated by juxtaposition and cross-
reference, the discernible sequence of the narrative, by which the
book may be divided into two corresponding sections, draws us
gradually to the most terrifying disorder of all, which is expressed
by Nancy's madness. The comparatively orderly pain and punishment of Florence's story is thus replaced by the meaningless discord attendant upon the destruction of innocence.

In placing the burden of interpretation on the reader through the
consciousness of Dowell, Ford has succeeded admirably in producing the effects of limited vision; but to achieve a corrective impression, in the reader, of understanding the whole nevertheless, he has

been obliged to arrange his presentation in such a way that Dowell has access to information that could not have been his. He has Dowell repeatedly refer to the source of his knowledge, or admit that he is drawing inferences:

Leonora, as I understand, would answer something like . . . (72)

I find, on looking at my diaries, that . . . (98)

That of course is only conjecture but I think the conjecture is pretty well justified. You have the fact that . . . (116)

And that evening Edward spoke to me. (202)

I don't know what it [the letter from Nancy's mother] contained. I just averaged out its effect on Nancy . . . (211)

I am not going to make up speeches. To follow her psychological development I think we must allow that . . . (213)

Leonora told me these things. (214)

Yet in dealing with the feelings of the two destroyed "girls" of the story, Dowell is made capable of remarkable imaginative reconstruction. In Maisie's case, during his description of the scene when Leonora boxes "the child's" ears, Dowell gives us Maisie's innocent reasons for going into Edward's room, and her behaviour while there (65-66) neither of which he could possibly have known. In Nancy's case, a complete omniscient intrusion occurs at some length (222-29). Although we are told that Nancy and Leonora talked together repeatedly, talked all night in fact, it seems incredible that Nancy would describe to a mother-figure such excesses of longing as are described in this passage. "The bed reeled beneath her; she gave way to the thought that she was in Edward's arms; that he was kissing her on her face, that burned; on her shoulders, that burned; on her neck, that was on fire" (225). But if we accept that she did, it becomes equally incredible that Leonora would report this to Dowell. Not even Leonora could report such an extremity as is described in these pages and then maintain with sang-froid that "the girl didn't love Edward" (245). These revelations, made possible only through a fantasizing Dowell, are glaringly at odds with his repeated insistence that he knows nothing of the human heart.

At one level then, Ford adheres to the narrative method he has formalized in the words of his created narrator:

I have, as I am aware, told this story in a very rambling way so that it may be difficult for anyone to find his way through what may be a sort of maze. I cannot help it. I have stuck to my idea of being in a country cottage with a silent listener, hearing between the gusts of the wind and amidst the noises of the distant sea the story as it comes. And, when one discusses an affair — one goes back, one goes forward. One remembers points that one has forgotten and explains them all the more minutely since one recognizes that one has forgotten to mention them in their proper places and that one may have given, by omitting them, a false impression. I console myself with thinking that this a real story and that, after all, real stories are probably best told in the way a person telling a story would tell them. They will then seem most real. (183)

But at another level such discursive, associative patterns of memory are really only a *rationale*, for the rambling method is under the author's careful control. It is a working out of his *progression d'effet*.[17] Ford works through Dowell's agency to combine all the effects of the narrator's impaired analysis, cumulatively, into a coherent resolution. The master stroke is that the resolution, in this case, is "irresolution"; it is the inevitable result of an impasse of sympathy for all sides. It is the quasi-authorial mind that relates the two wooings of Dowell, that slips into the account of the deathbed of Maisie the implication of "You understand she had not committed suicide" (76), and that insinuates into Dowell's perception that superb hidden insight, "We had got married about four in the morning and had sat about in the woods until then the eight o'clock breakfast with the Hurlbird aunts, listening to a mocking-bird imitate an old tom-cat" (86).

When all traces of authorial control have been accounted for, however, the reader finds himself listening to a distinctive monologuist, whose prevailing characteristic seems to be inconsistency. The self-styled eunuch, incapable of passion, is nevertheless capable of emphatic realization of passion in others. He whose own sex is ambivalent, and who has only once experienced the embrace of a woman (83), is capable of descanting authoritatively upon the relationship between the sexes (113-17). He who shows obsessive concern for minutiae like dates, distances, and timetables (77, 22, 47) can discern large encompassing patterns (237). He who provides

---

[17] Robert F. Haugh, in *Joseph Conrad: Discovery in Design* (Oklahoma: University of Oklahoma Press, 1957), p. 7, defines this difficult term as follows: "The term employed by Conrad and Hueffer in their conversations on the art of fiction, embraces growth, movement, heightening of all elements of the story: conflict and stress if it is a dramatic story; intensity and magnitude of image if it is a poetic story; complexity of patterns; balance and symmetry; evocations in style used for mood and functional atmosphere."

bathetic asides to the most solemn observations of death and dis-integration (76, 253) is nevertheless able to project himself beyond the comic analogies of the passing moment into sublime visions of eternity (70-71, 252). Consistent inconsistencies in both the sub-stance of narration and the person of the narrator prepare us for the paradoxical resolution we find in the picture of Nancy at the end, beautiful, physically healthy, poised, and proper, signifying nothing, a "picture without meaning" (254). Against this is balanced the ultimate picture of the novel, the culmination which Ford held should reveal "the psychological significance of the whole," which is of the doomed good soldier, "sober, quite quiet," gently requesting "a bit of a rest" as he takes out the small penknife (255-56). Both pictures display the "English good form" which the Philadelphian seeks still to emulate. It is perfectly correct, and perfectly appalling, like the "most horrible performance" Dowell has ever seen — the expressionless farewell between these two at the railway station, dur-ing which the bright red signal for the train's departure provided as passionate a statement as Dowell could get into the scene (250).

Dowell takes his leave of Edward with an unexpressed benedic-tion. The unresolved abyss between appearance and reality might have been bridged had the "God bless you" of the final paragraph been spoken. But it can be spoken only in retrospect — by Dowell in his vision of the embracing figures in the Land of God, and by Ford in the epigraph from Psalm 119 — "Blessed are those that are blameless." The reader also, labouring with Dowell to reconcile the screams, imbecilities, deaths, and agonies of "good people" (238) with "their appearance of calm pococurantism" (248), comes from the account with the stony feeling that it is indeed "all a darkness," and the only light that can illuminate it will be the light of Divine Judgement, since all human judgements fail. Dowell's awareness of his own confusion, his frequent contradictions and consistent inabil-ity to take a decisive stance, mirror the response of his silent listener. His narrative tone accomplishes three related functions: it renders his personality; it helps readers to recognize through his perceptions the bewilderment of his companions; and it embodies a commentary on the nature of human knowing and judging. Speaker and listener can only look up at the great moon together.

Different as they are, both Marlow and Dowell struggle to pene-trate beyond the evidence of their experience. In creating them, Conrad and Ford have sought to extend the boundaries of the fic-tional world, and to entice the reader to seek a meaning beyond the purview of the narrator — an awareness beyond the vision. This task, the aim of the impressionist novel, was the legacy of Henry James, and it was to James that Ford acknowledged his greatest debt. We have already noted how James, through example and especially through theory, developed the literature of perception and created the narrative strategies to embody it. One such narrative strategy was the eyewitness monologue.

I-narration occurs rarely in the works of Henry James, and is reserved for shorter fictions. In his Preface to *The Ambassadors* James expresses his distrust of the "romantic privilege" of "the first person," and eschews it for Strether on the grounds that it is, in the long piece, a form "foredoomed to looseness" (*The Art of the Novel*, p. 320). Looseness, he adds, is never much his affair. He later describes the risk of the I-narrator as being "the terrible *fluidity* of self-revelation," and one can understand how in this case it posed a threat to the "grade of intensity" he strove for in *The Ambassadors*.

However, where the matter deserving scrutiny is smaller in scale than Strether's undertaking, as in *The Sacred Fount* or *The Aspern Papers*, James is prepared to accept the risks of having his eyewitness speak in the first person. In both of these narratives there is an element of exploitation. The narrator seeks knowledge, and consequent gain in self-esteem or public fame, at the cost of others. In *The Sacred Fount* the anonymous house guest pursues a self-imposed "high application of intelligence"[18] in order to discover and decipher reciprocal relationships which seem to him to enrich one partner by depleting the other. In his relentless tracking down of "a law which would fit certain given facts" (230), his obsessive inquiries so harass and exasperate his fellow guests that he is understandably avoided, and finally charged, by his redoubtable antagonist Mrs. Brissenden, with being "crazy." The reader grasps what the narrator misses, namely that in his dealings with a woman who seems capable of draining others he has lost not only his palace of cards, but his own former youthful vigour. "I didn't, after all — it appeared part of my smash — know the weight of her husband's years, but I know the weight of my own. They might have been a thousand, and nothing but the sense of them would in a moment, I saw, be left me" (318). It is a curious, labyrinthine monologue which is bent, it seems, on exemplifying within itself the narrative of conjecture, and on conveying a warning that the endlessly refining

[18] *The Sacred Fount* (New York: Grove, 1953), p. 66. All page numbers in parenthesis are to this edition.

153

imagination feeds itself on others at grave personal cost. For this reason it has been considered James's singular act of self-parody. Whatever it is, self-revelation on the part of the narrator is not its chief effect.

Neither is self-revelation paramount in *The Aspern Papers*. The unnamed "publishing scoundrel" who rationalizes his way through an account of his own unscrupulous duplicity shows an avidity and dishonour of which he is fully aware, and as with all rogues, his disclosures of motive and method have their own fascination:

> I can arrive at the papers only by putting her off her guard, and I can put her off her guard only by ingratiating diplomatic practices. Hypocrisy, duplicity are my only chance. I am sorry for it, but for Jeffrey Aspern's sake I would do worse still.[19]

However, despite the reprobate charm of this bounder, the story is essentially Miss Tita's. Her ingenuous honesty is the heart of the account; her "force of soul" is the true dénouement. Poets and papers lose all significance in the light of her "infinite gentleness" (124), and if the narrator suffers defeat, she achieves victory. Wayne Booth has shown by his analysis of James's revision of this story that in each case the second version intensifies the narrator's awareness of his own baseness; and culminates in a suggestion that he has lost more than he bargained for (*The Rhetoric of Fiction*, pp. 357-59). Certainly in his account of his dealings with Miss Tita, he evaluates more than property, and leaves the reader pondering a kind of love poets seldom celebrate.

The moral concerns of truth and value found in *The Sacred Fount* and *The Aspern Papers* give place to a spiritual concern with good and evil in *The Turn of the Screw*. The proliferation of critical interpretations of this, James's most controversial eyewitness monologue, makes any fresh consideration of its meaning an exercise in filtration if not futility. Nevertheless the governess merits her place in any gallery of I-narrators, and we should consider what it is.

Attitudes are polarized. As Booth has it, the subject of the work is either "two evil children as seen by a naïve but well-meaning governess or two innocent children as seen by a hysterical, destructive governess" (*The Rhetoric of Fiction*, p. 346). Either the narrator is "reliable," as he understands the term, or she is not. And since

---

[19] *The Aspern Papers* (New York: Dell, 1959), p. 27. All page numbers in parenthesis are to this edition.

the tale she tells is one of supernatural visitation, the crucial question has become whether she saw what she claims to have seen — apparitions of creatures she never knew in her life. Consequently, the dispute has been what has been called "the distinguished discord between the apparitionist and non-apparitionist readers of *The Turn of the Screw.*"

Salient viewpoints may be summarized as follows: Edgar finds that "the story is concerned with the malign influence exercised on two exquisite and brilliant children ... by two dead servants," and Hoffman that the "ghosts are real and the children are corrupt and evil." Leavis considers Quint and Miss Jessel "the consistently bad ghosts of bad persons," and Heilman is "convinced that ... the story means exactly what it says: that at Bly there are apparitions which the governess sees, which Mrs. Grose does not see but comes to believe in ... and of which the children have a knowledge which they endeavour to conceal." On the other side, Edna Kenton believes that it is not the children, but the governess, who shows "a flair for evil," and Edmund Wilson gives the first explicit Freudian interpretation of the governess as "a neurotic case of sex repression" whose visions are "hallucinations." Osborn Andreas proposes that she subjects the children "to all the vagaries of her progressively more and more deranged mind," and Muriel West suggests that it is her physical violence, pure and simple, which causes Miles's death.[20]

More and more twists have been provided since the controversy erupted in flyting between F. R. Leavis and Marius Bewley in the pages of *Scrutiny* in 1950. Supporters of Wilson's theories have sought corroboration from the case histories of Freud and from the mental illness of James's sister Alice. Testifiers to the veracity of the governess have sought the real villain in the persons of the uncle

---

[20] Pelham Edgar, *Henry James: Man and Author* (London: Grant Richards, 1927), pp. 188-89; Charles G. Hoffman, "Innocence and Evil in James's *The Turn of the Screw*," *The University of Kansas City Review*, XX, 2 (Winter 1953), 98-105; F. R. Leavis, "The Appreciation of Henry James," *Scrutiny*, XIV, 3 (Spring 1947), 229-37; Robert B. Heilman, "*The Turn of the Screw* as Poem," *The University of Kansas City Review*, XIV, 4 (Summer 1948), 277-89; Edna Kenton, "Henry James to the Ruminant Reader: *The Turn of the Screw*," *The Arts*, XVI, 5 (November 1924), 245-55; Edmund Wilson, "The Ambiguity of Henry James," *The Triple Thinkers* (New York: Harcourt and Brace, 1938), pp. 122-64; Osborn Andreas, *Henry James and the Expanding Horizon* (Seattle: University of Washington Press, 1948), pp. 46-50; Muriel West, "The Death of Miles in *The Turn of the Screw*," *PMLA*, LXXIX (June 1964), 238-88.

and of Mrs. Grose.[21] And the most recent "case-book" has gone outside the work so completely that it has found corroborative evidence for hauntings in the papers of the Society of Physical Research and a model for Peter Quint in the person of George Bernard Shaw.[22]

Perhaps it is to be expected that a tale comparable — as James himself suggested in the Preface to *The Aspern Papers* — to the fairy tales of our childhood should evoke some highly imaginative, and even fantastic, reconstructions in response to its own mystery. It is common for the more adventurous commentators to discount James's own comments on the tale as ambiguous and vague, or to claim that his own subconscious desires — and neuroses — found expression in his "*jeu d'esprit.*" In view of the earnestness of contradictory critical opinions in the past seven decades, there is irony in James's assertion that his "perfectly independent and irresponsible little fiction rejoices, beyond any rival on a like ground, in a conscious provision of prompt retort to the sharpest question that may be addressed to it," and that its "perfect homogeneity" renders it "least apt to be baited by earnest criticism." There is a danger that the ingenuity of the sharp questions that have been addressed to both tale and teller may distract the reader from participation in the experience of Bly. Therefore the wise introduction of Leon Edel sounds a necessary caution:

> Readers coming fresh to the story are best advised to flee the commentators and read as one reads the fairies and ghosts of one's childhood — in all innocence and with a willing suspension of disbelief. . . . Every scene can be interpreted in several ways; only the governess feels "certitude" and the reader, uncontaminated by the obsessed exegetes,

21 C. Knight Aldrich, "Another Twist to *The Turn of the Screw*," *Modern Fiction Studies*, XIII (Summer 1967), 167-78. For good measure this author speculates that the iniquitous Mrs. Grose is actually the mother of the children, as the absentee "uncle" is the father. He approves John Clair's suggestion that Miss Jessel is alive — though demented — and sequestered at Bly, because it further implicates Mrs. Grose in deceit. It seems that the governess's employer is keeping a harem — though at a safe distance. Clair's theory in *The Ironic Dimension in the Fiction of Henry James* (Pittsburgh: Duquesne University Press, 1965) is that both Quint and Jessel are alive at Bly, and that Jessel, the maniac mother, is kept locked in the tower under the inefficient surveillance of Quint. It is a reading which appears to owe more to Charlotte Brönte's story than to Henry James's.

22 E. A. Sheppard, *Henry James and "The Turn of the Screw"* (Oxford: Oxford University Press, 1974). This extraordinary study also relates the tale to *Jane Eyre* and the plays of Ibsen (particularly *The Lady from the Sea* and *Little Eyolf*); the governess to Mlle. Henriette Duluzy; Miss Jessel to Annie Besant; and Bly to Ford Castle.

can capture the horror and ghostliness, and discover in the story all the evil he is capable of feeling.[23]

Edel's advice is rooted in James's own description of the fairy-tale nature of his "improvisation," and further in his expressed pleasure in the exercise of the imagination allowed by the writing — and therefore by the reading — of the tale. In James's mind this exercise of the imagination was meant to be "unassisted" and "unassociated." The only concession he makes to the agency of his eyewitness is found in an oblique reference to her tragic, yet exquisite "mystification," and its outcome in her expression:

> It was *déja très-joli* in "The Turn of the Screw," please believe, the general proposition of our young woman's keeping crystalline her record of so many intense anomalies and obscurities — by which I don't of course mean her explanation of them, a different matter; and I saw no way . . . to exhibit her in relations other than those; one of which, precisely, would have been her relation to her own nature. We have surely as much of her own nature as we can swallow in watching it reflect her anxieties and inductions. . . . She has 'authority', which is a good deal to have given her. . . . (*The Art of the Novel*, pp. 173-74)

The greater part of James's reflections upon the story is concerned with the impression of evil he wished it to make upon the reader, dependent upon the appreciation, speculation, and imagination provided by that reader. Edel has, therefore, presented James's own arguments with admirable economy and clarity.

To make "the reader's general vision of evil intense enough" is, as James wryly asserts, itself a charming job. To elucidate his problem in this regard one digression from the work becomes necessary. As inheritors of twentieth-century humanism and relativism, modern readers are a long way from the Swedenborgian doctrine of good and evil spirits James knew from his father. We seek psychological explanations of "acceptable or non-acceptable behaviour," and discredit the existence, let alone the agency, of manifestations of absolute evil. For an expression of the legacy of Swedenborg's *Heaven and Hell* we might turn to an autobiographical account of his own childhood by James's friend and contemporary William Dean Howells:

The Swedenborgian religion was not much understood by their neighbours. . . . But the boy [Howells is speaking of himself] once heard his father explain to one of them that the New Church people believed in

[23] *The Complete Tales of Henry James*, Vol. 10, ed. Leon Edel (New York: J. B. Lippincott, 1964), pp. 7-8. All page numbers in parenthesis are to this edition.

a hell, which each cast himself into if he loved the evil rather than the good, and that no mercy could keep him out of it without destroying him, for a man's love was his very self. It made his blood run cold, and he resolved that rather than cast himself into hell, he would do his poor best to love the good. The children were taught when they teased one another that there was nothing the fiends so much delighted in as teasing. When they were angry and revengeful, they were told that now they were calling evil spirits about them, and that the good angels could not come near them if they wished while they were in that state.[24]

Without attributing active adult belief in Swedenborg's dualism to either Howells or James, one can infer that early imaginative exposure to such ideas as these is partly responsible for the interest of both men in supernatural tales. This interest sets them squarely in the tradition of Hawthorne, whom they both admired.

The "authority" with which James has invested his narrator derives largely from the frame he has provided for her story. Others have noticed the artfulness of this introduction to deduce from it some mystery of tacit communication between Douglas and the anonymous narrator (who finally gives the story to the world at third hand); to notice significance in names and in the similarity of Douglas's circumstances to Miles's in the story; or to ponder the emphasis laid upon "love" in the case of both Douglas and the governess. All of these observations have their evidence, but to me the three remarkable features of the frame appear to be these. First, Douglas asserts of the tale confidently, "Nobody but me, till now, has ever heard [it]" (16). In view of the governess's circumstances at the end of the account, with one of her charges despatched in company with Mrs. Grose to report on the happenings at Bly to the mysterious uncle, and the other of her charges a corpse in her arms, this is an extraordinary statement. The imagination of the reader is forced to fashion for itself a sequel to the tale that will fit what he is given, or at least to admit that Rubin's conjectures that it is a fictional cloak for the governess' posthumous declaration of love to Miles-Douglas have some slight merit.[25] They would have more were it not for James's stated purpose to convey "portentous evil" — a love story, however tragic, hardly does this. The second is the tonal emphasis on "seeing." When Douglas first struggles to express the

24 *A Boy's Town* [1890], in *Selected Writings of William Dean Howells*, ed. Henry Steele Commager (New York: Random House, 1950), pp. 718-19.

25 *A Casebook on Henry James's "The Turn of the Screw,"* ed. Gerald Willer (New York: Crowell, 1969), pp. 350-66.

horror of the story he has heard he passes his hands over his eyes, and makes "a little wincing grimace." The account continues thus as he brings out the first words:

"For dreadful — dreadfulness!"
"Oh, how delicious!" cried one of the women.
He took no notice of her; he looked at me, but as if, instead of me, *he saw what he spoke of*. "For general uncanny ugliness and horror and pain . . ." (16; my italics)

Douglas continues in what follows alternately to face the fire, as if to avoid looking at the group watching him, and to fix the anonymous narrator with his eyes as if willing him to see something. He says again:

"She had never told anyone. It wasn't simply that she said so, but that I knew she hadn't. I was sure; *I could see*. You'll easily judge why when you hear."
"Because the thing had been such a scare?"
He continued to fix me. "You'll easily judge," he repeated: "you will."
I fixed him too. "*I see*. She was in love."
He laughed for the first time. "You *are* acute. Yes, she was in love. That is, she had been. That came out — she couldn't tell her story without its coming out. *I saw it*, and she *saw I saw it*." (17)

As my italicized references show, the emphasis upon seeing, on the part of Douglas in the past and his favoured guest in the present, is strong. It prepares us for the insistence upon the act of seeing in the monologue, where the governess frequently expresses the horror of the visitations through this simple verb: "Two hours ago, in the garden . . . Flora *saw*!" (56). "The more I saw, the less they would" (53). "What it was most impossible to get rid of was the cruel idea that, whatever I had seen, Miles and Flora saw more —" (89). "You see, you see, you *know* that you do and that you already quite suspect I believe it; therefore why not frankly confess . . . ?" (73). "That she now saw — as she had not, I had satisfied myself, the previous time — was proved . . ." (75). "I don't know what you mean. I see nobody. I see nothing. I never *have*" (116). "It came to me in the very horror of the immediate presence that the act would be, seeing and facing what I saw and faced, to keep the boy himself unaware" (133). "The more I go over it, the more I see in it, and the more I see in it, the more I fear" (57). The third important feature of the frame is Douglas's attestation to the authority of the governess. He describes her, at thirty, as "a most agreeable woman

159

... worthy of any position whatever ... awfully clever and nice" (17).[26] He admits to having liked her extremely, and to being glad that she liked him too. She emerges in his introduction to her story as being, at twenty, ingenuous and impressionable, but brave and eager to learn. There is therefore no suggestion before or after her terrible experience, according to Douglas, of incipient derangement or of retrospective self-dramatization. The prologue serves to introduce her as a narrator we can fully trust, as does the opening of her story.

It remains therefore to examine the narrator's telling of her story for discrimination between the "crystalline record" of "anomalies and obscurities," and "her own explanation of them," since my thesis is that confusion of those two, and that alone, is the trap which James concedes he has set for the unwary (172). And to illuminate further James's differentiation between the subject of the tale and its treatment by the narrator we should notice a reference to *The Turn of the Screw* in his preface to *The Altar of the Dead*, where he says, in adaptation:

The apparitions of Peter Quint and Miss Jessel ... are matters as to which in themselves, really the critical challenge (essentially nothing ever but the spirit of fine attention) may take a hundred forms. ... Our friend's ... mind about them, on the other hand [is] a different matter — challengeable, and repeatedly, if you like, but never challengeable without some consequent further stiffening of the whole texture. ... The moving accident, the rare conjunction, whatever it be, doesn't make the story ... the human emotion and the human attestation, the clustering human conditions we expect presented, only make it. (*The Art of the Novel*, p. 257)

"The clustering human conditions we expect presented" in the governess's tale, as Douglas has introduced it, are her sense of mission, her desire to satisfy her employer in every particular, her readiness to learn, and her awareness of her own naïve limitations. All these are presented clearly in the beginning of the account, as is her

26 James's careful time scheme shows that the governess was ten years older than Douglas when he must have himself been around twenty; therefore, the events at Bly were ten years behind her when they met. She has sent him the written copy of her story at least twenty years before he discloses its existence to others, and the guests infer that the meeting of the two must have taken place forty years ago. This distancing allows for her maturity at the time of writing, and for an enlarged experience of life which is reflected in her account: e.g., a young girl who has never seen an actor has since noticed the appearance of an empty theatre (47, 86); an untried governess has since had several consecutive positions of responsibility (26, 40).

hovering fear of being in some way unequal to her task because of some ominous circumstance outside her own shortcomings. She is, however, quickly mollified by Mrs. Grose's obliging courtesy and Flora's beatific radiance. Her observations are lucid, and if they are imaginative — the child resembling one of Raphael's holy infants (25) and the antique house resembling a drifting ship (27) — they are not unhealthily so.

A "tone of suspected and felt trouble" develops rapidly in the second chapter. It is from this point on that the revisions to which Edel has drawn attention occur. James seems to have taken pains to emphasize the strength of his narrator's feelings by expunging terms such as "perceived," "I understood," "I observed," and replacing them repeatedly with "I felt" and "I fancied." The governess now begins to respond to mysteries such as the boy's dismissal from his school and Mrs. Grose's reticence by showing herself sensitive to implications and ready to imagine their significance. Her explanation of obscurities, to Mrs. Grose and to herself, has begun.

It might be added that during the first enchanting weeks at Bly the governess is not without self-knowledge, and admits herself to be at this time fanciful, prim, and vain (24, 27, 34). But with the fall come the strange visitants, and all her imaginative energies are now bent upon explaining the evidence of her senses. Such meagre information as she elicits from the housekeeper she uses to augment and flesh out the explanations that seem to fit both her visions and the behaviour of the children. Indeed, so ready are her explanations that Mrs. Grose is scarcely permitted to finish a sentence, and the governess's narrative interpretation obscures much of the action which has inspired it. Is it true that "Flora saw!"? The declarative style is seductive, impeding the listener's attempts to distinguish the "crystalline record" from the teller's "explanation." We are left with what the governess has seen — and feared — as the only certainty. Even this certainty is clouded over by her maidenly reticence, leaving us to wonder why she is convinced, with the speed of light, that the male demon seeks out the boy and the female demon the girl. Buried sexual awareness seems to link Quint, Miles, and the uncle (who share the same waistcoats and possess the same potential power over women, or at least over the governess) on the one hand, and Miss Jessel, Flora, and the hapless governess — also a "lady" — on the other. Though she expresses it only in hints and telling associations, the governess's explanation of the ghosts' mission is couched in terms of sexual threat.

I have called the eight appearances of the ghosts, demons, or what you will — four times for each partner and never the two together — evidence of the governess's senses, and so I account them. Her record cannot be open to any doubt in this regard; she sees them, and whatever has conjured them forth, they are real to her. They do not appear solely at her own instigation, nor always in places where she expects them. They offer her nothing but an appearance of evil, pale, ravaged, and hungry, and a seeking gaze — in each case bent, she fancies, on finding and "fixing" someone else (38, 58).[27]

But of course it is her imagination which provides her with this supposition, and a survey of her behaviour after each encounter shows how much her fancy supplies her with. The first encounter she is able to dismiss, after much thought, as an intrusion by some unscrupulous traveller. But the second, in which she reads mutual recognition, produces a conviction where the first produced only mystification.

> On the spot there came to me the added shock of a certitude that it was not for me he had come there. He had come for someone else.
>
> The flash of this knowledge — for it was knowledge in the midst of dread — produced in me the most extraordinary effect . . . of duty and courage. (42)

Her conviction that "it was not for me he had come there," formed on the instant, remains unshaken. In the governess's edifice of assumption, she builds carefully on each premise as it forms, never revising or replacing any explanation that has occurred to her. And it is immediately following this first "certitude" that James offers, through her perception, a suggestion that the careful reader notes. The governess, finding no one on the terrace, presses her face to the glass as the apparition had done, and gives Mrs. Grose, entering the room, something of the shock the governess had received earlier. "I wondered why *she* should be scared" (43).

Is it, I wonder, a coincidence that the face which the governess presents through the glass is "white as a sheet" and "awful"; and that the face that Peter Quint presents to her through this same window in the final terrible scene is "the white face of damnation"? One of the features of the governess's narrative which has disturbed readers disposed to exonerate the children is the repeated evidence that she herself behaves in ways calculated to inspire terror. She

---

[27] Here is a clear example of duplication, in the monologue itself, of the language of the frame-narrator, who has spoken of being "fixed" by the gaze of Douglas (17).

frequently notes the terrible appearance she must have, in the extremity of her dread or anguish; she speaks of her wild sounds and her desperate grip on her charges; she many times embraces them with unwonted fervour. The thought that never occurs to her is that the awful evil threatening the children may be, at least in part, operating through her; and that she may be, however involuntarily, an agent of evil purpose. The power of Evil, an absolute Evil, is never doubted in the mind of the clergyman's daughter. To her it exists as a corruptive force, exerted through demons (82) bent on the destruction of innocence and a sharing of damnation (99). This is, as we have noted, a tenet of Swedenborg. There is grave irony in the fact that the governess, while passionately entertaining ideas of damnation, cannot appreciate the ominous aspects of her own behaviour — as, for example, when she excuses herself from church a second time to reflect on the "fulness of meaning" in recent events while sitting on an appropriated tombstone. "I only sat there on my tomb . . ." (94).

The explanations which the governess provides for her experiences carry a Swedenborgian connotation at every turn of the screw. This is suggested at the outset in her reconstruction of the reason for Miles's expulsion — which can only have been that he was an injury to others, a "corruption" (30). Mrs. Grose's joking reference to the governess's own susceptibility to corruption she dismisses at once. A close reading of the conversation of the two women at this point raises an interesting suggestion, for when the governess, thinking of her employer, laughs, "He seems to like us young and pretty!" Mrs. Grose, thinking of Peter Quint, answers, "Oh, he *did* . . . it was the way he liked everyone." Then she corrects herself. "I mean *his* way, the master's." Non-apparitionists have seen this as the first seed planted in the governess's subconscious, a direct lead to her hallucination on the tower. It is, however, possible to see another implication in the reference to the master who likes them young and pretty. Diabolists, take note.

After the second appearance, the governess, fortified by her inquiries in the village, pronounces the strange visitant "a horror" (45). Her declaration, "God help me if I know *what* he is" is followed ironically by, "I'm not fit for church." Her imagination contributes to the record of her senses that the stranger is "an actor," dressed up in the clothes of the "gentleman" he is not. And in recapitulation of the first conversation about Peter Quint she asserts — again an explanation — that he was looking for little Miles.

163

A portentous clearness now possessed me. *"That's* whom he was looking for."

"But how do you know?"

"I know, I know, I know!" My exaltation grew. "And *you* know, my dear!"

She didn't deny this, but I required, I felt, not even so much telling as that. She resumed in a moment, at any rate: "What if *he* should see him?"

"Little Miles? That's what he wants!"

She looked immensely scared again. "The child?"

"Heaven forbid! The man. He wants to appear to *them*." That he might was an awful conception, and yet, somehow, I could keep it at bay; which, moreover, as we lingered there, was what I succeeded in practically proving. I had an absolute certainty that I should see again what I had already seen, but something within me said that by offering myself bravely as the sole subject of such experience, by accepting, by inviting, by surmounting it all, I should serve as a expiatory victim and guard the tranquillity of my companions. (49-50)

From this point forward the governess never wavers in her conviction that the children are the intended victims and that she is the intended screen. All her explanations of her own experience implicate the children. What we read as evidence that Flora has not observed Miss Jessel, the governess interprets as evidence that she has (55-56). What the governess states as the intention of Miss Jessel, to get hold of Flora (58), we see as the governess's obsession. "I've done my best, but I've lost you" (117). What she sees as "a kind of fury of intention" (58), we see as the governess's own "absolute certainty" in contending for her principles mirrored in the haunting gaze. What she sees as brave attempts to guard the tranquillity of her companions, we watch, with mounting horror, become unbearable torments and harassments to them. Whether the children are "possessed" by the demons directly cannot be proved, so carefully does the record adumbrate evidence both for and against the theory. But there is no doubt that the governess, in being "possessed by a portentous clearness" as she explains her haunting to herself, is also, never knowingly, "possessed" by the evil that has come for *her*, "the sole subject of such experience."

The last conversation with Mrs. Grose sets the seal upon this interpretation.

"Leave us, leave us" — I was already, at the door, hurrying her off. "I'll get it out of him. He'll meet me — he'll confess. If he confesses, he's saved. And if he's saved —"

"Then *you* are?" (124)

And the last words of Miles endorse it. He calls the devoted guardian of his soul a "devil," and while she exults that *she* has him, he dies. His life, it seems, is the price of her exorcism (138).

In reading the governess's monologue as a retrospective account of her own devil-possession I, too, am trying to explain, as all critics do, the evocation of evil it holds for me. Theories of hallucination attendant upon Freudian repression do not seem to capture the actuality of evil that the tale bodies forth. The apparitions have too much power to be invented, and it is they, working through the possessed governess, that do indeed accomplish the impairment of Flora and the death of Miles. If the governess herself is unimpaired — indeed rather strengthened, as Douglas's account of her suggests — it is because, having unwittingly housed the conjunction of evil forces, she has passed through a fire and emerged like Cassandra. Evil has used her, and departed from her because she was an instrument and not an agent. This, perhaps, is what James meant when he wrote to Dr. Louis Waldstein, "Where there is life, there's truth, and the truth was at the back of my head." James's teasing truth may never be known for sure, because it is the truth at the back of the reader's head which shapes his response to the story. And this too, of course, the master acknowledged:

There is for such a case no eligible *absolute* of the wrong; it remains relative to fifty other elements, a matter of appreciation, speculation, imagination — these things moreover quite exactly in the light of the spectator's, the critic's, the reader's experience. Only make the reader's general vision of evil intense enough, I said to myself — and that already is a charming job — and his own experience, his own imagination, his own sympathy (with the children) and horror (of their false friends) will supply him quite sufficiently with all the particulars. Make him *think* the evil, make him think it for himself, and you are released from weak specifications. (*The Art of the Novel*, p. 176)

The triumph of the governess's monologue is precisely this, that in reading it we are forced to "*think* the evil." It is only afterwards, when we descend to thinking about the evil, that "weak specifications" are likely to occur. James seems to make, in his statement of narrative strategy, a psychological observation more cogent than any that has been found in the work itself. In using her own imagination and her own supposition, the governess thinks the evil for herself and incorporates it into her very efforts to protect the children from it. The thought evil is, she twice acknowledges, her "obsession" (87, 101). We can never be sure, totally and exclusively, what she

165

"saw" at Bly, but we can be sure that in undertaking to wrestle with a perceived blight she demonstrated those elements of possession and violation that culminated in shocking injury and destruction.

James, therefore, goes much further than Conrad and Ford. In *Heart of Darkness* and *The Good Soldier* the emphasis tends to be on the monologuists, their apprehension of truth through a clutter of impressions, appearances, conventions, accidents, and coincidences. In *The Turn of the Screw* the emphasis is rather on the unseen and the unstatable. This emphasis is disturbing, in retrospect, to all but the most casual of readers because it involves them in a struggle against, rather than with, the narrator; their acceptance of the narrator's authority can be accomplished only at the cost of abdicating their own responsibility as careful readers. The doubts, however, occur only when the spell is broken. For while he participates in the fairy-tale as an innocent listener to a powerful monologue, the reader is indeed under a spell, sharing a nightmare world with the governess and the children, and as driven, as fixed, as possessed, as they.

As eyewitness monologuists, Marlow, Dowell, and the governess share the ability that Aristotle notes of story-tellers, an ability to substitute the power of words for the power of action so that character and event may be obscured rather than revealed. Such power, a psychiatrist remarks, "has a peculiarly directive influence over us," placing us in "states of mind" which arouse our expectations while keeping us ignorant "for a long time about the precise nature of the conditions" in the experience recounted.[28] Thus there is a double effect for the participant in an eyewitness monologue: dramatic involvement in the events as they are disclosed (or obscured), and a fascinated sharing of the narrator's attempts to make meaning from them by the power of words. The variety of critical response to all the eyewitness monologues considered here testifies to the accuracy of the observatiton that such narrations "create in the reader an intricate play of emotion and a rich conflict of sympathy and judgement, a provisional bafflement in the face of experience which turns out to be more complicated than we ever would have dreamed" (Guerard, *Conrad the Novelist*, p. 127).

Knowing oneself baffled, however provisionally, can be one of the pleasures of reading. When we are engaged in a psycho-moral drama which has no easy solution we can take delight in our own attempts to arrive at increased understanding. For this reason we may re-read

[28] Sigmund Freud, "The 'Uncanny'," *Collected Papers*, IV (trans. Alix Strachey, London: Hogarth, 1934), pp. 405-06.

an eyewitness monologue many times, for whereas our enjoyment of dramatic involvement may remain static, our struggle to understand is dynamic. Insights change with a changing experience of life. The challenge of seeing something hitherto hidden continually motivates the participating reader of the eyewitness monologue, for each monologuist seems, above all else, to say, "Here is my experience of life. Bring yours to it, and make of it what you will."

CHAPTER SIX

Confessional Monologues

"Did I bring all this on myself? Have I relished it? Did I make the rules, design the pattern of events? For God's sake, or my own, am I to blame?" — PENELOPE MORTIMER, *Long Distance*

In the monologues discussed thus far the speakers have revealed themselves in the course of contemplating the sequence and significance of their own lives, or of seeking to understand experiences they have shared with others. The kind of monologue we now consider is not so much a recollection or a record as it is an inquiry into the meaning of personal experience. The confessional monologue springs from the need to explore and to share the most private places of a suffering psyche and therefore forms itself around the question of individual identity and concomitant questions of responsibility. "Who am I?" resolves itself into "Could I have been, or done, otherwise?"

Given this centre of self-searching, there are two defining characteristics of the confessional mode in monologue. One is a principle of selection, which distinguishes such from the interior monologues we have seen in Joyce or Faulkner. The monologues of Molly Bloom or Quentin Compson create an impression of random thought, of minds assailed by associative ideas over which they exercise no powers of selection. The control over sequence, the form which contains the flow, we have seen to be exercised and designed in these cases by the implied author. In the confessional monologue the speaker appears to create his own design. He makes his choices and defines them as he speaks; he considers certain events and people only as they are important to his self-searching; he traces and retraces his past only as it impinges on his present; he examines those compulsions that seem to have shaped his decisions; and in all of this he continually acknowledges, and frequently expounds upon, his own selective process. The second distinguishing mark of the confessional monologue is the expressed need for a "significant other" in the listener, through whom a purgation, if not an absolution, may be achieved. Every confessional monologuist is an Ancient Mariner. This, again, differentiates his monologue from its likeness among stream-of-consciousness variants. In both the communication can be described as intra-personal, but the confessional speaker also seeks out his counterpart and makes of him a mirror for the unburdening self.

Since the confessional monologuist speaks always from a condition of guilt and suffering,[1] he cannot aspire to the complacency of Felix Krull, the cheerfulness of Gulley Jimson, or the self-sufficiency of Hagar Shipley. Nor can he interest himself, as does Marlow or Dowell or the governess, in the perceptions of any other consciousness for their own sake. His suffering does not originate in the injustice or chaos of the external world but in the waste and confusion he apprehends within himself. His expressions of doubt, anger, regret, and frustration proceed, as they have begun, in anguished introspection. The sequence of his reflections, while under his conscious control, is not likely to be linear or chronological, but, like the "shuffle, fold and coil" of Sammy Mountjoy's memory,[2] it seems rather to inscribe endless circles with the self at both centre and circumference. In the words of one of the most memorable of confessional speakers, Nabokov's Humbert Humbert:

> When I try to analyze my own cravings, motives, actions and so forth, I surrender to a sort of retrospective imagination which feeds the analytic faculty with boundless alternatives and which causes each visualized route to fork and re-fork without end in the maddeningly complex prospect of my past.[3]

Confessional statements, attempting to create some kind of order or personal redemption out of a welter of painful and disordered experiences, invite readers to consider, likewise, the maddeningly complex prospect of their past, and to contemplate paradox.

[1] The Underground Man, spokesman for all who have over-acute sensibilities, says that "suffering . . . is the sole cause of consciousness." Dostoevsky, *Notes from Underground* (trans. Serge Shishkoff, New York: Thomas Crowell, 1969), p. 42. All page numbers in parenthesis are to this edition.

[2] William Golding, *Free Fall* (London: Faber, 1961), p. 6. All page numbers in parenthesis are to this edition.

[3] *Lolita* (New York: Berkeley, 1971), pp. 15-16.

In his examination of Montaigne's "personal essays," Auerbach has pointed out that experimentation is a necessary component of an introspective method:

> [Montaigne] means it seriously and emphatically when he says that his representation, however changeable and diverse it is, never goes astray and that though perhaps at times he contradicts himself, he never contradicts the truth. Such words mirror a very realistic conception of man based on experience and in particular on self-experience: the conception that a man is a fluctuating creature subject to the changes which take place in his surroundings, his destiny, and his inner impulses. Thus Montaigne's apparently fanciful method, which obeys no preconceived plan but adapts itself elastically to the changes of his own being, is basically a strictly experimental method, the only method which conforms to such a subject.[4]

Confessional heroes, exploring uncharted depths within themselves, are similarly driven to an experimental method — the only method which conforms to the subject of emergent self-understanding. They may choose the comparatively orderly form of the journal, as does Mauriac's Louis, or the typed document, as does Golding's Sammy Mountjoy. They may "speak" in a present tense continuum, as do Dostoevsky's Underground Man and Camus's Judge Penitent, or they may write a carefully constructed memoir, as do Nabokov's Humbert and Iris Murdoch's Bradley Pearson (*The Black Prince*). But whatever the form of the confession, it will convey immediacy to the reader, who finds himself directly addressed with a disarming intimacy. Whatever the content of the confession, it will unfold like a dream, the processes of the mind operating without necessary external stimulation. The oneiric quality of the monologue draws from the reader an imaginative as well as an intellectual response; in sharing an archetypal experience with the man for whom he has become confessor, he shares both the dream and the interpretation.

Thus it is in the confessional monologue that the author can be said to have disappeared most completely for the reader while he is reading. In other kinds of monologue authorial selection and authorial voice may still be detected to a lesser or greater extent behind the person speaking. But in the confessional monologue the illusion of immediacy and singularity is seamless.

The internalization of experience may be found, of course, outside fiction. The confessions of St. Augustine and of Rousseau have their place as progenitors of the confessional novel as much as do

---

[4] *Mimesis*, pp. 291-92.

the essays of Montaigne. The confessional form is found in the French Romantics, in Gogol, Turgenev, and Kafka. But Dostoevsky most notably develops the idea of self-scrutiny into a vehicle for "corrective punishment."[5] His "anti-hero," speaking from "the underground," is the prototype of the twentieth-centry model, the alienated introvert. *Notes from Underground* exemplifies the mind's recoil upon itself in an endless, never-to-be-concluded outpouring, internally and eternally circular. Whether the flow appears as dialogue with an assumed audience, as in Part One, or as monologue, as in most of Part Two, the Underground Man can never terminate his attempts to come to terms with the self which he conceives as a trapped rodent:

> There, in its miserable, stinking underground, our wronged, beaten-down and ridiculed mouse immediately plunges into cold, venomous, and most important, everlasting spite. For forty uninterrupted years it will remember the insult to the last, most shameful detail and add to it each time still more shameful details, maliciously taunting and provoking itself by its own imaginings, yet it will remember everything, go over everything, dream up a lot of slander against itself under the pretext that this too might have happened, and will forgive nothing. . . . On its deathbed it will once again remember everything, together with the interest that has accumulated. (11)

The effect of the "our" in the first sentence goes deeper than a royal plural. Perhaps in accompanying this miserable creature through its maze of rationalization and self-laceration the reader-listener will learn something about himself. Who then is this speaker who can "never start or finish anything" (18)?

We never know his name. We know only his nature, as he himself describes it. He begins his monologue with three statements. "I am a sick man . . . I am a nasty man. A truly unattractive man" (3). At first one may construe these statements as three ways of saying the same thing, but a close look at the Russian original shows that already the psychological process of rationalization and qualification has begun. A literal translation of the Russian would be "I man sick . . . I spiteful (malicious) man. Repulsive i man." All three clauses are stylistically correct in Russian, but the shift in emphasis and tone resultant from the changed word order is untranslatable. Also the first person singular is not usually capitalized in Russian

---

[5] The Russian noun in this phrase is the term used in the title *Crime and Punishment*; it has been translated also as "correction," the phrase thereby becoming "penal correction," and as "expiation."

except at the beginning of a sentence. Therefore the capital at the beginning of the second clause, following interpunctuation, is more clearly a new beginning in the original. It is, however, a new beginning which follows a pause. The three dots, which are part of the original, signal a side-glance at the reader, as if the speaker were watching for the effect of his first three words. Lest they produce pity, he continues with two defiant corrections. In what follows the quoted opening, the speaker reverts to his initial clause to blame his liver for his sickness. Immediately he qualifies this diagnosis; he does not really know the origin of his symptoms, because he has not consulted a doctor. This leads to another qualification, for he respects the science of medicine and its exponents. At once he corrects the impression this statement gives. Lest he appear unknowingly naïve, he adds a jest, "I am superstitious to the extreme; well, at least to the extent of respecting medicine." But the jest also may be misinterpreted. Suppose the reader were to assume him ignorant? Another jest corrects this impression. "I am sufficiently educated not to be superstitious, but I am." And since the reader might well question his refusal to see a doctor, he must prepare a shocking answer to the anticipated question. "No sir, it's out of nastiness [spite, as in the opening clause] that I don't want to see the doctor." Again, he anticipates the reaction. "You, my dear sir, probably don't understand that. Well, I do." So he continues to trap his listener into responses which he immediately forestalls or frustrates. The whole opening sequence embodies the attitude which he later describes in himself, "When petitioners looking for information happened to come to the desk where I sat, I gnashed my teeth at them, and I felt an insatiable delight when I succeeded in upsetting someone" (4).

Every phrase in Part One of the Underground Man's monologue is designed to upset his listener. He engages in polemic with an imaginary petitioner, "looking for information," by treating him derisively at every turn. There are constant disproofs of the supposed opinions of the other person or persons, alternate evasions and self-justifications, and repeated implications of indifference towards others which merely prove his essential dependence upon them. This is the fundamental paradox of his confession. In order to free himself from the image reflected in the consciousness of others, the Underground Man strives himself to distort and besmirch that image in every imaginable way.

This is the role-playing of despair. The image of the self must be made into a mask behind which the real self hides forever undiscovered. If the Underground Man can hide behind an ever-changing mask he can be free, rid of witnesses, forever immured in his underground existence. Therefore even the most categorical of affirmations is open to further qualification. "But I swear to you, gentlemen, that I do not believe a word, not even one little word of all that I have just dashed off! That is, I believe, perhaps, but at the same time, I don't know why, I feel and suspect I am lying like a trooper" (36).

This style of expression, endlessly rebutting definitive statement, has been called the "loophole" device, and has been shown operating in the speech of other heroes of Dostoevsky, all of whom are characterized by confessional monologues.[6] The paradoxes produced by contradictions between the speaker's analyses and his behaviour are more than the eccentricities of some half-demented creature, they are a revelation of man about man. This we see worked out in the progression of the monologue, for the speaker finally imagines, and expresses as direct speech, the response of listeners to his "logical mish-mash" — a response which articulates everything the reader has been feeling as he reads (36-37). Then:

It goes without saying that I just dreamed up all those words of yours. That too comes from the underground. For forty years on end I kept my ear to the crack listening to those words of yours. I thought them up myself, for that's about all that came to me. Small wonder that they were learned by heart. . . .

But are you, are you really so gullible that you imagine I might publish all this and, what's more, give it to you to read? And here is another puzzle for me: why, actually, do I call you "gentlemen," why do I address you as if I were really addressing readers? Confessions of the kind that I intend to begin setting forth are not published and are not given to other people to read. I, at least don't have that much firmness in me. . . .

In the reminiscences of every man there are some things that he does not reveal to anyone except possibly to friends. Then there are some that he will not reveal to friends, but only to himself, and even so in secret. But finally there are some that a man is afraid to reveal even to himself, and every man accumulates a good number of such things.

6 See, for instance, M. M. Bakhtin, *Problemy Poetici Dostoevskgo: Problems of Dostoevsky's Poetics* (trans. Richard Balthazar, Moscow: 1963). Bakhtin builds his theory of Dostoevsky's poetics from what he calls a "two-voiced word," a word which is both self-referring and also substituting for the voice of a listener, and finds its most consistent exponent in the Underground Man.

I'll even venture this: the more decent a man is, the more of them he has. (37-38)

In this way the Underground Man approaches the second part of his confessions, which is a narrative account of his dealings, sixteen years earlier, with a prostitute, Lisa, to whom he has made a false confession before using her as a means of proving his own despicability. This is the truth about himself he is afraid to reveal even to himself, the "corrective punishment" by which he can become "honest to God (124). Its sequel is a broadening from the "I" and the "you" of the dialogue to a universal "we":

... all this will produce a very disagreeable impression, because we have all become estranged from life, we all hobble to a greater or lesser degree. We have become so estranged that at times we even feel disgust for the real "living life," and that's why we can't stand being reminded of it. (124)

Thus the consciousness of the exacerbated mouse becomes human consciousness in general, and far from being a nineteenth-century Russian nihilist, the Underground Man becomes the spokesman of mankind. *Notes from Underground* is not merely a "Confession," as Dostoevsky's original title named it, but it is also a work about confession and about the universal need for "corrective punishment" if man is to become reintegrated into life.

The final irony unveiled by the Underground Man is that even as he voluntarily undergoes his corrective punishment a man is likely to perpetuate fraud, dramatizing himself in the way Heine alleges Rousseau did in his *Confessions* by accusing himself of crimes out of "vanity" (38). This is precisely what we may see subsequent confessional monologuists doing. Indeed, one of them seems to be elaborating, point by point, each of the notes offered from Dostoevsky's underground:

... I navigate skillfully, multiplying distinctions and digressions, too — in short, I adapt my words to my listener and lead him to go me one better. I mingle what concerns me and what concerns others. I choose the features we have in common, the experiences we have endured together, the failings we share — good form, in other words, the man of the hour as he is rife in me and in others. With all that I construct a portrait which is the image of all and of no one. A mask, in short, rather like those carnival masks which are both life-like and stylized, so that they make people say: "Why, surely, I've met him!" When the portrait is finished, as it is this evening, I show it with great sorrow: "This, alas, is what I am!" The prosecutor's charge is finished: But at the same time the portrait I hold out to my contemporaries becomes a mirror.

... I stand before all humanity recapitulating my shames without losing sight of the effect I am producing, and saying: "I was the lowest of the low." Then imperceptibly I pass from the "I" to the "we." When I get to "This is what we are," the trick has been played.[7]

This is Jean-Baptiste Clamence speaking, towards the end of his "mirror" monologue in *The Fall*. The "Judge Penitent," we see at once, is a maker of masks who confronts his listener with an image of himself, and thereby incorporates him into the universal "we." But this is not the only similarity between *Notes from Underground* and *The Fall*. Camus used his admired Dostoevsky as a source for both structural imitation and ambiguous satire. The latter he achieved by attributing to his monologuist a confessional twist, for Clamence accuses himself for the ultimate purpose of being thereby justified in judging others. If *Notes from Underground* is about confession, *The Fall* is about judgement achieved through confession. If the Underground Man is a creature who sees himself as an insect or as vermin, Jean-Baptiste Clamence is a creature who sees himself as God. In the course of his history as he spasmodically recounts it he has been provided with the masks of the penitent, the judge, and the pope; the final role he sees himself as playing is that of the highest Judge of all.

How intoxicating to feel like God the Father and to hand out definitive testimonials of bad character and habits. I sit enthroned among my bad angels at the summit of the Dutch heaven and I watch ascending toward me, as they issue from the fogs and the water, the multitude of the Last Judgment. They rise slowly; I already see the first of them arriving. On his bewildered face, half hidden by his hand, I read the melancholy of the common condition and despair of not being able to escape it. And as for me, I pity without absolving, I understand without forgiving, and, above all, I feel at last that I am being adored! (143)

The arrogance of this vision is mitigated by the accompanying sardonic humour of self-parody. One of Clamence's avowed intentions is to amuse his listener (9), and the levity he displays when he is introducing himself continues in ironic underplay, with mounting savage intent, throughout his monologue. At first the wit is epigrammatic:

[7] Albert Camus, *The Fall* (trans. Justin O'Brien, New York: Random House, 1956), pp. 139-40. All page numbers in parenthesis are to this edition.

Anyone who has considerably mediated on man, by profession or vocation, is led to feel nostalgia for the primates. (4)

... style, like sheer silk, too often hides eczema. (6)

A single sentence will suffice for modern man: he fornicated and read the papers. (6)

When one has no character one *has* to apply a method. (11)

But this self-assured humour, designed to impress the listener with the speaker's urbanity, gradually gives place to less consciously witty observations in which the comedy continues to be black. Thus in speaking of two women, a mature prostitute and a well-born unmarried girl, with whom he once lived contemporaneously, he comments that he played the gallant with the first and gave the second an opportunity to learn the realities. He continues, "Unfortunately the prostitute had a most middle-class nature; she since consented to write her memoirs for a confessions magazine quite open to modern ideas. The girl, for her part, got married to satisfy her unbridled instincts and make use of her remarkable gifts" (104). And in speaking of the many criminals he has defended, he remarks, "To achieve notoriety it is enough, after all, to kill one's concierge. Unhappily, this is usually an ephemeral reputation, so many concierges are there who deserve and receive the knife" (26).

The careful formulations of the Judge Penitent, delivered with an air of having been rehearsed, if not perfected, by habitual enactment, are a far cry from the unresolved incoherencies of the Underground Man. Yet many features of his existence remind us of his predecessor. Clamence has immured himself in an "underground" of his own choice, the dank canals of Amsterdam (43) which resemble the concentric circles of hell (14), a place utterly removed from the "lofty places" he delighted in before his penance (23). Later he calls it "a soggy hell, indeed! ... universal obliteration, everlasting nothingness made visible" (72). He is in his forties (8), a man "who has seen everything." He has no friends (73). His remembered past includes humiliation by a malicious servant (34) and utilization of prostitutes (102, 103). In all these circumstances he resembles the Underground Man, and like him he has discovered "the frivolity of seriousness," because he also is a paradoxicalist who has come to see his life as the playing out of chosen roles (87). The form of his disclosures is similar too. He moves from verbal fencing to the recollection of incidents which opened his eyes to his own duplicity, culminating in the fall which was the occasion of his fall

176

(70). His finally announced urge to go out, like that of the Underground Man, is inspired by the falling snow, with its promise of a blanket of peace and silence. And his last recorded words are a testament to complicity.

The satire of the judge's monologue reveals itself in his mocking and derisive humour and also in the edifice of motive which he gradually reveals to his listener. He discloses his need to look down on others from the heights of his own perfection. He has always been a monster of pride, and when a series of discoveries about his true nature has forced him to abdicate his sense of superiority, he has assumed the function of Inquisitor so that in forcing others to share guilt with him he can continue to despise them. "You see in me, *très cher*," he says to his listener, "an enlightened advocate of slavery" (132). It is in this respect that he becomes, as the epigraph from Lermontov suggests, "the aggregate of the vices of a whole generation in their fullest expression." Both his former good intentions to be of service to others and his later obsession to convince others of their guilt are expressions of that desire to enslave others which critics have discerned in Camus's major criticism of contemporary man.[8]

His confession, however, shows that Clamence's self-styled advocacy of slavery is not such a simple matter. He has arrived at his bitter self-knowledge by a road of humiliation which he carefully traces; his failures in dignity and compassion are both symbolized by the twin episodes of the bridge — the mocking laughter which continues to haunt him and the splash of a suicide to which in thought and vision he continues to return. His fear of bridges is the product of these experiences as it is the witness of his own loss of freedom, and it is this loss which compels him to deprive others of theirs.

But on the bridges of Paris I, too, learned that I was afraid of freedom. So hurray for the master, whoever he may be, to take the place of heaven's law. . . . The essential is to cease being free and to obey, in repentance, a greater rogue than oneself. When we are all guilty, that will be democracy. . . . Death is solitary, whereas slavery is collective.
. . . This is why, *très cher*, after having solemnly paid my respects to freedom, I decided on the sly that it had to be handed over without delay to anyone who comes along. And every time I can, I preach in

---

[8] Thus, for example, Philip Thody, *Albert Camus 1913-1960* (London: Hamish Hamilton, 1961); Thomas Hanna, *The Thought and Art of Albert Camus* (Chicago: H. Regnery, 1958); John Cruikshank, *Albert Camus and the Literature of Revolt* (Oxford: Oxford University Press, 1959).

my church of *Mexico City*, I invite the good people to submit to authority and humbly to solicit the comforts of slavery, even if I have to present it as true freedom. (137)

The reader is "anyone who comes along," but he is more specifically the *cher compatriote* who is constantly addressed. As in the dramatic monologue, and as in the first part of *Notes from Underground*, the audience is incorporated into the action of this confession as a tacit participant in a running dialogue. Clamence indicates the answers he receives just sufficiently to maintain an uninterrupted flow of monologue. The artfulness of this device is most clearly seen in the "social conversation" of the opening:

Are you staying long in Amsterdam? A beautiful city, isn't it? Fascinating? There's an adjective I haven't heard in some time. (6)

Here is our gin at last. To your prosperity. Yes, the ape opened his mouth to call me doctor. In these countries everyone is a doctor, or a professor. . . .
But allow me to introduce myself: Jean-Baptiste Clamence, at your service. Pleased to know you. You are in business, no doubt? In a way? Excellent reply! (8)

You're leaving already? Forgive me for having perhaps detained you. No, I beg you; I won't let you pay. I am at home at *Mexico City* and have been particularly pleased to receive you here. I shall certainly be here tomorrow, as I am every evening, and I shall be pleased to accept your invitation. Your way back? — Well — (10)

The signposts continue in this way, precisely locating the time and place of each meeting, but as Clamence becomes progressively more self-disclosing the interjections of his interlocutor are less in evidence. The terms of address become more intimate, from the *"monsieur"* of the opening to the *"mon cher"* and *"très cher"* of the later meetings, until finally, and significantly, the listener is addressed as *"cher maître"* (147) at the moment that identification between speaker and listener is accomplished. But the manner of this accomplishment produces a shock of recognition in the reader, for up to the last page of the monologue he has assumed the identity of the confessor. Now he finds that Clamence's confessor is truly his double, and that the feverish occupant of the bed which is so like a coffin is talking to himself. Delineation between parody and reality is seldom so blurred as it is in *The Fall*. Does the reader, ultimately, stand accused? Only the individual reader can answer that question.

Inevitably this ambiguity produces diverse interpretations of the work. Roman Catholic critics, intrigued by the references to Christ, the implications of the title, and the clear parallels between Clamence and Elijah (and therefore John the Baptist), offer a Christian exposition. A humanist view traces the rise of Clamence's self-knowledge counteracting his fall from virtue, thereby making him a fuller human being after his confession than he was before. Henri Peyre finds that the inherent satire makes the meaning by denying that any true confession can ever be made:

> The hero of *The Fall* is an embittered, sarcastic nihilist, a garrulous talker merging his own guilt in the guilt which he instills in all those whom he forces to listen to him. If anything, that baffling tale should be read as a satire of the self-indictment practised by Christians and atheistic Existentialists alike.[9]

Whatever their ultimate significance, however, Clamence's accusations remain as haunting to his listener as the laughter and the cry on the bridge are to Clamence. The confession presupposes a community of guilt and articulates an uncertainty about human values which may, after all, inspire the reader to an answering confession of guilt, or to a vindication of certainty. And if it does not involve the reader in any responsive way, it remains, as has been said before, an indictment of indictment. Like *Notes from Underground* it is what it is about, and content and mode are inseparably fused.

The monologues created by Dostoevsky and Camus are unusually organic. In other confessional monologues of this century the circumstances and the character of the speaker are more readily separated from his style of address, and traditional novel components such as plot, theme, and setting can be discerned and discussed in a more traditional way. Thus we can see the journal of Mauriac's Louis as a study in avarice with a clearly redemptive outcome, and the memoirs of Humbert Humbert as a case history of aberration with an inevitable sequel of madness. In *Viper's Tangle* and *Lolita*, both Mauriac and Nabokov have provided the reader with more than the monologue *per se*. They have added a framework which allows an external, albeit ironic, view of their speakers, and their artistic purpose goes in each case beyond the confession itself. Both Louis and Humbert write their confessions over a long period of

---

[9] Germaine Brée, ed., *Camus: A Collection of Critical Essays* (New Jersey: Spectrum, 1962. In a representative Christian opinion, Bernard C. Murchland, C.S.C., places Camus in the Mauriac-Greene tradition, and sees the confession as a means of the lawyer's redemption. A humanist interpretation is found in R. W. B. Lewis, *The Picaresque Saint* (Philadelphia: Lippincott, 1961). Henri Peyre, "Camus the Pagan," *Yale French Studies*, No. 25 (Spring 1960), p. 23.

time, and reflect over what they have written, so that the immediacy of the speaking voice is dissipated. Thus Louis writes:

> Tonight I woke, fighting for breath. I felt a compulsion to get up. I dragged myself to my chair, and sat, reading over, to the accompaniment of a howling wind, the last few pages I had written. I was appalled by the light they shed on my deepest self.

And Humbert, on the fifty-sixth day of his incarceration, writes:

> This then is my story. I have reread it. It has bits of marrow sticking to it, and blood, and beautiful bright-green flies. At this or that twist of it I feel my slippery self eluding me, gliding into deeper and darker waters than I care to probe.[10]

The monologuist, in each case, is aware of the confession he has created and consciously evaluates his success or failure at his task of self-scrutiny. The confessional act has become an end, rather than a means for these writers. The same is true of Iris Murdoch's Bradley Pearson, who is himself a novelist, and whose consuming concern for art shapes his memoirs more pervasively than does his need to understand his own guilt in the tragic experience he unfolds:

> So we live on together here in our quiet monastery, as we are pleased to call it. And so I come to the end of this book. I do not know if I shall write another. You have taught me to live in the present and to forswear the fruitless anxious pain which binds to past and to future our miserable local arc of the great wheel of desire. Art is a vain and hollow show, a toy of gross illusion, unless it points beyond itself and moves ever whither it points. You who are a musician have shown me this, in the wordless ultimate regions of your art, where form and substance hover upon the brink of silence, and where articulate forms negate themselves and vanish into ecstasy. Whether words can travel that path, through truth, absurdity, simplicity, to silence I do not know, nor what that path can be like.[11]

Since Bradley's imaginative propensities are everywhere evident in his confessions, Murdoch provides corrective points of view in the prefatory notes of an "editor" (cf. *Lolita*) and in "Four Postscripts by Dramatis Personae" which culminate in the editor's assertion that "Art tells the only truth that ultimately matters."

Other examples could be offered of the use made by twentieth-century novelists of the confessional monologue for the purpose of

[10] Francois Mauriac, *Le Noeud de Vipères*, trans. Gerard Hopkins, in *A Mauriac Reader* (New York: Farrar, Strauss and Giroux, 1968), p. 353. Nabokov, *Lolita* (New York: Berkeley, 1971), p. 280.

[11] Iris Murdoch, *The Black Prince* (Harmondsworth: Penguin, 1975), p. 392.

examining the intrinsic truth of isolated or universalized experience.[12] But there is one recent novel in which the confessional monologue stands alone, in the tradition fathered by Dostoevsky, and in which it is comparable in tone, rhetoric, and effect to the monologues of the Underground Man and the Judge Penitent.

William Golding's *Free Fall* has earned less acclaim than his other "fables," and this may be partly the result of Golding's avowed purpose of presenting a contemporary and known world in place of a mythopoeic one, and partly the result of the confessional mode. For, as Stephen Medcalf expresses it:

> ... the resolution remains thick and uncertain: and, perhaps because Sammy has already tried to do it for us, the second reading of the book provides nothing new. Alone among Golding's novels *Free Fall* is more of a puzzle fragmentarily solved than a mystery to be known, though it has long illuminating stretches.[13]

This is not a critical opinion with which I find it easy to agree, but it is cited here as a fairly representative response. All of Golding's novels are interrelated thematically and structurally, but *Free Fall* is the most readily separable from the corpus; its distinguishing and, to many readers, daunting characteristic might be expressed in Sammy's own words as he mutters in his cell: "I? I? Too many I's, but what else was there in this thick, impenetrable cosmos? What else? A wooden door and how many shapes of walls?" (169-70).

In common with other confessional monologuists, Sammy Mountjoy continually asks discomfiting questions. Perhaps the most pertinent ones for critics occur in his introduction, when he asks: "And who are you anyway? Are you on the inside, have you a proof-copy? Am I a job to do? Do I exasperate you by translating incoherence

---

[12] A partial list shows some interesting variants. In Alan Sillitoe's *The Loneliness of the Long Distance Runner* the speaker reveals himself as a hardened criminal whose aim in life — the outwitting of governors of every kind — is encapsulated in the re-enactment of a long-distance race. In John Fowles's *The Collector* the confession of the perverted lepidopterist is supplemented by the diary of his victim. In Margaret Drabble's *The Waterfall*, the narrator's story and self-description alternate, the same speaker employing both objective third person reporting and subjective confessional analysis. In David Storey's *A Temporary Life* the speaker unfolds his experiences in the present tense, incorporating both confession and description. In his *Molloy, Malone Dies*, and *The Unnamable*, Samuel Beckett's grotesques hobble through long examinations of their own deprived existences and ruminations about human suffering in general. In Philip Roth's *My Life as a Man*, the created spokesman is a novelist who writes a couple of "useful fictions" before the "true" account of his life.

[13] *William Golding* (Essex: Longman, 1975), p. 30.

into incoherence?" (8). But the implied admonition to the reader is fleeting. Although he is writing, and not speaking, Sammy Mount-joy, like the Underground Man and the Judge Penitent, is really making his confession for himself: "Perhaps reading my story through again I shall see the connection between the little boy, clear as spring water, and the man like a stagnant pool. Somehow, the one became the other" (9). The reader can only give assent, and read on. He has been drawn into the confession, and he can share Sammy's search.

For many readers, Golding's derivativeness has become an intellectual game. The inspirations he drew from Ballantyne, Wells, Bierce, Eliot, Conrad, Burroughs, Ibsen, Trollope, Browning, *et al.* have been frequently discussed. The ironic inversion of Dante's *Vita Nuova* found in *Free Fall* has been exhaustively noted.[14] It is more material to this study, however, to note the possible influence of Camus's *The Fall*, which was first published in English in 1956, on Golding's fourth novel, which appeared in 1959.

Similarities extend beyond the titles of the works.[15] In both there is quasi-religious paradox in nomenclature. In the case of Camus's hero, "Jean-Baptiste" recalls the voice crying in the wilderness, the prophet whom men thought was Elijah come again to prepare the way of the Lord by preaching repentance and baptizing the penitent by immersion in the waters of Jordan. The water motif in *The Fall*, coupled with the speaker's references to himself as Elijah, elaborates the Biblical significance of his given name. The surname "Clamence" echoes clemency, and ironically undergirds the judge's self-imposed function to "pity without absolving." In the case of Golding's hero, "Samuel" recalls the infant Samuel of the Old Testament, given by his mother into the care of a priest who trains him to serve at the altar and to become judge over himself and pro-

14 Mark Kinkead-Weekes and Ian Gregor, *William Golding: A Critical Study* (New York: Harcourt Brace, 1967), p. 174 f.; Virginia Tiger, *William Golding: The Dark Fields of Discovery* (London: Calder and Beyars, 1974), pp. 155-83.

15 Golding's title adds scientific to theological connotations. The adjective supplies the noun with an implication of both free will and the condition of neutralized gravitational pull in space. The author has said of it:

... the poignancy of the modern intellectual is that he is literally in this state of free fall ... it is in fact a scientific term. It is where your gravity has *gone.* . . . There is also the Miltonic idea; there is also the Genesis idea; there is also the ordinary daily life idea of something which is for free and something which is also fall. "Free" and "fall" are both caught up in it.

claimer of kings. The Biblical implications are both extended and corrected in the second name, "Mountjoy," which may be associated with the Mount of Transfiguration and also with the joyful reaches of the Mons Veneris. As their names suggest, both are accomplished and articulate heroes. Both are also sensualists who confess to having exploited and debased a woman after securing her love and loyalty. In Sammy's case the violation of Beatrice has a stronger Dostoevskian colouring than does the lawyer's conquest (which is one of many debaucheries) because Sammy seeks a penetration of the self more than possession; and whereas both men link their own "fall" with the unprevented destruction of a woman, for Sammy that same woman is the Beatrice of his passion.

The most significant analogue linking the two confessions, however, is the experience of a German prisoner-of-war camp and associated torments. Clamence remembers playing "pope," and drinking water which might have saved the life of a "significant other." Sammy remembers a nightmare terror, tinged with betrayal, which prefaced his most significant experience of others. At the heart of his confession, the torture cell has offered him the two kinds of torment which the lawyer describes in the course of his *récit*, that of the "little-ease" and that of the "spitting-cell." An examination of the texts will illuminate this analogue:

The "little-ease" was distinguished from others by ingenious dimensions. It was not high enough to stand up in nor yet wide enough to lie down in. One had to take on an awkward manner and live on the diagonal; sleep was a collapse, and waking a squatting. (*The Fall*, 109)

Have you at least heard of the spitting-cell, which a nation recently thought up to prove itself the greatest on earth? A walled-up box in which the prisoner can stand without moving. The solid door that locks him in his cement shell stops at chin level. Hence only his face is visible, and every passing jailer spits copiously on it. The prisoner, wedged into his cell, cannot wipe his face, though he is allowed, it is true, to close his eyes. (*The Fall*, 111)

Sammy's torment occurs in a cell in which darkness, unknown dimensions, and wetness all contribute to his terror. As he relives this punishment he says:

Who could have told me . . . that the darkness before my blindfolded eyes would take on the likeness of a wall so that I would keep lifting my chin in order to look over it? . . . I lifted my chin again to see over the wall which rose with me. A kind of soup or stew of all the dungeon

183

stories flew through my head, oubliettes, walls that moved, the little ease.

... I squatted, then crouched and worked my way to the right, I found an angle and then wood. All the time I was trying to hold a new diagram in my head without displacing the old, conjectural one of a bench and a judge.   (166-68)

Hutching and crawling his blind way around the confined space, Sammy discovers from his tracing of the walls that he is in a cell.

How large a cell? I began to move and break up the granite of my immobility, stretched myself carefully along my own wall; but before my knees were straight my feet came against the concrete of the other wall; and hutching round through what might be ninety degrees until my body lay along by the door I found the same. The cell was too small for me to stretch myself out.   (172-73)

The thing that his hand finds in the centre of the cell is "Smooth. Wet. Liquid," and tears of strain join the water already on his face (179). When his agony is over and he walks again the transfigured outdoors, companions are embarrassed to notice, he says, "the water on my face" (187).

The dungeon cell and the walled-up box evoked by Jean-Baptiste Clamence as illustrations of the Last Judgment are realities which Sammy Mountjoy, also obsessed with the idea of judgement, knows experientially. Both are prefigured in the paradox of pleasure in pain as it is enunciated by the Underground Man:

... the pleasure involved here comes precisely from an all too acute consciousness of your own degradation, because you yourself feel that you have reached the last wall; that it was vile all right, but that it could not be otherwise; that you no longer had a way out, that you could never become a different man, that even if you had the time and the faith to change yourself into something else, you probably would not have the desire to change; even if you had the desire, you could do nothing even then, because, in reality there might be nothing to change into. ... Here's what happens, for example, as a result of intensified consciousness: you know you are a wretch, as if it were a consolation to a wretch that he himself already realizes that he actually is a wretch.   (*Notes from Underground*, 8)

The "word-weaving" of the Underground Man embroiders the metaphor of the incarcerated consciousness. His metaphysics of despair finds a ready echo in the intransigence of Clamence. But Sammy's confession takes a different turn. *In extremis* he cries out for help; in a spiritual victory which is never explained he "bursts the door" before external hands open it, and in his willed breakthrough of what the Underground Man calls "the last wall" is a vindication of the freedom he thought he had lost.

The narrative technique of Sammy Mountjoy itself exemplifies the dichotomy which troubles him, and which he seeks to attribute to his two schoolteachers, Rowena Pringle and Nick Shales (217). Two styles of rhetoric inform his monologue in much the same way that we have noted in the narrative of Joyce's *Portrait*. For, like Stephen Dedalus, Sammy is two people; his problem, perhaps, is that like Halde he does not understand plurality (253). He is the artist whose visions, couched in the vivid pictorial terms appropriate to one whose portraits hang in the Tate (7), are rendered in highly charged images; and he is *l'homme moyen sensuel* whose lowly origins and whose questionable morality find a paradigm for identity in a metaphor as humble as a "row of useless hats" (6). The reiterated question, "When did I lose my freedom?" (5) which Sammy uses as a structural principle for the ordering of his retrospection is not, therefore, the crucial question to be answered by such self-scrutiny. Instead, his confession moves inexorably towards the refutation of his statement "There is no bridge" (253). We will perhaps see this more clearly if we juxtapose two dichotomous accounts at the centre of the monologue to find the bridge between them.

There is a distinct relationship between the highly wrought and emotion-charged description of Sammy's pivotal terror in the cell and the elliptical and factual account of his visit to the hospital which presumably followed his return home after the war. In expression the passages are as different as is imaginable:

I could see everything now except the slug-thing because there was almost no darkness left. There was light falling away in a torrent, there were shouts and screams visible as shapes, long curves that shone and vibrated. But the shape of the thing on the floor was communicated to me through one enslaved finger... (182)

The receptionist traced out a route on a plan. Not at all, it was a pleasure to her, professionally smooth, helpful and untouched... Kenneth's office was empty. There were green filing cabinets, papers, pen, blotter, ink and a couch for confidences. (238)

But in content the echoes abound. Sammy walks the once magical gardens aware that the "sense of institution" lies over house and gardens "like the greyness of a prison camp" (238). Beatrice Ifor is here incarcerated, in a state "rather like experiencing continual and exaggerated worry" (247). As he walks to meet her for the first time since he abandoned her seven years before, Sammy remembers, most of all, her terror (241). The terribly changed Beatrice sits facing the right-hand wall, which, Sammy notes, is in the darkest corner of the large bare room. He also notes, as a brief signal from the past, that she appears to be posed. When the nurse tries to attract her attention, Beatrice turns painfully, with a series of small lurches, "jerk by jerk through ninety degrees" (243). Her "entombed eyes" are "nittering" at Sammy through his tears and sweat, and then she urinates. "The pool splashed and spread."

Although he is writing this memory in his most economical prose, Sammy must be conscious of the echoes that pervade it, the corner, the wall, the blindness, the hutching movements, the ninety-degree turn, the water on the face, the fetid liquid on the floor. He is aware of an intermittent extraneous sound, a woman crying "like a marsh-bird," as in the cell he was aware of his own voice muttering and crying to punctuate the silence with meaningless sound. He must surely connect Beatrice's involuntarily urination with his own lowered trousers in the cell, with the nightmare of the imagined dismembered organ lying in the centre of the stinking pool there. In the cell he had tried to remember a name. "Muriel, Millicent, Molly?" (180). In the sequel to his meeting with poor Beatrice ("Down, down, forced down in the fetor") he tries again to recall the name of the child who had pissed on the schoolroom floor. "Maisie, Millicent, Mary?" (245). And in the "flashback" ending of the monologue we learn why it was that Sammy had been reminded of the befouled nursery in the cell, for later he discovers it to be a cupboard which customarily housed buckets and floor cloths — no doubt slop buckets and urinal mops.

So the two accounts are related, bound together by one of the unclean odours of mortality. But Beatrice cannot burst her door. She has no voice to cry for help, and she will know no apotheosis. Sammy, it is clear from Kenneth's Hippocratic remonstrances, will never know if or when he walled her in. He is left with no answer for remorse.

There is a further analogy to be pursued. The interrogation Sammy suffers at the hands of Dr. Halde is strongly reminiscent of Sammy's persecution of Beatrice, so reminiscent that during it Sammy recalls his previous probe: "Do you feel nothing then? Maybe" (142). "Maybe" has been Beatrice's answer to all his urgent questions, frustrating his every attempt to get inside her head.

This brings us to consider the fundamental error in Sammy's reconstruction of his history in the light of loss of freedom. He has associated his conquest of Beatrice with the sexual decision he made after his headmaster's warning: "If you want something enough, you can always get it provided you are willing to make the appropriate sacrifice" (235). The decision was made in an odour of musk, after a healing immersion in waters that confirmed his manhood (236). He thinks therefore that the "white unseen body" of Beatrice Ifor is his object, and that her "utter abjection this side of death" can be realized in physical terms. It is a common human mistake. But as the headmaster has pointed out, "What you get is never quite what you thought." And in Sammy's case what he thinks he wants at this moment of his "fall" is not what he really wants (117).

A review of his pursuit of Beatrice confirms this. Sexual desire is subordinate to the true goal of identification. "Above all else, even beyond the musky treasures of your white body . . . what is your mystery? . . . Even if you do not know what you are at least admit me . . . I want fusion and identity . . . I want to be you" (104-05). Musk wins, but it is Sammy the painter, not Sammy the lover, who comes close to the realization of Beatrice's identity, and even then (as in the real-life portrait of the utterly abject Beatrice [242]), the head and face are in shadow and only the body is illuminated (120, 124). "There was nothing that would give us a unity and substantial identity." The catechism rituals gradually cease, the "black central patch" which is Beatrice continues in another mode, never to be known by another mind or body.

With all this in the background we can see the function of Dr. Halde as Sammy's double. Not only does the German interrogator insist that there are similarities between himself and his victim:

"We are neither of us ordinary men, Mr. Mountjoy. There is already a certain indefinable sympathy between us." (137)

"I made my choice with much difficulty but I have made it. . . . For you and me, reality is in this room. We have given ourselves over to a kind of social machine. . . . We are both degraded by this, Mr. Mountjoy, but there it is." (140)

"Oh, I agree, we're in the sewer together — both of us up to the neck." (146)

but also he attempts to penetrate Sammy's consciousness in ways which echo Sammy's earlier attempts to know Beatrice. Dr. Halde says he has been studying his prisoner, "putting myself in your place" (141). Overriding Sammy's protestation that he knows nothing, that he cannot answer, Dr. Halde persists. "Well?" "Think . . .

Think . . . Think." "Tell me!" Step by step, from the overtures ("What is it like to be you?" [103]) to the threat of destruction at the end (". . . I will kill you" [152]), Halde's ruthless interrogation follows the kind of pattern Sammy has used, and meets the same kind of equivocation (in place of Beatrice's "I don't know" and "Maybe" Sammy's ultimate answer is: "I don't know whether I know anything or not [151]). This gives one of several possible meanings to the Sphinx's riddle which closes the confession. If Sammy can see himself in Dr. Halde, then the statement "The Herr Doctor does not know about peoples" reflects back to himself. No amount of probing and remembering will penetrate the mystery of "other." Sammy cannot know about people, himself or anyone else. And therefore he asks himself the wrong questions. But he can discover peoples, or peoplehood. He can, in the blessed vision that sings and shines, see man transfigured, and know himself transfigured — or resurrected — also.

Such mountain-top experiences are fleeting. Man has to descend to the valley of everyday life again; his only way of recapturing the apotheosis is the way Sammy takes, the way of confessing it, of painting it in words.

And here was a point, a single point which was my own interior identity, without shape or size but only position. Yet this position was miraculous as everything else since it continually defied the law of conservation of energy, rule one as it were, and created shapes that fled away outward along the radii of a globe. These shapes could be likened to nothing but the most loathsome and abject creatures, continuously created, radiating swiftly out and disappearing from my sight; and *this was the human nature I found inhabiting the centre of my own awareness.* The light that showed up this point and these creatures came from the newly perceived world in all its glory. (190; my italics)

Furthermore, as in the opening paragraph of the confession, where Sammy has concentrated his total experience into a paragraph of highly charged rhetoric, the descent too finds its equivalent expression. Throughout his "shuffle and coil" of memory, Sammy has alternated his two contrasting styles of speech, the correlatives of the two worlds, golden and grey, of spirit and flesh. Thus the lyrical cadence of "I have understood how the scar becomes a star, I have felt the flake of fire fall, miraculous and pentecostal," has turned into the flat statement, "I lived on Paradise Hill, ten minutes from the station, thirty seconds from the shops and the local" (5). Consequently, the bald narrative of the coda brings the reality of a now distanced consciousness into balance once more. Read alongside the ecstatic description of his resurrection, Sammy's discovery of the "we" of "peoples" makes colder, more normal sense of his pentecostal breakthrough and explains the symbolism of the second door. "The commandant indicated the door back to the camp dismissively" (253). As we read the curt description we are reminded that before his agony Sammy had been offered a choice of two doors. "You saw the door to your left because you came through it. There is another door to your right. Don't look round. Choose, Sammy. Which door is going to be your exit?" (151). When Halde accepts that Sammy will not give him information, he says, "Your exit is a better one than mine." Sammy's better exit leads him to the horror "too searing for the refuge of madness" and to the unimaginable steps "destructive of the centre" (185). He bursts the door. Then the physical door is opened by the commandant. Sammy remembers, in his final memory, that before reaching the Traherne-like vision of trees, mountains, and Kings of Egypt, he passed back through the door on the side of the concrete corridor, the door to the camp. Whereas there is no bridge from the utterly interior to the communal, there are doors; this is why Sammy speaks the language of the Underground man: "To communicate is our passion and our despair" (8).

In Sammy Mountjoy, Golding has stood the world of appearances on its head, reached in and down, destroyed savagely and recreated for the very concrete creation itself (102). But Sammy says: "My darkness reaches out and fumbles at a typewriter with its tongs. Your darkness reaches out with your tongs and grasps a book. There are twenty modes of change, filter and translation between us." This is the bridge offered by the confessional monologue, and only insofar as the reader also reaches in and down to destroy savagely and recreate is the internal landscape of the psyche realized. "What we know is not what we see or learn but what we realize" (149).

The necessary *entente* between speaker and listener renders explication of the confessional monologue unusually difficult. Other monologues may be approached through what we see and learn. The confessing hero is unable, by the very nature of his self-examination, to actualize objective data. For him, the mind is its own place.

If we compare the three speakers we have examined, certain characteristics emerge in common. Each man speaks compulsively from his own centre of consciousness, and draws the listener into the ambiguities of his experience by a process of mystification. Each

189

discloses himself as an unsympathetic, even an odious character, well aware of his own nature and ready to expose the baseness he acknowledges. Each is preoccupied with the double and divided world of self and other, and finds no acceptable simple solution to the problems of relationship. Each uses the language of the ego as it is described by Northrop Frye, issuing from "a consciousness imprisoned in the restrictive self . . . which, being conscious, knows that it is imprisoned."[16] Related to the concept of incarceration is the imagery of imprisonment, judgement, and corrective punishment which colours each man's account of his past. Each voluntarily undertakes a reliving of his own most anguished moments, brooding upon incidents which have produced humiliation and self-loathing. For each the worlds of empirical observation and imaginative vision separate and coalesce. For each the act of confession is a means of masochistic exploration of guilt. And since each knows himself to be a part of the main, the guilt is imputed to the listener, who must share it.

The confessional monologue, therefore, demands not understanding so much as empathy. The reader is required to see with the eyes of the speaker, to know what he knows of suffering, and to realize with him the meaning of the human condition. Confession provides the most intimate of communications, and the most immanent of discoveries. For as each speaker — the Underground Man, the Judge Penitent, and Sammy Mountjoy — uses an other as a mirror of the self, so the reader also confronts a mirror; nor can he see what the protagonist sees without seeing himself also by reflection.

[16] *The Well-Tempered Critic* (Bloomington: Indiana University Press, 1963), p. 97.

CHAPTER SEVEN

Regarding Readers

A novel is like a bow, the violin which makes the sounds is the reader's soul. — STENDHAL, *La Vie de Henri Brulard*

The aim of the foregoing discussion has been to isolate and examine a number of modern monologue novels, according to suggested categories to which they are seen to belong, in order to note the various ways in which novelists have used the monologue form, either to achieve a many-faceted speaking voice for themselves or to give full dramatic life to the speaking presences they have created mimetically. Although certain similarities in mode, structure, or imagery lend credence to the broad classifications I have indicated, distinctive features in each monologue novel set it apart from every other, each novel proving as uniquely memorable as its speaking voice. As Bakhtin says of Dostoevsky's work, the basic principle is "to affirm the other's 'I' not as object, but as another subject," and thus to proclaim the worth of personality.[1] Thus each novelist discussed in this study has transformed his faith in the self-sufficiency of a single consciousness into a formal and structural entity which I have called the monologue novel.

Not every novelist, however, has sought to affirm the other's "I" through psychological mimesis in the mode of Dostoevsky. In formalized monologues, we have seen writers creating speakers as channels for their own philosophical and metaphysical expression. Faulkner and Woolf choose to create monologuists as the means of contributing facets to a total design; consequently each has developed a form which contains a multiplicity of voices speaking sequentially or contrapuntally. This seems to be a desirable design for

[1] *Problems of Dostoevsky's Poetics*, p. 8.

novelists whose need to communicate "felt life" is comparable to that of lyric poets, but whose interest in the variety and interdependence of humanity is comparable to that of dramatists. Formalized monologues, therefore, engage the listener in ways similar to the drama, yet leave him savouring the distinctive voice and quality of mind of the original teller — the novelist himself.

Autobiographical monologues offer the reader access to a personality whose discernible characteristics are very different from any that might be ascribed to his creator. The *fiat* of the novelist, in each case, is a creature of memorable voice who creates his own world by a series of verbal gestures. As the writer's first and main concern is the figure of his monologuist, so the reader's lasting impression is also that of the figure as a speaking presence. This form of monologue seems to attract artists who, having excelled in the more conventional realistic novel forms, welcome the challenge offered by systematic and cohesive impersonation.

Eyewitness monologues are by their nature impressionistic. Writers who are fascinated by the blurring of distinction between illusion and reality find an I-narrator a satisfying means of probing the nature and meaning of experience, and particularly of unusually harrowing experience. The eyewitness monologues considered here have all been produced by highly conscious artists who have elsewhere theorized on the techniques of fiction, and who have sought to present their monologuists in such a way — by corroborative frame or by direct address — that the reader will readily accept his role as audience.

Confessional monologues are so rootedly subjective that they risk losing the ear of a reader who is unable to identify himself with the ego compulsively perpetuating and compounding his self-examination. For this reason the more compelling confessional monologues are compact, and threaded with an imagery which endorses the universal elements in the individual experience of guilt. One of the problems faced by a confessional speaker is that of bringing his inquiry to an end, since his search for absolution conducts him along essentially circular, if convoluted, paths of memory and extrapolation. Sammy Mountjoy is the least typical exponent of the confessional monologue because his creator has substituted the form of a typewritten document for the progenitive style — "a compulsive babble" — found in the monologuists created by such authors as Dostoevsky, Camus and Beckett. An interest in psychological probing, however, motivates all the creators of confessional monologues, and needs to be met by a matching interest, and an empathetic response, on the part of the reader.

Though the style of each kind of monologue is declarative, its effect is always interrogative. The monologue poses questions that only the individual reader can answer, and requires of him the twin acts of "listening" as he reads, and of visualizing and thus concretizing the figure of the speaker to whom he listens, as he listens. Other fictive forms, of course, may make similar requirements, but in no other form is so much freedom offered the reader to imagine, and thence to create, as he engages in that subjective relationship with the speaker which is made possible by the monologue form.

Monologue novels have a long history. Groupings can be neither exclusive nor inclusive. More and more monologues, of more and more kinds, seem to be appearing in the twentieth century. Some notable modern variants offer the monologuist as a mental patient (Penelope Mortimer's *Long Distance*), as a subject for behavioural conditioning (Anthony Burgess's *A Clockwork Orange*), as an undiscovered murderer (Joseph Kell's *One Hand Clapping*), as a psychic receptor (L. P. Hartley's *Poor Clare*), and as a myth-maker (Margaret Atwood's *Lady Oracle*). In addition to the many examples of monologues from men tracing their development as artists or criminals, there is a considerable body of monologues from lonely, deranged, and usually menopausal women. It seems that what T. S. Eliot called "the third voice" of the poet, "when he is saying, not what he would say in his own person, but only what he can say within the limits of one imaginary character addressing another imaginary character,"' is becoming the increasingly preferred voice of the novelist.

Why should this be? To support my contention that the monologue novel will continue to fascinate many writers and readers of this century I offer two main reasons, both of them socio-historical. The first has to do with the growth of the media, and the second with developments in psychological theory, particularly in the realm of communicology.

There are many today who share the pessimistic views of Marshall McLuhan that the Gutenberg era is at an end; reading and writing are fast becoming obsolete practices and the art of the novel, in particular, is increasingly superseded by the arts of the media. One feels a little foolish pointing out how many novels, in the past few

---

[2] Quoted by Edel, *The Psychological Novel*, p. 138, from Eliot's lecture on *The Three Voices of Poetry*.

decades, have been redesigned for a mass audience through cinema and television. A stronger feeling, and one likely to inspire activism among teachers of English, takes hold when one discovers in more and more "literature" classrooms the substitution of film for text.

Feelings apart, however, there is little doubt that the telling of a story, once the prerogative of the *histor* or the writer, has in the twentieth century become increasingly the domain of the comic strip and the cine or video camera. In a somewhat gloomy prevision at the close of their study of narrative art, Scholes and Kellogg consider the advent of the motion-picture film "with its attendant devices of synchronous sound track and videotape, and its flexible means of presentation in theater or home, direct or via television" (*The Nature of Narrative*, p. 280). Their findings are ominous. They see the lyric and the drama, old and honoured forms, as continuing serenely untroubled by change as they have done for centuries. But they allow that the main impetus of narrative art may well pass from book to cinema, which they rightly describe as a narrative rather than a dramatic medium. Their concern, however, is for the older forms of storytelling, and for the narrative art produced in the novel's golden age — the nineteenth century. I suggest therefore, that the writers of modern monologue novels, freed from the sequence and suspense inherent in other forms of story, and free likewise from typological characterization, have found in their creation of monologues an art form that continues not only viable, but relatively unthreatened by the tentacles of the media.

Twenty years ago Nathalie Sarraute was making a similar claim, although her dissatisfaction with contemporary psychological novels led her into some subjective absolutes. Sarraute, as a practising advocate of the French *nouveau roman*, is hardly a disinterested critic, but her conclusions are suggestive. In speaking of Faulkner's *The Sound and the Fury*, she says that Faulkner's "bold and very worthwhile experiments" force the reader to be constantly on the alert, "he is obliged, in order to identify the characters, to recognize them at once, like the author himself, from the inside . . . to plunge into them as deeply as the author, whose vision he makes his own."[3] She goes on to note that the author seeks thus to entice the reader into his territory, and that "I" narration is the simplest and most effective means of securing this enticement.

[3] Nathalie Sarraute, *The Age of Suspicion: Essays on the Novel* (trans. Maria Jolas, New York: Brazillier, 1963), pp. 70-71.

Sarraute considers the novelist's use of "I," moving imperceptibly from Faulkner to the kind of generalized figure she customarily evokes, and links I-narration to Post-Impressionism in painting, which she calls "first person" painting. She continues:

Thus, in a movement analogous to that of painting, the novel, which only a stubborn adherence to obsolete techniques places in the position of a minor art, pursues with means that are uniquely its own a path which can only be its own; it leaves to the other arts — and, in particular, to the cinema — everything that does not actually belong to it. In the same way that photography occupies and fructifies the fields abandoned by painting, the cinema garners and perfects what is left by the novel.
The reader, instead of demanding of the novel what every good novel has more than often refused him, i.e., light entertainment, can satisfy at the cinema, without effort and without needless loss of time, his taste for "live" characters and stories.

These statements seem to express clearly the degree to which motion pictures and television are replacing written fiction. The passive viewer does not seek participation in a creative act so much as an escapist entertainment somewhere between the poles of the sensationally fantastic and the comfortably familiar. The great works of earlier novelists can still swim into his ken, and frequently do, as films, but when they do he receives them merely. He does not help to create them. They become a substitute for reading, and offer a diversion so relatively effortless that the Gutenberg galaxy seems indeed an outmoded aggregate of dead and dusty stars.

Those who embrace the monologue novel do so, I submit, at least in part because they choose to resist this erosion of their responsibility, as readers, to collaborate with the writer in a creative act. A contemporary writer, Kurt Vonnegut Jr., has expressed the thought that everything which has been filmed of his work has been one character short; it has lacked himself.[4] As Vonnegut sees it, the movie, and only the movie, accomplishes the disappearance of the author. To this thought he adds:

The worst thing about film, from my point of view, is that it cripples illusions which I have encouraged people to create in their heads. Film doesn't create illusions. It makes them impossible. It is a bullying form of reality, like the model rooms in the furniture department of Bloomingdale's.
There is nothing for the viewer to do but gawk. For example: there can be only one *Clockwork Orange* by Stanley Kubrick. There are tens

---

[4] Kurt Vonnegut, Jr., *Between Time and Timbuktu* (New York: Dell, 1972), pp. xv-xvi. "In a movie, somehow, the author always vanishes."

of thousands of *Clockwork Oranges* [*sic*] by Anthony Burgess, since every reader has to cast, costume, direct and design the show in his head.

There are several examples of the accuracy of Vonnegut's contention. One apposite to this study occurs in the filmed version of *The Turn of the Screw*, drawn from a dramatization entitled *The Innocents*. The ambiguity discussed in Chapter Five as a chief source of interest for the reader of James's novella is diluted by the film. Since the camera, and not the governess, narrates, the apparitions are made visible to the viewing audience. Their authenticity cannot be challenged, and neither can the exactitude of the governess's "explanation" of their appearance to Mrs. Grose. Not only does the governess indubitably see them, but the audience sees her seeing them, and shares her horror of them. What for a reader was an evocation of evil, subjectively inchoate, becomes for a viewer an exercise in suspense, objectively explicit. Moreover, the loss suffered when reading is replaced by viewing is exacerbated by the persistence of an after-image which, in the case cited, lends to each re-reading of the text the memory of those visual details which the camera has, often gratuitously, provided. And in place of the haunted features of an unidentifiable governess, one sees the haunting face of the lovely Deborah Kerr.

Both *A Clockwork Orange* and *The Turn of the Screw* are monologue novels. However, even when the narrative content of the adaptation to film is not monologue, and when the camera does not so evidently do violence to the delicacy of the text, the imagination of the spectator is inevitably frustrated. Such a case, in my opinion, occurred in a televised version of *Madame Bovary*. As dramatization this was faithful and sensitive, the only significant loss was the voice of the narrator. Nevertheless, the Emma and Charles that once took form only in the reader's mind are now forever imprinted, for the viewer, by the physical presences of the actress and actor he has watched on the screen. The valid filling in and fleshing out of characters which is performed as we read a novel can change each time we read it, so that our experience of Molly Bloom, for example, is to some extent new with each re-reading of *Ulysses*, and is never finally crystallized into a single configuration of features or reduced to the sound of a single human voice. All of this I understand to be inherent in Vonnegut's deceptively simple statement.

In his analysis of the reading process, Iser examines ways in which the skilful novelist activates the reader's imagination, and deduces that the film of a novel frequently leaves a reader feeling "cheated":

With the novel the reader must use his imagination to synthesize the information given him, and so his perception is simultaneously richer and more private; with the film he is confined merely to physical perception, and so whatever he remembers of the world he had pictured is brutally cancelled out.[5]

This recent statement is in perfect accord with one made in the earliest days of the novel by an I-narrator:

... no author, who understands the just boundaries of decorum and good-breeding, would presume to think all: The truest respect which you can pay to the reader's understanding, is to halve this matter amicably, and leave him something to imagine, in his turn, as well as yourself. For my own part, I am eternally paying him compliments of this kind, and do all that lies in my power to keep his imagination as busy as my own.[6]

Sterne's Tristram conceives his monologue as the half of a conversation, as a game of the imagination which he shares with his listener; it follows that Sterne is, in fact, doing just what Eliot had said the "third voice" of the poet does. It is hardly possible for the camera, as narrator, either to assume the limits of one imaginary character or to address another imaginary character.

The phenomenological theory of art stresses the "virtuality" of a literary work, which, it postulates, is not to be identified as an objective text nor as an awakened response within an individual reader, but as a dynamic continuum of realization between the poles of the artistic (the text created by the author), and the aesthetic (the concretization accomplished by the reader). If a novel were no more than a static object for contemplation there would be nothing lost should it be transformed from book to film. If the realization of the reader were easily and completely effected, there would be nothing gained by a second reading of the work. Slatoff has shown, however, that the qualities of a work can become radically transformed for the reader with each successive reading, until those very structures which had once served to fragment experience can be found to pull it together. He cites the technique of progressive disclosure in *The Sound and the Fury* as an example of initial mystification promising

[5] Wolfgang Iser, *The Implied Reader* (Baltimore: The Johns Hopkins University Press, 1974), p. 283.

[6] Laurence Sterne, *The Life and Opinions of Tristram Shandy* (Harmondsworth: Penguin, 1967), p. 127.

increased satisfaction for the reader who returns again and again to the work. From this example he moves inductively towards the re-reading experience of any great work to note that:

> ... as the effects of sequence and novelty wear off ... one gains more and more sense of the work as a spatial entity. Beyond this are the countless subtle alterations of one's experience that occur with each rereading. I am not merely repeating the truism that all experiences are shaped and altered by preceding experiences. Insofar as the literary entity is a structure of relations and emphases and proportions, one must say that the work itself undergoes a transformation as one rereads it. One can, of course, say that the form of the work remains constant and that it is only one's experience of it which changes ... but there is no *human* way of defining that form without assuming some sort of perceiving act. (*With Respect to Readers*, p. 20)

Slatoff's analysis of the dynamics of literary response leads me to consider the second reason I offer for the increasing number of monologue novels being written today. His emphasis on the reader as participant rather than spectator indicates a communicological approach to the experience of reading. For him, it seems, the reading of a novel is a communicative act in which the reader not only receives and decodes the message sent him through the printed page, but also enters and maintains an inter-personal relationship with the sender. This is a way of regarding the transaction between teller and listener which seems to stem from communications theory, and such theory stems in turn from more recent philosophy. In the terminology of Martin Buber, an "I-Thou" relationship replaces an "I-It" one.[7]

Buber's philosophy of dialogue has had far-reaching effects upon existential thinking in the twentieth century, both in philosophy and in psychology. Together with theories of self-transcendence found in Kierkegaard, Tillich, and Gabriel Marcel, Buber's concept of "meeting" has laid the foundation for the development of the humanist psychology which pervades modern thought, and has led to the

---

[7] Martin Buber, *I and Thou* (New York: Scribner, 1958). The significance of Buber's general concept has been well described by Will Heberg:

> The term I-Thou points to a relation of a person to person, of subject to subject, a relation of reciprocity involving "meeting" or "encounter," while the term I-It points to relation of person to thing, of subject to object, involving some form of utilization, domination or control, even if it is only so-called "objective" knowing. The I-Thou relation, which Buber usually designated as "relation" *par excellence*, is one in which one can enter only with the whole of his being, as a genuine person. *The Writings of Martin Buber* (New York: Meridian, 1956), p. 14.

basic tenet of communicology that each communicant recognizes himself in the other:

> The fact is that we can understand ourselves by starting from the other, or others, and only by starting from them; . . . it is only in this perspective that a legitimate love of self can be conceived.
>
> You must participate in a self in order to know what it is.[8]

Such assumptions seem to underlie the creation of monologue. The writer of a monologue novel starts from an *other* which he creates, and in seeking to participate fully in that self he invites the reader to create and participate with him. His act is a complex combination of involvement and self-consciousness which requires a similar empathetic identification from the reader as listener. Indeed, I suspect that a reader's fullest and deepest engagement as the respondent in such a communication may well bring to him also a heightened sense of self. Many important kinds of involvement require, in literature as in life, a combined sense of self and a recognition that the other is not-me. Shakespeare can be Othello while at the same time pitying and judging him. So can the reader.

In speaking of "empathy," whether between writer and monologuist or between monologuist and reader, it is important to understand that the related terms "projection" and "sympathy" do not apply. Empathy denotes a lending of oneself to the character, whereas projection denotes a substitution of the self or part of the self for the character, and sympathy denotes affectionate regard and compassion for the character. Far from always promoting concern and commiseration, empathy can at times bring about a condition in which the reader finds himself implicated or accused, as we have seen in the confessional monologues we have noted. The reader's response to a monologuist need be no more indulgent than the writer's has been.

In treating monologuists to whom my own response, whether of recognition or mystification, of delight or guilt, has been readily empathetic, I have thus far ignored a significant corollary. In all communication our response to the personality addressing us may be guarded, ambivalent, or openly hostile. Leon Edel has noted that the reader's positive or negative attitude to the psyche revealed in a psychological novel is not necessarily unaccountable. Communica-

---

[8] Gabriel Marcel, *The Mystery of Being*, Vol. II (Chicago: Gateway, 1960), p. 9; Paul Tillich, *The Courage to Be* (New Haven: Yale University Press, 1959), p. 124.

tion may fail, and it "may sometimes be the fault of the artist," or it may be the fault of the reader; but "generally it must be recognized rather as the failure of the two consciousnesses involved to establish a harmonious relationship. This happens often enough in life; there is no reason why we may not expect it to happen sometimes in our relationship to certain novels that we read."[9] Where the monologue novel is concerned, similar failures in communication may occur, and may be signalled by the reader's positive distaste for the person he meets as he reads.

Consequently it is easy to understand Wayne Booth's concern for the morality of a monologue such as Céline's *Journey to the End of Night* (*The Rhetoric of Fiction*, p. 379). However, his desire for moral certainty in a relativistic age betrays the widely read critic's nostalgia for the norms of previous centuries. It discounts the susceptibility of the artist to his own immediate environment, which may be all he has. William Golding has said that "Men don't write the books they should, they write the books they can." Similarly, if I am right in the premise that writer and reader reciprocally share a single enterprise, it may be said that readers read the books they can rather than the books they should. As a twentieth-century reader, I find monologuists who offend me deeply as Céline's Bardamu offends Booth. My hostile response limits my capacity for understanding their values and extinguishes my desire to re-enter their world. As audience for a monologue, readers may surely give a bored or mystified hearing without applause, or if they fear incipient corruption they can cease to listen. It is easier to close a book than it is to leave a public lecture or to shut out subliminal propaganda from a bombardment of visual stimuli.

My thesis that the monologue invites or necessitates reader participation asserts the insistence of the reader's own creative imagination as he "listens." Once again Golding has a valuable word. "Now I have a standard remark that I make for students when they write me letters. I write back and I say, 'What is in a book is not what the author thought he put in it, but what the reader gets out of it; so your guess is as good as mine'. That is really what I tell them, and I think it is true."[10] This is another way of saying that within the frame of reference provided by a novelist, the reader has

[9] *The Psychological Novel*, p. 139.

[10] Jack Biles, *Talk: Conversations with William Golding*, p. 58. This represents an about-face on Golding's part, after an argument with Frank Kermode and much reflection.

200

the last word. It is entirely appropriate that he should, since he concretizes the telling of the tale by the power of his respondent imagination. In the monologue, this means that possibilities for empathy are conceived by the author, but not prescribed. The reader as audience and the writer as monologuist are involved in humanity together. Their shared perceptions become the focus of the work; what has already happened, or what will happen next, cease to have importance save in the light of who we are. To paraphrase W. H. Auden, a monologue novel reads the reader.

We return therefore to what Scholes and Kellogg call the soul of narrative, its embodied quality of mind. There are film directors who seem to be exploring ways of conveying this through their medium; one thinks of the superlative achievements of Antonioni, Fellini, Bergman, and Renoir. But in my limited experience of film I have yet to have been drawn into an I-Thou relationship, or to have felt myself collaborating with the teller in the realization of a tale.

For to perceive a beholder must *create* his own experience. And his creation must include relations comparable to those which the original producer underwent. They are not the same in any literal sense. But with the perceiver, as with the artist, there must be an ordering of the elements of the whole that is in form, although not in details, the same as the process of organization the creator of the work consciously experienced. Without an act of creation the object is not perceived as a work of art.[11]

Without an act of re-creation, communication fails. The "I-Thou" contract integral to the monologue novel is beautifully described by Ford Madox Ford in his musings about his "ideal" narrative mode:

What is to be aimed at in a style is something so unobtrusive and so quiet — and so beautiful if possible — that the reader shall not know what he is reading, and be conscious only that he is living in the life of the book. . . . a book so quiet in tone, so clearly and so unobtrusively worded, that it should give the effect of a long monologue spoken by a lover at a little distance from his mistress's ear — a book about the invisible relationships between man and man; about the values of life; about the nature of God — the sort of book that nowadays one could read in as one used to do when one was a child, pressed against a tall window-pane for hours and hours, utterly oblivious of oneself, in the twilight.[12]

[11] John Dewey, *Art as Experience* (New York: Minton, 1934), p. 54.

[12] "Literary Portraits XIII: Fyodor Dostoievsky," *Outlook*, February 14, 1914, pp. 206-07.

Thus the "I" of the writer speaks. What then may we say of the "Thou" thus envisaged, the reader-listener who finds the terms of the contract inverted as he "re-creates" the work, himself now the "I" for whom the monologuist has become "Thou"?

Roland Barthes has provided a neat epigram: *dans le texte, seule parle le lecteur*.[13] The progress of his thinking as a structuralist critic has led him to renounce the traditional view that there can be a clear and single message passed from the writer of a novel to its reader. The chart of this progress is an interesting one to note.

Forty years ago Russian Formalists began an attempt to describe fiction much as the linguist describes a sentence, structurally rather than semantically. Along with other modern structuralists, Barthes built upon their premises to produce a complicated machinery for use in analyzing the *nouveau roman*. But he found "scientific description" of texts, even of such texts as those provided by Robbe-Grillet, less viable than the neo-Formalists had assumed. Consequently, he came to see the novel no longer as a structural model, but as an invitation to the reader to *structurate* it himself.

The five codes devised by Barthes as a means of analyzing Balzac's story *Sarrasine* are an attempt to describe, at least in part, the process of reading a text. Application of the codes endorses the reader's prerogative; he must, as it were, produce rather than consume the text which, because it is *scriptible* and not *lisible* in the mode of classic texts, is "stereoscopic" in its effect. Barthes deduces from his analysis of *Sarrasine* that estimable novels of the past resemble modern fiction precisely in this, that they are pluralistic enough to bear any number of "structurations" by the reader.

That "structurations" are increasingly evident in modern fiction seems to be borne out by the monologue novels under discussion. Novelists such as James, Conrad and Golding have long made use of the hermeneutic gap in several modalities of fiction, questioning the truths they seem to assert even as they assert them, and disclosing through the manifest merely that the manifest discloses nothing. Significantly, however, each of these authors has been drawn to the monologue as a form in which indeterminacy is most satisfyingly evinced through the "I-Thou" contract. They and all other creators of monologue novels invite their readers into tacit dialogues through the poetics of open form.

During the past decade, what is called "open form" has received

13 S/Z, trans. Richard Miller (New York: Hill & Wang, 1974).

considerable critical attention. Umberto Eco has related it to sophisticated concepts of indeterminacy both in physics and in the cognitive process. His theory is that the reader's collaboration as creator, tacitly invited by our most cherished older works of fiction, is in many modern works positively demanded, for

> ... every work of art, even though it is produced by following an explicit or implicit poetic of necessity, is effectively open to a virtually unlimited range of possible readings, each of which causes the work to acquire new vitality in terms of one particular taste, or perspective, or personal performance.[14]

In the modern monologue novel, personal performance on the part of the reader meets and matches the personal performance of the monologuist so that the I-Thou relationship, itself essentially dependent upon the singularity of both performers, may be realized.

This study began with the words of one of the monologuists it has undertaken to describe, words in which Sammy Mountjoy pronounced himself the "only teller" of his tale. It ends, as it must, with the unfinished testimony of an "only listener" — *dans le texte, seul parle le lecteur*. Within the restraints of my own particular taste, perspective, and performance as a reader, I have sought to show the I-Thou contract at work, believing that whenever we find ourselves engaged in communication with a fictive other, the life we re-create is essentially our own.

[14] "The Poetics of the Open Work," *20th. Century Studies*, 12 (1974), 21.

Bibliography

PRIMARY SOURCES

Austen, Jane. *Emma*. Boston: Houghton Mifflin, 1957.

Camus, Albert. *La Chute (The Fall)*. Trans. Justin O'Brien. New York: Vintage, 1956.

Cary, Joyce. *Herself Surprised*. London: Michael Joseph, 1941.

——. *The Horse's Mouth*. Harmondsworth: Penguin, 1948.

——. "The Way a Novel Gets Written." *Adam International Review*, 18, Nos. 212-213 (November-December 1950), 3-11.

Conrad, Joseph. *Heart of Darkness*. New Jersey: Prentice-Hall, 1960.

——. *Under Western Eyes*. Kent ed. Vol. XXII. New York: Doubleday, 1925.

Defoe, Daniel. *Moll Flanders*. London: Oxford University Press, 1971.

——. *Robinson Crusoe and Other Writings*. Boston: Houghton Mifflin, 1968.

Dostoevsky, Fyodor. *Crime and Punishment*. Trans. Princess Alexandra Kropotkin. New York: John Winston, 1953.

——. *Notes from Underground*. Trans. Serge Shishkoff. New York: Thomas Y. Crowell, 1969.

Faulkner, Williams. *As I Lay Dying*. New York: Random House, 1957.

——. *Essays, Speeches and Public Letters*. Ed. James B. Meriwether. New York: Random House, 1965.

——. *The Sound and the Fury*. New York: Random House, 1946.

Fielding, Henry. *Tom Jones*. New York: W. W. Norton, 1973.

Flaubert, Gustave. *Selected Letters*. London: Weidenfeld and Nicolson, 1950.

Ford, Ford Madox. *The Good Soldier*. New York: Vintage, 1957.

————. *Joseph Conrad: A Personal Remembrance.* Boston: Little, 1924.

————. *Henry James: A Critical Study.* New York: Dodd, 1916.

————. "Literary Portraits XXIII: Fyodor Dostoievsky." *Outlook,* February 14, 1914.

————. *Mightier than the Sword.* London: Allen and Unwin, 1938.

————. *Return to Yesterday.* New York: Horace Liveright, 1932.

————. "Techniques." *The Southern Review,* I (1935), 35.

————. *Thus to Revisit.* London: Chapman and Hall, 1921.

Forster, E. M. *Aspects of the Novel.* London: Arnold, 1927.

Golding, William. *Free Fall.* London: Faber, 1961.

Hopkins, Gerard Manley. *A Hopkins Reader.* Selected with introduction by John Pick. London: Oxford University Press, 1953.

James, Henry. *The Ambassadors.* New York: W. W. Norton, 1964.

————. *The Art of Fiction.* New York: Oxford University Press, 1948.

————. *The Art of the Novel.* Ed. Richard P. Blackmur. New York: Scribners, 1947.

————. *The Aspern Papers.* New York: Dell, 1959.

————. *The Portrait of a Lady.* London: Macmillan, 1882.

————. *The Sacred Fount.* New York: Grove, 1953.

————. *The Spoils of Poynton.* Norfolk, Conn.: New Directions, 1924.

————. *The Turn of the Screw. The Complete Tales of Henry James,* Vol. 10, Ed. Leon Edel. New York: J. B. Lippincott, 1964.

Joyce, James. *A Portrait of the Artist as a Young Man.* Harmondsworth: Penguin, 1969.

————. *Stephen Hero.* New York: James Laughlin, 1944.

————. *Ulysses.* Harmondsworth: Penguin, 1968.

Laurence, Margaret. *The Stone Angel.* Toronto: McClelland & Stewart, 1968.

Mann, Thomas. *Confessions of Felix Krull, Confidence Man.* Trans. Denver Lindley. New York: Alfred A. Knopf, 1955.

————. *Stories of Three Decades.* Trans. H. T. Lowe-Porter. New York: Alfred A. Knopf, 1936.

Mauriac, François. *Le Noeud de Vipères (Vipers' Tangle).* In *A Mauriac Reader.* Trans. Gerard Hopkins. New York: Farrar, 1968.

Mortimer, Penelope. *Long Distance.* London: A. Lang, 1974.

Murdoch, Iris. *The Black Prince.* Harmondsworth: Penguin, 1975.

Nabokov, Vladimir. *Despair.* New York: Capricorn, 1970.

————. *Lolita*. New York: Berkley, 1971.

Proust, Marcel. *A La Recherche du Temps Perdu (Remembrance of Things Past)*. 2 vols. Trans. Frederick A. Blossom and C. K. Scott Moncrieff. New York: Random House, 1932.

Sartre, Jean-Paul. *La Nausée (Nausea)*. Trans. Lloyd Alexander. London: Hamilton, 1962.

Smith, Stevie. *Novel on Yellow Paper*. London: Cape, 1969.

Stendhal. *Le Rouge et le Noir (The Red and the Black)*. Trans. C. K. Scott Moncrieff. New York: Heritage, 1947.

————. *La Vie de Henri Brulard (The Life of Henri Brulard)*. Trans. Catherine Alison Phillips. New York: Vintage, 1955.

Sterne, Laurence. *The Life and Opinions of Tristram Shandy*. Harmondsworth: Penguin, 1967.

Tolstoy, Leo. *Anna Karenin*. Trans. Leo Wiener. Boston: Dana Estes, 1904.

Trollope, Anthony. *Barchester Towers*. New York: Scribners, 1923.

Vonnegut, Kurt, Jr. *Between Time and Timbuktu or Prometheus 5*. New York: Dell, 1972.

Woolf, Virginia. *Mrs. Dalloway*. London: Hogarth, 1933.

————. "Modern Fiction." *Collected Essays*, Vol. 2. London: Hogarth, 1966, 103-10.

————. *A Writer's Diary*. Ed. Leonard Woolf. New York: New American Library, 1968.

————. *The Waves*. London: Hogarth, 1943.

SECONDARY SOURCES

Adams, Richard P. *Faulkner: Myth and Motion*. Princeton: Princeton University Press, 1968.

Aldrich, C. Knight. "Another Twist to *The Turn of the Screw.*" *Modern Fiction Studies*, 13 (Summer 1967), 167-78.

Allen, Walter. *The English Novel: A Short Critical History*. New York: Dutton, 1954.

Andreas, Osborn. *Henry James and the Expanding Horizon*. Seattle: University of Washington Press, 1948.

Auerbach, Erich. *Mimesis: The Representation of Reality in Western Literature*. Trans. Willard Trask. Princeton: Princeton University Press, 1953.

Axthelm, Peter M. *The Modern Confessional Novel*. New Haven: Yale University Press, 1967.

Baernstein, Jo-ann. "Image, Identity and Insight in *The Good Soldier.*" *Critique*, 9 (1966), 78-95.

Baker, Joseph E., ed., *The Reinterpretation of Victorian Literature.* Princeton: Princeton University Press, 1950.

Bakhtin, M. M. *Problems of Dostoevsky's Poetics.* Trans. Richard Balthazar. Moscow: Soretskij Pisatel, 1963.

Barth, J. Robert, S.J., ed. *Religious Perspectives in Faulkner's Fiction.* Indiana: University of Notre Dame Press, 1972.

Barthes, Roland. *S/Z.* Trans. Richard Miller. New York: Hill & Wang, 1974.

Beach, Joseph Warren. *The Twentieth Century Novel: Studies in Technique.* New York: D. Appleton-Century, 1932.

Bentley, Phyllis. *Some Observations on the Art of Narrative.* London: Home and Van Thal, 1946.

Biles, Jack R. *Talk: Conversations with William Golding.* New York: Harcourt, 1970.

Blackstone, Bernard. *Virginia Woolf: A Commentary.* New York: Harcourt, 1949.

Bleikasten, André. *Faulkner's* As I Lay Dying. Trans. Roger Little. Bloomington: Indiana University Press, 1977.

Booth, Wayne C. *The Rhetoric of Fiction.* Chicago: The University of Chicago Press, 1961.

Bowling, Lawrence E. "What is the Stream of Consciousness Technique?" *PMLA*, 65 (1950), 333-45.

Brée, Germaine, ed. *Camus: A Collection of Critical Essays.* New Jersey: Spectrum, 1962.

Buber, Martin. *I and Thou.* 2nd ed. Trans. Ronald Gregor Smith, New York: Scribner, 1958.

Cassell, Richard A. *Ford Madox Ford: A Study of His Novels.* Baltimore: Johns Hopkins, 1962.

———, ed. *Ford Madox Ford: Modern Judgments.* New York: Macmillan, 1972.

Clair, John A. *The Ironic Dimension in the Fiction of Henry James.* Pittsburgh: Duquesne University Press, 1965.

Comfort, Alex. *The Novel and Our Time.* London: Phoenix House, 1948.

Commager, Henry Steele, ed. *Selected Writings of William Dean Howells.* New York: Random House, 1950.

Cranfill, T. M., and R. L. Clark, eds. *An Anatomy of "The Turn of the Screw."* Austin: University of Texas Press, 1965.

Cruikshank, John. *Albert Camus and the Literature of Revolt.* Oxford: Oxford University Press, 1959.

Cruttwell, Patrick. "Makers and Persons." *Hudson Review*, 12 (Winter 1959-60), 487-507.

Daiches, David. *Virginia Woolf*. Norfolk, Conn.: New Directions, 1942.

Dewey, John. *Art as Experience*. New York: Minton, c. 1934.

Dreiser, Theodore. "The Saddest Story." *New Republic*, 3 (June 1915), 155-56.

Eco, Umberto. "The Poetics of the Open Work." *20th. Century Studies*, 12 (1974), 6-26.

Edel, Leon. *The Psychological Novel*. London: Rupert Hart-Davis, 1955.

————, ed. *The Ghostly Tales of Henry James*. New Brunswick: Rutgers University Press, 1948.

————, ed. *The Complete Tales of Henry James*, Vol. 10. New York: J. B. Lippincott, 1964.

Edgar, Pelham. *Henry James: Man and Author*. London: Grant Richards, 1927.

Engelberg, Edward. *The Unknown Distance: From Consciousness to Conscience, Goethe to Camus*. Cambridge: Harvard University Press, 1972.

Evans, Oliver. "James's Air of Evil: *The Turn of the Screw*." *Partisan Review*, 16 (February 1949), 175-87.

Evans, Robert O. "Conrad's Underworld." *Modern Fiction Studies*, 2 (May 1956), 56-62.

Fant, J. L., and R. P. Ashley, eds. *Faulkner at West Point*. New York: Random House, 1964.

Freedman, Ralph. *The Lyrical Novel: Studies in Herman Hesse, André Gide, and Virginia Woolf*. Princeton: Princeton University Press, 1963.

Freud, Sigmund. *Standard Edition of the Complete Psychological Works of Sigmund Freud*. Trans. James Strachey. London: Hogarth, 1957.

————. *Collected Papers*, Vol. 4. Trans. Alix Strachey. London: Hogarth, 1934.

Friedman, Alan. *The Turn of the Novel*. New York: Oxford University Press, 1966.

Friedman, Melvin J. *Stream of Consciousness: A Study in Literary Method*. New Haven: Yale University Press, 1955.

Friedman, Norman. *Form and Meaning in Fiction*. Athens: University of Georgia Press, 1975.

————. "Point of View in Fiction." *PMLA*, 70 (1955), 1166-68.

Frye, Northrop. *Anatomy of Criticism: Four Essays*. Princeton: Princeton University Press, 1957.

————. *The Well-Tempered Critic*. Bloomington: Indiana University Press, 1963.

Garnett, Edward, ed. *Letters from Joseph Conrad 1895-1924*. Indianapolis: Bobbs-Merrill, 1928.

Goldknopf, David. *The Life of the Novel*. Chicago: The University of Chicago Press, 1972.

Graham, J. W., ed. *Virginia Woolf:* The Waves: *The Two Holograph Drafts*. Toronto: University of Toronto Press, 1976.

Gray, Paul. "James Joyce's *Dubliners*: A Study of the Narrator's Role in Modern Fiction." Diss. University of Virginia, 1965.

Green, Peter. "The World of William Golding." *Transactions and Proceedings of the Royal Society of Literature*, 32 (1963), 37-57.

Gross, Seymour. "A Further Note on the Function of the Frame in 'Heart of Darkness'." *Modern Fiction Studies*, 3 (Summer 1957), 167-70.

Guerard, Albert J. *Conrad the Novelist*. Cambridge: Harvard University Press, 1958.

Guiguet, Jean. *Virginia Woolf and Her Works*. London: Hogarth, 1965.

Gwynn, F. L., and J. L. Blotner, eds. *Faulkner in the University*. New York: Random House, 1965.

Hafley, James. *The Glass Roof: Virginia Woolf as Novelist*. Berkeley: University of California Press, 1954.

Hamilton, Kenneth. "Boon or Thorn? Joyce Cary and Samuel Beckett on Human Life." *The Dalhousie Review*, 38 (Winter 1959), 433-42.

Hanna, Thomas. *The Thought and Art of Albert Camus*. Chicago: H. Regnery, 1958.

Hardy, Barbara. *Tellers and Listeners: The Narrative Imagination*. London: Athlone, 1975.

Hartley, L. P. *The Novelist's Responsibility*. London: Hamish Hamilton, 1967.

Hatfield, Henry, ed. *Thomas Mann: A Collection of Critical Essays*. New Jersey: Prentice Hall, 1964.

Haugh, Robert F. *Joseph Conrad: Discovery in Design*. Oklahoma: University of Oklahoma Press, 1957.

Heberg, Will. *The Writings of Martin Buber*. New York: Meridian, 1956.

Heilman, Robert B. "*The Turn of the Screw* as Poem." *The University of Kansas City Review*, 14, No. 4 (Summer 1948), 277-89.

Hoffman, Charles G. "Innocence and Evil in James's *The Turn of the Screw*." *The University of Kansas City Review*, 20, No. 2 (Winter 1953), 97-105.

Hoffman, Frederick J. *Freudianism and the Literary Mind*. Baton Rouge: Louisiana State University Press, 1945.

―――. *William Faulkner*. 2nd edn. New York: Twayne, 1966.

Hollingdale, R. J. *Thomas Mann: A Critical Study*. London: Rupert Hart-Davis, 1971.

Howe, Irving. *William Faulkner: A Critical Study*. 3rd edn. Chicago: University of Chicago Press, 1975.

Humphrey, Robert. *Stream of Consciousness in the Modern Novel*. Berkeley: University of California Press, 1955.

Iser, Wolfgang. *The Implied Reader: Patterns of Communication in Prose Fiction from Bunyan to Beckett*. Baltimore: Johns Hopkins, 1974.

Jelliffe, Robert A., ed. *Faulkner at Nagano*. Tokyo: Kenkyusha, 1956.

Johnstone, J. K. *The Bloomsbury Group: A Study of E. M. Forster, Lytton Strachey, Virginia Woolf, and Their Circle*. London: Secker and Warburg, 1954.

Kahler, Erich. *The Orbit of Thomas Mann*. Trans. Krishna and Richard Winston. Princeton: Princeton University Press, 1969.

Karl, Frederick. *A Reader's Guide to the Contemporary Novel*. New York: Noonday, 1967.

―――. *A Reader's Guide to Joseph Conrad*. New York: Noonday, 1960.

Kennedy, Margaret. *The Outlaws on Parnassus*. London: Cresset, 1958.

Kenner, Hugh. "Conrad and Ford." In *Gnomon: Essays on Contemporary Literature*. New York: McDowell, Oblensky, 1958, 162-70.

Kenton, Edna. "Henry James to the Ruminant Reader: *The Turn of the Screw*." *The Arts*, 6, No. 5 (November 1924), 245-55.

Kinkead-Weekes, Mark, and Ian Gregor. *William Golding: A Critical Study*. New York: Harcourt, 1967.

Langbaum, Robert. *The Modern Spirit: Essays on the Continuity of Nineteenth and Twentieth Century Literature*. New York: Oxford University Press, 1970.

―――. *The Poetry of Experience: The Dramatic Monologue in Modern Literary Tradition*. New York: Random House, 1957.

Langer, Susanne. *Feeling and Form*. Boston: Routledge and Kegan Paul, 1953.

Leavis, F. R. "The Appreciation of Henry James." *Scrutiny*, 16, No. 3 (Spring 1947), 229-37.

Lee, Hermione. *The Novels of Virginia Woolf*. London: Methuen, 1977.

Lehmann, John. *The Whispering Gallery: Autobiography I*. London: Longmans, 1955.

Le Sage, Laurent. *The French New Novel*. University Park, Pennsylvania: Pennsylvania State University Press, 1962.

Lewis, C. S. *The Allegory of Love: A Study in Mediaeval Tradition.* Oxford: Clarendon, 1936.

Lewis, R. W. B. *The Picaresque Saint: Representative Figures in Contemporary Fiction*. Philadelphia: J. B. Lippincott, 1961.

Lodge, David. *Language of Fiction: Essays in Criticism and Verbal Analysis of the English Novel.* New York: Columbia University Press, 1966.

Lubbock, Percy. *The Craft of Fiction*. London: Jonathan Cape, 1921.

Macauley, Robie. "The Good Ford." *Kenyon Review*, 11 (1949), 269-88.

Malin, Irving. *William Faulkner: An Interpretation*. Stanford, Calif.: Stanford University Press, 1957.

Marcel, Gabriel. *The Mystery of Being*. 2 vols. Chicago: Gateway, 1960.

Medcalf, Stephen. *William Golding*. Essex: Longman, 1975.

Meixner, John A. *Ford Madox Ford's Novels: A Critical Study*. Minneapolis: University of Minnesota Press, 1962.

Merleau-Ponty, Maurice. *Phenomenology of Perception*. Trans. Colin Smith. London: Routledge and Paul, 1962.

Muir, Edwin. *The Structure of the Novel*. London: Hogarth, 1957.

Ohmann, Carol B. *Ford Madox Ford: From Apprentice to Craftsman.* Connecticut: Wesleyan University Press, 1964.

Peyre, Henri. "Camus the Pagan." *Yale French Studies*, No. 25 (Spring 1960), 20-25.

Richter, Harvena. *Virginia Woolf: The Inward Voyage*. Princeton: Princeton University Press, 1970.

Roussel, Royal. *The Metaphysics of Darkness: A Study in the Unity and Development of Conrad's Fiction.* London: Johns Hopkins, 1971.

Rubin, Louis D., Jr. *The Teller in the Tale*. Washington: University of Washington Press, 1967.

Sarraute, Nathalie. *The Age of Suspicion: Essays on the Novel*. Trans. Maria Jolas. New York: Brazillier, 1963.

Scholes, Robert, ed. *Approaches to the Novel: Material for a Poetics.* California: Chandler, 1961.

————, ed. *Learners and Discerners: A Newer Criticism. Discussions of Modern Literature by Henry Levin.* Virginia: University Press of Virginia, 1964.

————. *Structuralism in Literature*. New Haven: Yale University Press, 1974.

Scholes, R., and R. Kellogg. *The Nature of Narrative*. London: Oxford University Press, 1966.

Schorer, Mark. "The Good Novelist in *The Good Soldier*." *Horizon*, 20 (August 1949), 132-38.

————. "Technique as Discovery." In *Forms of Modern Fiction*. Ed. William Van O'Connor. Bloomington: Indiana University Press, 1959, pp. 9-29.

Scott, Evelyn. *On William Faulkner's* The Sound and the Fury. New York: Cape and Smith, 1929.

Shepard, Leslie. *William Faulkner's* As I Lay Dying: *A Critical Commentary*. New York: Simon and Schuster, 1965.

Sheppard, E. A. *Henry James and "The Turn of the Screw."* Oxford: Oxford University Press, 1974.

Sherry, Norman. *Conrad and His World*. London: Thames and Hudson, 1972.

Slatoff, Walter J. *With Respect to Readers: Dimensions of Literary Response*. Ithaca: Cornell University Press, 1970.

States, Bert O. *Irony and Drama: A Poetics*. New York: Cornell University Press, 1971.

Stein, Jean. "Interview with William Faulkner." *Paris Review*, No. 4 (Spring 1956), pp. 28-53.

Stein, William Bysshe. "The Lotus Posture and 'The Heart of Darkness'." *Modern Fiction Studies*, 2 (Winter 1956-57), 235-37.

Surmelian, Leon. *Techniques of Fiction Writing: Measure and Madness*. New York: Doubleday, 1968.

Tate, Allen. *On the Limits of Poetry: Selected Essays, 1928-1948*. New York: Swallow Press, 1948.

Thody, Philip. *Albert Camus 1913-1960*. London: Hamish Hamilton, 1961.

Tiger, Virginia. *William Golding: The Dark Fields of Discovery*. London: Calder and Beyars, 1974.

Tilford, J. "James the Old Intruder." *Modern Fiction Studies*, 4 (Summer 1958), 157-64.

Tillich, Paul. *The Courage to Be*. New Haven: Yale University Press, 1959.

Tillotson, Kathleen. *The Tale and the Teller*. London: Oxford University Press, 1959.

Tindall, W. Y. "Apology for Marlowe." In *From Jane Austen to Joseph Conrad*. Ed. R. C. Rathburn and M. Steinmann, Jr. Minneapolis: University of Minnesota, 1958, pp. 274-85.

Van Ghent, Dorothy. *The English Novel: Form and Function*. New York: Harper and Row, 1953.

Van O'Connor, William, ed. *Forms of Modern Fiction*. Bloomington: Indiana University Press, 1959.

Vickery, Olga W. *The Novels of William Faulkner: A Critical Interpretation*. Baton Rouge: Louisiana State University Press, 1959.

Waggoner, Hyatt H. *William Faulkner: From Jefferson to the World*. Lexington: University of Kentucky Press, 1959.

Wasserman, Jerry. "Narrative Presence: The Illusion of Language in *Heart of Darkness*." *Studies in the Novel*, 6 (1974), 324-31.

Watt, Ian. *The Rise of the Novel*. Harmondsworth: Penguin, 1957.

Wellek, René, and Austin Warren. *Theory of Literature*. 3rd edn. New York: Harcourt, 1956.

West, Muriel. "The Death of Miles in *The Turn of the Screw*." *PMLA*, 79 (June 1964), 238-88.

Wiley, Paul. *Novelist of Three Worlds: Ford Madox Ford*. Syracuse: Syracuse University Press, 1962.

Willer, Gerald, ed., *A Casebook on Henry James's "The Turn of the Screw."* New York: Thomas Y. Crowell, 1969.

Wilson, Edmund. *Axel's Castle: A Study in the Imaginative Literature of 1870-1930*. New York: Scribner's, 1959.

Wilson, Edmund. *The Triple Thinkers: Twelve Essays on Literary Subjects*. New York: Harcourt, 1938.

Wright, Andrew H. *Joyce Cary: A Preface to His Novels*. London: Chatto & Windus, 1958.

Index

The Bibliography, which includes some authors and titles not mentioned in the text, is not indexed here.